The Making of the Modern State

D1548518

The Making of the Modern State

A Theoretical Evolution

Brian R. Nelson

palgrave
macmillan

THE MAKING OF THE MODERN STATE
© Brian R. Nelson, 2006.

First published in 2006 by
PALGRAVE MACMILLAN™
175 Fifth Avenue, New York, N.Y. 10010 and
Houndmills, Basingstoke, Hampshire, England RG21 6XS
Companies and representatives throughout the world.

PALGRAVE MACMILLAN is the global academic imprint of the Palgrave Macmillan division of St. Martin's Press, LLC and of Palgrave Macmillan Ltd. Macmillan® is a registered trademark in the United States, United Kingdom and other countries. Palgrave is a registered trademark in the European Union and other countries.

ISBN 1–4039–7189–7
ISBN 1–4039–7190–0

Library of Congress Cataloging-in-Publication Data

Nelson, Brian R.
    The making of the modern state : a theoretical evolution / Brian R. Nelson
        p. cm.
    Includes bibliographical references and index.
    ISBN 1–4039–7189–7—ISBN 1–4039–7190–0 (pbk.)
    1. State, The I. Title.

JC11. N44 2006
320.1′1—dc22   2005051248

A catalogue record for this book is available from the British Library.

Design by Newgen Imaging Systems (P) Ltd., Chennai, India.

First edition: March 2006

10 9 8 7 6 5 4 3 2 1

Printed in the United States of America.

For
Susan and Jennifer

Contents

Preface

If one were to ask, "Why study the state?" the most obvious answer would be because we live in one. Less obvious, but more interesting, would be because political thinkers have been debating about exactly what it is, and how best to conceptualize it, since classical times. Since the form of the state has changed over historical time, the debate has itself taken different forms, a fact that adds another level of interest to the topic. And when American political science decided early in its formation as an academic discipline that the state was not a theoretically useful concept, that made the state, that is the modern state, exceedingly interesting for those whose thinking tends toward the longer historical view of things. Since political theory first arose as an attempt to understand the state, and has always reflected in some manner the existing form of polity, a science of politics that rejects what heretofore had been its essential subject matter clearly raises some fascinating issues.

Hopefully, this book will capture all of these levels of interest. While it is framed as a critique of the stateless perspective of American political science, its intent is in fact much broader: to attempt to understand our modern political consciousness within the context of the modern state. Contemporary social and political science is the theoretical form of this consciousness, but one need not be a specialist in these disciplines to appreciate the impact of the modern state on our most basic political assumptions and ideological beliefs. Indeed, it is not really possible to understand fully our own ideological proclivities without understanding their connection to the state. I doubt, for example, that most libertarians realize that the individualism they defend against the state could hardly exist outside of it.

To attempt to grasp the nature of modern political consciousness in these terms, however, requires a historical understanding of the theoretical evolution of the modern state itself. This, in turn, requires an understanding of earlier state formations and ideologies that, directly or indirectly, influenced that evolution. It is this broad historical framework that constitutes the main portion of this book. It is a book, above all, about the state and state theory, from the archaic to the modern period. And quite apart from the narrower issue of the relevance of the state to contemporary social and political science, the historical evolution of the state to its modern form is a fascinating subject in its own right.

It must be admitted from the outset, however, that such a broad and complex subject cannot be given its due justice in one short book or, for that matter, in many. Nor can one person alone provide it, certainly not myself who, having studied the state and taught about it for many years, am all too aware of how much more is to be learned. Fortunately, for those who find the state as interesting a subject as myself, there are many books dealing with the more specialized aspects of the theory of the state. Some of these, the most useful or, at any rate, the most interesting, are cited. In addition, I have provided fairly extensive notes on some of the narrower technical aspects of the subject that would otherwise disrupt the more general narrative. At the same time, I have attempted in both text and notes to make the subject accessible to the nonspecialist.

Finally, thanks are due to the many students who have taken my seminar on the political theory of the modern state. Their interest in the subject spurred me to write this book, and their criticisms have helped me to clarify my own thinking on the subject. Thanks are due in particular to Ms Gaye Gungor for her fine editorial assistance, and for sharing with me her expertise on the subject of the European Union.

Chapter One

State and Ideology

The state has in recent years become a focus of interest to American political scientists, as well as to others within the historical and social sciences. That interest was ever lost is itself interesting, a uniquely American phenomenon. In Europe, at least until the postmodern period, interest in the state never really waned, and for good reason. Not only did the modern state first emerge there and thus initiate and sustain a state tradition of political thought, but also its subsequent history of violence and, in the last century, totalitarianism made the state a very real presence in European consciousness. The two world wars and all that was associated with them further confirmed the reality of the state. In Europe, few thinkers doubted that the horrors of the last century were rooted in a political reality that went much deeper than the ideologies or insanities of a few particular leaders.

All the more paradoxically, therefore, that in the United States the state ceased to be a primary focus of theoretical interest precisely when one would think interest would be highest: in the immediate postwar era. What explains this paradox? To be sure, the American intellectual soil has always produced odd hybrids of political consciousness, but this alone does not explain the postwar loss of interest in the state. Despite the terrible reality of state power manifested so clearly in the last century, there existed certain historical and cultural factors that supplanted this reality in American political consciousness with a more benign and stateless view of politics.

One of these has been there from the beginning. Although we have had a state in the formal sense ever since the adoption of the constitution, and in a more or less real sense since the end of the Civil War, until at least the New Deal and World War II, it has not looked much like a state in the European sense. In Europe, the state was formed by absolute monarchs who early on centralized a permanent, and for the subjects quite visible, structure of legal and administrative power. In this country, the state was formed by a variety of factions into what was originally a loose knit federal and quasi-democratic structure. American citizens recognized that they possessed a government, or rather governments, but had little sense of the existence of a centralized state.

Other factors unique to American political life also contributed to a lack of state consciousness, most notably the dominance of the liberal ideology. Liberalism's emphasis on individual rights and limited government has conspired against a state-centrist view of political life. To the American mind politics appears to be little more than competing groups and individuals, and the state, to the extent it is thought of at all, as a mere umpire established to insure the political game is played fairly.

More profoundly, the early or classical liberal ideology, no less than later Marxism, viewed the state as subordinate and epiphenomenal to civil society, and liberal democracy the ideal political structure for capitalist accumulation. Indeed, capitalism came to be seen as the necessary prerequisite for a liberal-democratic system, an idea that, however theoretically suspect, remains the cornerstone of American foreign policy to this day. From this perspective, the state is at best a "necessary evil," an unfortunate necessity to insure the sanctity of contract and other legal requirements of a capitalist free market. In the classical liberal view, the state as such never possessed a purpose, a substance, a reality of its own.

But why, until quite recently, did postwar American political science so uncritically share the broader culture's stateless perspective? The answer appears to be as obvious it is perplexing. American political science was never able to escape its own cultural milieu. Despite its desire early on in its development, and particularly in the postwar period to found a genuine science of politics, its most fundamental theoretical tenets remained tied to the popular vision of politics. Hence, it carried into its theoretical frame-work much of the corpus of the American liberal ideology, not only a belief in the value of capitalism and liberal democracy, but also a focus on indi-viduals and interest groups rather than the larger legal and institutional framework we call the state. And when, subsequently, American political science did attempt to broaden its focus to include these factors, it did so by creating models of political analysis that explicitly rejected the state model.

Yet, while it is true that American political science has always been less tied to a state-centric view of politics than its European counterpart has, there was until the postwar period at least some interest in the institutional framework of government if not in a full-blown theory of the state. Interwar political scientists such as R.M. MacIver and Woodrow Wilson certainly did not consider the state an irrelevant topic.[1] But it became a matter of doctrine among postwar political scientists that the concept of the state is incompat-ible with a true science of politics.[2] In this, they drew upon some of the key thinkers of the interwar period who had already begun to break from the more institutional political science of MacIver and Wilson. Most notable among this group were Arthur Bentley, Charles Merriam, and David Truman who proposed that the scientific study of politics should focus not on the state, or on constitutional and legal institutions, but on the empirical processes of political activity.[3] This would mean, among other things, that individuals, groups, and political parties should be the basic subject matter of political science. Whatever value this may have had in the development of the discipline, there is little question that this new science of politics looked suspiciously American and liberal in its rejection of the state and in its concomitant focus on individual and group interests.

Given the new postwar science of politics, the assault upon the concept of the state was unrelenting. Most notably, it was criticized as metaphysical nonsense, a criticism directed largely at nineteenth- and early-twentieth-century German theories of the state, primarily but not exclusively those of Hegel, which saw the state as representing certain transcendent principles, or embodying spiritual ideals, or possessing a "higher personality" of its own. Since early American political science was largely shaped by German political thought, the "new science of politics" was in the first instance intent on divorcing itself from this type of, in Arthur Bentley's words, "soul stuff."[4] As a science, it was to be strictly empirical, rejecting all forms of theorizing that could not be given a definite empirical referent.

Thus, what had begun in the interwar period as an attempt to found an empirical discipline grounded in the political behavior of individuals and groups became a virtual rout of any perspective other than empiricism, which meant a rejection of such a metaphysically suspect concept as the state. For the state was not only implicated in normative issues, from Aristotle through nineteenth century German state studies, it was a concept, or so it seemed, without a clear empirical referent; indeed, an entirely unnecessary concept because political behavior is observable, measurable, and quantifiable without reference to the state at all.

Behavioralism, as this new "science of politics" came to be known, was the dominant mode of political analysis throughout the 1950s and 1960s. Its repercussions are felt to this day. Many contemporary political scientists were trained in the behavioral tradition which, given its radically antistate bias, has led to a pervasive resistance to the new initiatives in state studies.[5] This may indeed be the postbehavioral period, but it is a period in which the state is "brought back in" only with a great deal of theoretical struggle.[6]

Perhaps the most pervasive and influential theoretical framework premised upon the behavioral epistemology was pluralism. Politics, American politics at any rate, was to be understood as interest group competition to determine, in the words of Harold Laswell, a key interwar influence on the subsequent development of behavioralism, "who gets what, when, and how."[7] Indeed, this remains probably the most pervasive definition of politics in the discipline, and it is a definition that requires no concept of the state at all. As one commentator notes, "The relentlessly behavioralist concept of politics—who gets what, when, and how—does not need any corresponding notion of the state, for it might as easily apply to a family, a faction, a firm, or a farm."[8]

Indeed it might, and pluralist theories of politics were applied to just such groups without noticeable regard for the larger institutional structure of the state.[9] At most, the state was treated simply as another group; another "actor" in the inelegant terms of a discipline determined to create an ahistorical and value-neutral language as scientific as its methods. Since the state cannot "act," what was really meant here by the state was the specific individuals and groups that constituted the administration, in short, the government, which now was to be understood as itself simply another interest group in the political process. In this way, the state came to be conflated with government, and to this day one of the common definitions of the state is that it is simply another word for government, a definition that in the history of political thought is in fact retrograde. It took centuries for the crucial distinction between state and government to be made without which modern politics, even as understood by contemporary political science, would hardly be possible.

To be sure, attempts were made to construct a broader context of political analysis than individual and group processes, most notably in systems analysis and structural functionalism, theoretical constructs that essentially became combined into one general analytical framework.[10] The system's approach did direct attention to the larger social and political structures in which individual and group behavior are embedded, but in its more abstract formulation, at least, it tended to ignore the specifics of that behavior.[11] The "system," it was frequently charged, resembles a "black box" with inputs and outputs but devoid of any real empirical social and political content. The "system," in fact, was more abstract than the state concept it was to replace.

Although contemporary political science has gone beyond these particular theoretical frameworks, the methodological tradition of behavioralism continues to be extraordinarily influential. As a consequence, most political scientists continue to ignore the state as a valid unit of political analysis, and in some cases such as rational and public choice theory[12] the discipline has returned to an abstract individualism that is quite in line with liberal, and stateless, views on the nature of politics. Moreover, at the other albeit less influential end of the methodological spectrum, "postmodern" and post-structural forms of analysis within the discipline are perhaps even more biased against state theorizing than the more positivist traditions of the discipline. This is particularly true in the work of Michel Foucault whose focus is the social and cultural "microphysics of power" rather than its centralized state form.[13] As for the rest, the discipline is now broken into a multiplicity of theoretical perspectives without, it seems, any paradigmatic continuity at all, from forms of structuralism to cultural analysis of political phenomena.[14]

It is against this background of paradigmatic uncertainty that current interest in the state has emerged, although its roots go back to the late 1960s as Marxist and neo-Marxist modes of political theorizing began to infiltrate a small segment of the discipline. In response, neo-institutionalist theories of the state that objected to the "class reductionism" of neo-Marxism began to draw adherents. Much of the current theorizing on, and debates about, the state occurs within and between these two schools of thought. What is particularly interesting from the perspective of this book is that these theories and debates are themselves a historical by-product of the theoretical evolution of the modern state. They are clearly derivative of the debate early in the last century between Max Weber and the ghost of Karl Marx, a debate we reexamine in chapter seven.

Although the state has become once again a matter of theoretical interest within American political science, it is hardly the dominant interest.

Moreover, the state is largely conceptualized as the permanent administrative structure of governance, not as a totality of social, political, and ideological factors. This is more the case with the institutionalists than the Marxists, but it is generally true that most contemporary state theorists do not deal with the state in its historically given completeness. This, we would argue, is not only to fail to conceptualize the state in its true dimensions, but as a consequence, to fail to understand how the modern state shapes modern political consciousness, including modern political science.

The intent of this book, then, is not only to argue for the importance of the state concept in political analysis, but for its conceptualization as a totality of ideological and structural factors. More controversially, it is to suggest that when this is done, a paradoxical fact emerges: that the rejection of the state concept by mainline political science is in fact often an ideological reflection of what is being rejected. Indeed, it is difficult to imagine the forms of stateless political analysis that have emerged in the postwar era apart from the state. A subtle but illuminating example of this is revealed in the methodological individualism of early behavioralism and the subsequent attempt to contextualize political behavior within an abstract system ana- lytic approach. These two modes of political analysis in fact reflected the most notable and paradoxical feature of the modern state: an extraordinary centralization of abstract impersonal power coupled with an individualism and pluralism unknown in any previous form of polity.

Viewed historically, however, none of this should come as a surprise. Political theory has always reflected, positively or negatively, consciously or, in the case of American political science, unconsciously, the existing form of polity. This is apparent in even the most cursory review of the historical evolution of political ideas, and it is no less apparent in contemporary political science. It becomes more apparent when the connection between contemporary political science and the state is seen from the perspective of the actual development of the modern state. To understand the state is to understand it historically, a view shared as well by some in the field of soci- ology who have criticized their own discipline for ignoring the state and its historical evolution.[15] In this, the complaint that "American sociology has deliberately remained ahistorical"[16] could as easily be applied to American political science as, indeed, it frequently has been.

Here, in fact, lies the real reason for the rejection of the state by American political science. Its attempt to create a value free scientific methodology in line with prevailing positivist assumptions required, almost of necessity, an ahistorical approach. The object of science in this view is to establish uni- versally valid laws and explanations of empirical reality that, in the case of social science, transcend historical contingency, and the modern Western state is above all the product of historical contingency. It is the result of centuries of structural and ideological developments, none of which were predictable and, in retrospect, often improbable. Such a construct as the modern state, thus, presents enormous problems to the ideal of science in those terms desired by most in the social and political sciences. The issue of the state, in fact, is at bottom an issue of fundamental epistemological import.

What follows, then, is precisely a historical analysis of the evolution of the modern state, but in its political, sociological, and most importantly as we are dealing with the issue of theoretical comprehension, its ideological totality. This requires going back well before the modern state itself, not only to earlier types of state formations, but also to pre-state formations, for the modern state is not only shaped by earlier forms of polity but is best understood in contrast to them. Such a broad overview of the subject may at first seem far removed from contemporary debates about the state, but be assured it is not. These debates, as indicated, are more often than not unconsciously implicated in the ideological legitimations of the modern state, and can only be understood properly as they have evolved over historical time.

One final example may help make the point. A common critique of American political science, not made by Marxists alone, is that its focus on group and individual behavior fails to account for the importance of social class, that class is treated as simply another variable in the political process rather than as a constituative factor in the formation of any polity beyond the most primitive. Yet, it is inescapably clear that social class constitutes the sociological basis of any state formation, the modern state included. What makes the modern state unique is that its ideology of legitimation is premised upon a classless concept of political authority, a fact that can be comprehended only through a historical analysis of the ways in which that ideology evolved. When this is done, and contemporary political science viewed in those same historical terms, it becomes apparent that its stateless theoretical models and methodologies are reflective of the same classless concept of political authority.

The proceeding chapters, therefore, essentially parallel the actual theoretical evolution of the state, from pre-state formations to the modern state. Hence, the key social science theories of the state will be dealt with last since they emerge quite late in the development of the modern state and, in major part, are best understood as a reaction to this development. There is, however, one exception to this approach. We begin with contemporary anthropological theories of the state since they deal most fundamentally with beginnings, with the genesis of state formation.

Chapter Two

State Formations

No treatise on such a large subject as the state should begin without some attempt at definition, but it is difficult to comprehend in one definition the actual variety of states that have emerged over historical time.[1] At the same time, it is impossible to discuss the state without some common understanding of its major characteristics, however much they may vary in particular cases. Hence, what follows is a basic typology rather than a formal definition of the key elements of a state structure, including the modern state. This is to be understood as constituting an "ideal type" in the sense that Max Weber intended, as a purely formal construct that aids in ordering and comprehending empirical reality, not as a precise model of any particular existing social or political structure.

Perhaps the most immediately notable characteristic of the state is that it is a territorial form of political organization. This is not to be confused with the natural territorial demarcation that any group of humans, or animals, establish to mark off hunting grounds or living space. Such demarcation exists only as a vague and general separation between peoples, not as a definite and legally recognized line between one polity and another characteristic of the state. The legal demarcation of state territoriality is a unique development in the evolution of political society.

The state is a sovereign entity. This, when coupled with territoriality, may be said to be its defining characteristic. To possess sovereignty is to possess supreme coercive power and, when applied to the state, to possess it within a defined territorial boundary. In Weber's classic definition, the state is "*the monopoly of the legitimate use of physical force* within a given territory."[2] Moreover, sovereignty means not only that the governing authority is supreme within the state's territory, but that it is independent of all external authority as well.

We understand today that the state is an abstraction, a conceptual ordering of the locus and extent of sovereign authority. As such, it requires government of some form to transform the abstraction called state into the actual exercise of sovereign authority. What makes state forms of government unique is that they are the sole exerciser of sovereignty within the state's territory (government as such pre-dates the state, for all peoples have government of some type, even if highly undifferentiated, but not all have a state). Subordinate governments may exist, as in a federal system, but they remain subordinate to the authority of the central government. When more than one government claims sovereign authority, the state either does not exist or is in a condition of civil war.

The state exercises its authority through law, and the modern Western state is itself entirely a legal structure, in Weber's words again, a "rational-legal system." Even in very early forms of the state, where the basis of authority is personal or traditional rather than legal, the commands of the state (government) are given as law. The law may be little more than existing custom, but it is still law, that is, commands backed up by sovereign authority.

To these basic structural characteristics of territoriality, sovereignty, centralized government, and coercive law, must be added some corresponding form of state consciousness or ideology of legitimation. While theoretically a state could exist in the structural sense without it, in reality no state could survive without some operative myth that legitimized it. And it is characteristic of all states that the legitimizing ideology is framed in terms of some myth of foundation by which they were initially formed, by the Gods in the earliest states or, in the modern state, by an act of rational consent.

In addition to these explicitly political characteristics, all states, the modern state included, are based upon some system of class stratification. This is not the only kind of social stratification that exists in state societies, but it is unique to states, and is the most important. This is not to suggest that social and economic factors other than social class are not necessary to the existence of the state. A settled agricultural economy was a necessary precondition for the emergence of the earliest states, for example, as were a number of other related factors such as a certain population density. But we must distinguish here between necessary conditions and the specific mode of social cooperation through which people organize and regulate themselves in the performance of vital social and economic activities. Social class is not merely a condition for the state's existence in the passive sense that geographical or population factors are, but the active principle of social and economic ordering, control, and regulation that must occur through some system of permanent social stratification in any but the simplest of societies. As an inherent part of those mechanisms of control, the state cannot be understood apart from the class system, anymore than the absence of the state in simple societies can be understood apart from the absence of a class system.

That these social and political characteristics are unique to the state becomes immediately evident when contrasted with pre-state forms of society. Here the anthropological evidence is unambiguous. Politically, none of the features of state society exists, whether in simple band and tribal systems or even in more developed chiefdoms except perhaps in the most advanced types. There is no centralized government, no sovereign authority, no legally defined territory, and no system of codified law. What is even more striking is that the underlying social and economic structure is radically egalitarian. There is no private property in land, or in any other form beyond simple personal possessions, and the resources of society are shared communally.

Hence, beyond traditional age and gender distinctions, there is no class system.[3]

Governance of such socially and politically undifferentiated societies, wherein no centralized authority exists, much less the sovereign state, can only occur through mechanisms of kinship. Pre-state societies regulate themselves through gens, or clans, or other kin structures of social articulation, including the regulation of conflict, not through legal constraints imposed by a territorial sovereign.[4] And the rules of justice in kin based societies are always and everywhere customary rather than statutory. Custom is the pre-state equivalent of law, the sacred and immemorial mores of a people.[5]

Given the undifferentiated character of kin forms of governance, and the lack of any central authority, pre-state societies are composed of distinct, autonomous, and easily separable parts. Bands are made up of small family units that can easily separate from the band and form or join other bands that share a common lineage. Tribes are equally capable of this kind of organization. Indians of the American plains, for example, were little more than a dispersed collection of bands sharing a common language who gathered as a tribe infrequently for religious or military purposes, and usually only as convenience dictated. In certain cases, anthropologists have termed these societies "segmentary," and although the term has proven controversial, the concept underlying it remains useful.[6]

The concept is particularly important in understanding the formation of the modern state, for it was only in the destruction of the "segmentary" character of medieval society that the formation of a territorial sovereign authority became possible.[7] Clearly, state sovereignty cannot exist where real authority rests with subordinate social units. This is why many "third world" states today are states in name only. Created as legal fictions by colonizing powers in the last century, they are states attempting to rule essentially segmental societies based on tribal or other local units that are the locus of political loyalty and that strive to function independently of the state. These states are still in the state building process and face, in essentials, the same dilemmas that the modern Western state faced in overcoming the centripetal forces of their own segmental societies.

To be sure, the most advanced type of pre-state formation, what anthropologists characterize as chiefdoms, are less segmental and undifferentiated than band and tribal units.[8] Here there is some centralization of authority, particularly in what might be termed strong chiefdoms,[9] but it is far from a state form of sovereignty. Chiefdoms of the more advanced type may eventually lead to a class divided state society, but not inevitably so.[10] Indeed, the precise mechanisms by which state societies emerge out of chiefdoms or some other more basic social formation are not known, although anthropologists have put forward a number of competing theories. The difficulty is that there are a limited number of pristine states, that is, states that have arisen autonomously without the influence of other states, and these exist only in the archaeological evidence. Among these would be included the states of the ancient Near East including Egypt, the archaic states of Mesoamerica and Peru, and the earliest states in India and China.[11]

Broadly speaking, theories of (pristine) state formation are of two types: those that see the state emerging through processes of integration,[12] and those that see it as the outcome of conflict such as warfare.[13] There are a number of subtheoretical approaches in each category, although the conflict theorists appear to have the more persuasive position.[14] One thing is certain, however: class domination constitutes the ultimate coercive basis of all primary and secondary states (states emerging in response to, or in imitation of, other states).[15] This is not to imply any causative role to social class in the state's formation. What "causes" the state to emerge in the first place is hardly a settled matter. The empirical evidence is simply not there to assert with any confidence what the causative factors are. Indeed, some anthropologists maintain that the state is the "cause" rather than the effect of social class.[16] It is probable in most cases that the two emerged together as mutually reinforcing factors. All that we do know for certain is that state societies are class stratified and that the state is profoundly implicated in the class system.

The crucial importance of social class in the existence of the state, and the corresponding ideologies of legitimation, can best be seen through a comparative analysis of the different forms of state that have existed over historical time. While a variety of typologies of state formations have been proposed, for our purposes we focus on four historically given types: ancient city-states, ancient empire states, modern city-states, and the modern Western or "nation-state."[17] The term ancient here is meant to include both the archaic states of the Near East as well as the classical states of Greece and Rome. The archaic states that arose in Mesoamerica and elsewhere should also be included, but since they did not have an impact on the subsequent development of state thinking in the West, they will not constitute the focus of our analysis. The modern city-state refers to those city-states emerging out the disintegration of feudalism at the end of the Middle Ages and, most importantly, the city-states of Renaissance Italy that had the greatest influence on the subsequent ideological evolution of the modern Western state. Modern city leagues, of which the most famous and successful was the German Hanseatic League from the mid-fourteenth century on, were important as well, but did not constitute true territorial states.[18]

In the following chapters, we will analyze the major forms of state formation that have evolved from the classical city-states of ancient Greece to the modern period. It is only against this background that the theoretical evolution of the modern Western state becomes comprehensible. In this analysis, the link between the underlying structure of class stratification and the ideology of legitimation will be stressed, for it is this that has constituted the core of theoretical justifications of all historically given state formations, as well as the theoretical debates surrounding contemporary social scientific analysis of the modern state. In this chapter, however, we need to briefly review the role of class and ideology in the archaic states of the Near East, for it is here that the link between the two is most clearly revealed, much more clearly than in modern liberal democracies.

The earliest pristine states arose during the late neolithic period some five to six thousand years ago in the Nile valley and in Mesopotamia, the Fertile Crescent between the Tigris and Euphrates rivers. Geography was a crucial factor here. The potential fertility of these areas was more than capable of generating the surplus required for state formation. Without this, a settled mode of life would have been impossible. But the creation of the surplus required the building and maintenance of irrigation systems and, as a consequence, the necessity to impose some form of central control. Indeed, one notable, if controversial, theory of state formation, Karl Wittfogel's "hydraulic hypothesis," which asserts that complex irrigations systems require centralized forms of political control, perhaps best fits the circumstances of the ancient Near East.[19]

The Sumerians of Mesopotamia, until this century a people of shadowy historical existence, created the very first states in about 3500 BCE. These were all initially city-states, sometimes quite large ones even by today's standards, comprising tens of thousands of people. They were on the whole warlike and, in some cases, expansionary, resulting in the formation of early empire states, albeit rather disorganized and short lived ones. It was not until the Assyrians united the whole of Mesopotamia and the Fertile Crescent, including Egypt for a short period from 745–612 BCE, that we can speak of the formation of something resembling a true empire state.[20] In this, the Assyrians began what would become a distinct political form in the ancient and classical periods with the rise of the great empires of the Persians, Macedonians, and, particularly important for the subsequent development of the modern Western state, the Romans.

This much can be said with certainty: The basis of early state formation was the city, empires arising as purely secondary formations. The same may be said for the classical states of the Greco-Roman period and, indirectly, even of the modern state. So important has the city been in this regard that it constitutes the most important type of clearly definable premodern state. Indeed, along with empire states, which in the ancient world are everywhere the outgrowth of an expansionary city, they provide us with our basic typology of historically given state formations. City-states and empire states comprise the known forms of state until the advent of the modern state.[21]

The Egyptian state emerged at almost the same time as the Sumerian states, in 3100 BCE. In both cases, the absolute sovereign authority of the state was embodied in the king, the lugal in Sumeria, Pharaoh in Egypt, an authority that was at once political as well as religious.[22] The king was not only chief political authority, but chief priest as well. A key difference, however, was that the while the lugal represented God on earth,[23] Pharaoh was God on earth. Nonetheless, the power and majesty of both these archaic kings was enormous. They stood atop rigidly class divided societies as absolute theocratic rulers, and while in real political terms there were inevitably sources of resistance among the noble classes, the ideology of absolute kingship was never challenged.[24]

The essentially religious ideology of these theocratic rulers did not merely legitimize their absolute authority, however; it also defined the specific role they were to play. As God's representative on earth, or as God himself, the king was to maintain harmony between the social and natural orders; no small task, but one crucial to the survival of the state in the minds of people who understood all events to be ruled by the will of the Gods.[25] The crops grew because the rain fell or the Nile rose, to be sure, but these events occurred because the Gods dictated them, and a successful priest-king could sway the Gods for the good of the state through the appropriate rituals and sacrifices. When the rains ceased, the consequence was not merely the specter of hunger but a political crisis of the first magnitude.

In the same way, the king was responsible for the maintenance of a just state, for the Gods had decreed justice to be the foundation of the state as well as of the universe as a whole. Justice was an integral component of an implicate social and natural order ruled by the Gods and requiring the intervention of the king for its maintenance, no less than the recurrence of rain or the rising of the Nile.[26] And in the case of justice, it was expressed by the king in the form of law, a prime marker of the state, of which the most famous is the law code of Hammurabi, king of Babylonia (ca.1800 BCE).

The Hammurabic code, which profoundly influenced the legal systems of other Near Eastern states, most importantly the early Hebrew state, has come down to us as a model of archaic law, the essence of which is the concept of the theocratic king as dispenser of justice. Given the foundation myth that the Gods had created and were the proprietors of the city (the idea that the city and its lands were owned by the Gods was a common Mesopotamian belief), the code of Hammurabi proclaims "to establish justice in the earth."[27] And what is the most notable characteristic of the Hammurabic code, apart from the assertion of the divine origin of the state and law, is its clear justification of the prevailing class system typical of Mesopotamian state societies, that of king, priests, nobles, commoners, and slaves. Although the law was meant to protect all, it was not designed to protect all equally. The nobility and priesthood, for example, were penalized less for wronging a member of the lower orders than of their own caste, a principle that was reversed when the wrong occurred the other way around.[28]

It might appear from this brief overview that the archaic states of the Near East have little in common with the modern Western state. If we are focusing only on the particulars of social and political organization and the ideology of legitimation, this would be true enough. But if we expand our view to the general nature of the state as such, all of the key elements of the state, including the modern state, are there, from a centralized sovereign authority to the underlying structure of class stratification. Indeed, setting aside its religious content, even the ideology of legitimation is characteristic of the modern state in its affirmation of the existing class system. These general commonalities are important to bear in mind, for there is a tendency to treat the modern Western state as *sui generis*, as somehow different in essentials from earlier state formations. A not uncommon error, for example, is to think that a democratic form of government obviates the class basis of the state.

But what about the influence of the archaic states of the Near East on the development of the modern state? Certainly there is no direct influence, yet it can be said that they have indirectly contributed to the development of all states, including the Western state, in generating the "state idea" itself. More than this, the Near Eastern states influenced Roman imperial concepts of kingship, and these were to shape much of the medieval debate on the locus and extent of political authority, a debate that subsequently influenced the developing theory of the modern state. Still, the influence of the archaic states of the Near East is largely indirect, with one very important exception: the ancient Hebrew state.

There is in this a paradox, for the Hebrews were a tribal people living in the internices of great states and empires who established, at best, a relatively primitive and short lived state structure. Formed in about 1000 BCE when the force of external pressures, most notably the Philistine threat, compelled the twelve tribes of Israel to unite under a kingship,[29] it eventually split along tribal lines into two separate states, Israel and Judah. Subsequent invasions by Assyrians and others destroyed both.[30]

What was to make the subsequent influence of the Hebrew state so important was that its ideology of legitimation limited the power of the king more dramatically than in any other archaic state of the Near East. Unlike the polytheistic ideologies of earlier archaic states, the Hebrews knew but one God, Yahweh, who transcended the state no less than nature itself. Here there was no possibility that the king could speak for God, and it was unthinkable that he could ever assert godly attributes. The role accorded to other Near Eastern monarchs of maintaining harmony between the natural and social orders was denied to the Hebrew kings.[31] More than anywhere else in the Near East, the king played an essentially secular role. Religious functions devolved largely upon the priesthood and upon the prophets, a group unique to the Hebrews.[32]

Indeed, the prophets provide a clear indication of the relative autonomy of religion in the Hebrew state, and the consequent limitations on kingly authority. They freely criticized the king when he failed to heed the divine plan, the covenant between Yahweh and the Jewish people, something that would have been unthinkable in any other Near Eastern theocracy. Here the foundation myth posited a covenant between God and the people as a whole, not between God and the king. If the Egyptian foundation myth posited the state as the creation of a god-king, the Mesopotamian as the creation of the Gods in which the king became their voice on earth, the Hebrew mythology posited neither. The Hebrew king was the "arbiter of disputes and the leader in war"; he was not the spokesman for God.[33] Thus, while the king was the dispenser of justice, he was not, like Hammurabi or Pharaoh, the source of law. The Jewish law, the Torah, evolved from the Mosaic law of the Ten Commandments given to Moses by God during the exodus from Egypt. This law bound the king as much as anyone else, as the prophets were wont to remind him when he strayed from the path of righteousness. Pharaoh and lugal, as the source of law, were above it; the Hebrew king was at all times subject to it.

It was precisely this unique character of Hebrew kingship, however, that made it so important in the subsequent development of the state concept in the West. After the collapse of the Roman Empire, Davidic concepts of kingship (King David became the ideal model of secular kingship for the early Christians), along with imperial notions of rulership, were promulgated by a proselytizing Western Church to Germanic tribal chieftains. What this precluded in the development of Western kingship, and subsequently in the evolution of the state itself, was any notion that secular authority, while divinely ordained, was God on earth or possessed God-like attributes. Hence, even where the king was understood to be the source of law, as in later medieval views premised upon Roman imperial concepts of kingship, he was never believed to be above the ultimate source of law that was understood to be rooted in natural and divine (biblical) dictates of justice including the ancient Mosaic law. And while the eventual conflict between the developing Western state and the church revolved around the limits and extent of kingly authority in the religious sphere, it was never a conflict over these fundamental assumptions inherent in the Judeo-Christian tradition.

What in the final analysis is the common feature in the archaic states of the Near East is the fundamental role of religion in the formation and legitimation of the state. This was true, with the exceptions we have noted, even for the Hebrews. The ideologies of legitimation, the foundation myths, however much they may have varied in particulars, all rested upon religious assumptions that justified the rule of a noble-priestly class. These same assumptions, within the Judeo-Christian framework, prevailed throughout much of the medieval period until classical Greek thinking on the state began to infiltrate Western consciousness. It was these assumptions that the modern Western state ultimately shattered and, in its theoretical evolution, laid the basis for an entirely novel concept of political authority.

The following chapters attempt to trace this evolution, but it will be helpful first to specify the general characteristics of the modern Western state, those that make it a unique development in modern political history. Since the archaic states of the Near East are the most unlike the modern state, the contrast will help to clarify those aspects of the modern state that make it unique. It must be emphasized once again, however, that the basic structural and sociological characteristics of the modern state are identical to those of all earlier forms of state, including the archaic states, from territoriality and centralized sovereign authority to an underlying system of class stratification. To be sure, the specific manifestations of these factors are not the same—territorial size, type of legal system, and form of class stratification are different—but not the existence of these factors as such. What makes the modern state genuinely unique is the manner in which it theoretically conceptualizes these factors, that is, its myth of foundation, its ideology of legitimation.

That ideology is based upon an impersonal theory of sovereignty, one in which the state is conceived as an abstraction separate from both ruler and ruled, a view advanced by Quentin Skinner in his *The Foundations of Modern Political Thought*.[34] Sovereignty resides in the impersonal state, not in the ruler as commonly conceived in the archaic states and in much, though not all, classical and medieval political thought, or, in the case of popular sovereignty, in the people as a whole. In brief, state sovereignty replaces ruler sovereignty as the legitimizing ideology of the state, and this is true even with the development of the modern doctrine of popular sovereignty, for in this view the "sovereignty of the people" is itself abstract and impersonal and manifested only through the state.

In order for the concept of impersonal state sovereignty to exist, then, a clear distinction had to be made between the state and government. Where ruler sovereignty prevailed, this distinction could not be made since the state and government were one and the same. Louis the XIV's famous dictum *l'état c'est moi* perfectly captures this idea in its most extreme form. In the same way, it could not exist without a clear distinction between the state and society, one in which the state is conceived as separate from the broader social order over which it has authority. Such a conception can only occur where, at least in appearance, the state is not merely an extension of social and economic relationships, of the class system for example. A purely class state by definition would not be an impersonal state.

This explains why, with the partial exception of classical Roman political thought, there was no theory of the abstract impersonal state until the modern period. Political theories prior to then understood the polity, the classical Greek *polis* for example, in much less abstract terms, even though it possessed the form of what we now would call a state. The separation of government and society was much less clear in premodern states. That we frequently translate such terms as *polis* into "state" without carefully specifying the difference between the modern understanding of the term and its original meaning runs the risk of serious historical distortion.

The ideology of legitimation of the modern state is premised upon these crucial distinctions. And it is the inevitable contradictions between the ideology and the reality of the modern state that constitute the basis of so much contemporary political thought—and debate. If, for example, the modern state, no less than any other historically given form of state, is based upon some system of class stratification, then the concept of the impersonal state separate from society can be maintained only with the greatest difficulty, a difficulty compounded, as we shall see, with the emergence of the contemporary welfare state.

What is clear at this juncture is that the ideology of the modern state, and the theoretical evolution upon which it is based, could not occur so long as a concept of ruler sovereignty legitimized in religious terms prevailed. Rational modes of thinking would have to replace religious understandings of political authority, a process that began long before the emergence of the modern state, but that was crucial in its subsequent theoretical development. This process first began with the classical Greeks.

Chapter Three

The Ideal State

The contribution of the classical Greeks to state theory, and to political thought generally, is best understood against the background of the archaic states of the Near East. The key term here is theory, for until the Greeks a theory of the state did not exist. The Near Eastern states were legitimized by religious myth, and understood by the subjects in these terms. The Greeks alone in the ancient world subjected their political institutions to rational modes of analysis. In this, they bequeathed to the West theories of the state that would, in much later times, play a profound role in the theoretical formation of the early modern state.

Why the Greeks were able to break from purely traditional and religious modes of political thinking is speculative, but certainly a key element of the answer lies in the history and development of the ancient Greek city-state: The *polis*. Taking its essential form by the middle of the eighth century BCE, the *polis* was constituted from the various tribal communities (*ethnos*) to which the Greek peoples had heretofore given their allegiance. The precise reasons for this transformation are lost in myth, but Greek legend posited a foundation myth of a great lawgiver and, in fact, later developments of some of the *poleis* such as Athens and Sparta did rely on great legal reformers.[1]

The formation of the *polis* appears at first not to be notably different from that which occurred in the creation of the archaic states of Mesopotamia: Tribal units, for reasons not entirely understood, banded together to form a territorial polity. And, following the Mesopotamian pattern again, the city-state became the source of social and political identification rather than kinship. In the case of the Greek *polis*, this identification became intense, so much so that while tribal units were maintained for various political and religious purposes, kinship ultimately ceased to have any real political significance.[2]

But appearances would be deceiving, for the historical evolution of the Greek *polis* was entirely different from the pattern of development in Mesopotamia. Most notably, citizenship replaced kinship as the basis of political organization, real active citizenship, not merely that passive subjectship characteristic of the archaic states of the Near East. Moreover, while the various city-states of Mesopotamia came and went, became empires, or were absorbed into empires, the basic political structure of theocratic kingship remained from the Sumerian period onward. Not so in

Greece. Here the various *poleis* underwent a series of constitutional transformations between the eighth and fourth centuries, typically, though not universally, from kingship to aristocracy, oligarchy, tyranny, and democracy.[3] As a result, the citizen of the Greek city-state had within historical memory experienced a wide variety of political forms, and was thus confronted with the obvious question: Which constitution of the state is best?

This question was all the more easily raised given the absence of a religious ideology premised upon unquestioning faith. The Greek gods had essentially local political meanings and, while important to the average citizen and to traditional legitimations of the state, they did not possess the awe inspiring character of the ancient deities of the Near East. As a consequence, while Greek religious ideology was resistant to rational modes of social and political analysis (Socrates was put to death for, among other things, "religious impiety"), it did not possess the overwhelming authority characteristic of religion in other ancient states.[4] Men were thus free to speculate on the ideal form of the state, and on the nature of political life. They could, for the first time in the ancient world, theorize about politics rather than merely confirm the existing theocratic ideology of court and temple.

From both a structural and ideological point of view, then, the Greek *polis* provided an environment conducive to the development of political theory, something not remotely existent anywhere else in the ancient world. And nowhere was this truer than in Athens, which saw its political development encompass the entire range of constitutional forms. Most important was the establishment of a democratic regime that prevailed throughout most of the fifth and fourth centuries BCE. It was against this background that Plato and Aristotle, Athens' greatest political thinkers, first created comprehensive theories of the state.

Note that the term used to describe democratic Athens is "regime" (*politeia* or *politeuma*) rather than state.[5] This is a crucial distinction in any understanding of the classical Greek polity, for while the *polis* was a state in the broad anthropological sense of the term—it was territorial with a centralized structure of government—it was clearly not a state in the modern sense. This is because the classical regime was characterized by the absence of any clear distinction between state and society, something absolutely fundamental to the modern state. Hence, in Athens, and throughout the Hellenic world, the politically dominant class did not merely have a preponderance of influence in the state; it controlled all the key institutions of state power and authority. The dominant class, in short, was the state or, more precisely, the regime. Hence, a democratic Athens was a constitutional form in which the poorer classes constituted the political structure of the *polis*, as an oligarchic regime was one constituted by the wealthy.

The history of the creation of the Athenian democracy is illustrative of its regime character. Beginning with constitutional reforms by the great lawgiver Salon in the early sixth century BCE, which initiated the process of diminishing the economic and political power of the aristocracy, a radically democratic constitution was instituted by Cleisthenes in 508/507 BCE. While subsequent reforms of the democratic system occurred in the fourth century, as well as some short lived oligarchic reactions in 411 BCE and 404 BCE, its basic structure endured until the subordination of Greece to the Macedonian Empire under Philip II and Alexander the Great.[6] Even then, the outer form of democracy, if not its substance, remained.

It requires no background in ancient history to grasp the implications of a state in the form of a classical regime. Class conflict and often outright class warfare lay at the very core of the Greek *polis*, for the political stakes involved were enormous. The politically dominant class utterly controlled the state and, as such, possessed not simply that preponderance of influence in determining public policy typical in other state formations, but in determining the entire structure of polity and society as well. The subordinate classes had no choice but to submit or, not infrequently, to rebel and wrest the state from the hands of the class enemy. The result was an intensity of political life and citizen involvement, particularly in democratic regimes, that remains one of the most significant, and admired, aspects of the classical Greek experience, but it was also the source of that class violence and political instability that ultimately destroyed the *polis*. The tendency to romanticize the Athenian democratic regime as the paradigm of citizen involvement and democratic ideals, a tendency that remains to this day despite the fundamental differences between the modern state and the classical city-state,[7] overlooks this negative aspect of the Greek experience.

In the long run, the negative side prevailed. Neither the Athenian democracy nor the *polis* itself survived. Although the success of Athens in the Persian wars led to Athenian dominance in the Delian League of Greek city-states, and then to an empire which threatened the autonomy of other *poleis*, most notably Sparta and her allies, the dominance was short lived. The great Peloponnesian War that followed (431–404 BCE) spelled the effectual end of the *polis* experience as the subsequent absorption of the Greek *polis* into the Macedonian Empire spelled its actual end. And while the Peloponnesian War demonstrated the inherent inability of the Greek city-states to unite into a larger political unit (not until after Alexander's death were experiments in federal forms of organization even attempted, far too late to change anything),[8] it demonstrated something even more fundamental: the inability of the *polis* to transcend class interests.

It is against this turbulent history that the emergence of classical Greek political thinking on the state must be understood. The first thing to be noted is that Greek political theory was foremost and always state (regime) theory. While this may seem obvious, much contemporary political science in fact rejects the state as a valid basis for political analysis, something that would have been inconceivable to the classical Greek thinkers. For the Greeks, to think about politics was to think about the state, and once the Greek state or *polis* is understood as a regime structure, the various theories of the classical city-state that were to emerge during the fifth and fourth centuries BCE become entirely understandable, even predictable.

The first of these, framed by peripatetic teachers of ethics and rhetoric who appeared around the middle of the fifth century, the Sophists, is perhaps the most obvious. Given that the politically dominant class determines the constitution of the *polis*, the state and its laws must be entirely conventional. Justice, then, is whatever this class says it is; in short, whatever is in its class interest. Power alone is the basis of the state and its laws, and the political leadership's claim to rule by universal standards of justice is nothing more than an ideology of legitimation that enshrines the values and interests of the ruling class.[9] The astute political leader, it follows, is one who understands these facts and lives by them.

The Sophists, needless to say, were terribly popular with wealthy young men who wished to enter politics and who were willing to pay their teachers a handsome sum to learn the political ropes.[10] The problem was that the Sophists' views were a prescription for disaster, as events were to demonstrate. The tragedy of the Peloponnesian War that Thucydides documented in his great historical classic of the same name was the outcome of precisely that self-interested power politics the Sophists praised. It is not without reason that the traditionalists despised the Sophists and executed Socrates as one of them, not grasping the crucial difference between the two. But tradition is already moribund once it is questioned, and it no longer could adequately legitimize the *polis*, particularly under a democratic constitution that allowed for a manifold of social and political opinions. What was required was a theoretical response to the Sophists' theoretical challenge.

Plato's *Republic*, the first fully developed political theory in the Western world, constituted not only an uncompromising rejection of the Sophist view of the state, but of the entire theory of politics that corresponded to it. The essence of Plato's argument is that the state is natural and, as such, constitutes an ethical community premised upon the maintenance of justice. Justice, therefore, is itself natural, an inherent quality of humanness and, what is absolutely crucial to the Platonic theory of the state, knowable. It is not simply the opinion (*doxa*) of the politically dominant class, as the Sophists maintained, but an intellectually comprehensible and universally applicable transcendent standard or *form* of rightness.

Plato's argument revolves around two fundamental ideas key to the classical theory of the state: that it is possible to derive a knowable theory of justice, and that the intellectually ideal Form of justice allows the theorist to derive an idealized perfect form of the state by which to judge the relative justice of actual states. The early Greek theories of the state were thus based upon an initial conception of the "ideally best state" as an ethical standard of political justice applied subsequently to a theory of the "best possible state" in actual political practice. The *Republic* is a theory of the ideally just state premised upon the perfect form of justice. Its function, therefore, is not practical, but critical: to demonstrate the inadequacy of the Sophist theory of the state and the injustice of Athenian democracy that, to Plato, seemed to be the perfect expression of Sophistical theory. Subsequent works by

Plato, *The Statesman* and most notably his final work, *The Laws*, deal with the best possible state that might be created under actual circumstances.

Given Plato's underlying epistemology, that justice is a knowable form, his theory of the ideally just state is logically predictable: It is a state ruled by those who possess knowledge of the transcendent form of justice, that is, by philosophers. The constitution of the ideally best state, then, is one based upon the maintenance of a division of labor that insures the continued rule of a philosophic elite. This is accomplished by subordinating other classes—the military elite and those performing economic functions—to philosophic rulership, and by denying to the rulers the key objects of self-regardiness, the family and private property. Any other constitution of the state would by definition be unjust since justice requires in the first instance knowledge of what justice is, something that philosophers alone possess. The unjust state, it follows, is characterized by a breakdown in this division of labor. The greater the breakdown, the more unjust the state will be, as Plato's subsequent analysis of unjust constitutions demonstrates.[11]

Plato's political thought may be said to constitute the essential paradigm of the classical theory of the state, the essence of which is the presumed unity of ethics and politics.[12] Ethical principles such as justice are knowable universals that, as universals, apply both at the individual and at the collective level. A state that embodies these principles makes it possible for the citizen to become ethically virtuous, just as a state that fails to embody them produces unethical (unjust) citizens. Since in the Socratic (Platonic, Aristotelian) view human fulfillment and happiness are possible only with the acquisition of ethical virtue, the proper function of the state is precisely the inculcation of virtue (*arete*) in its citizenry, and this requires in the first instance a state that is itself constitutionally virtuous.

While subsequent Greek, and Roman, political thought would differ with Plato on various epistemological issues, the unity of ethics and politics would remain its defining characteristic. So too would its belief that the small city-state or *polis* constitutes the ideal form in which to effect this unity, even during the later age of empire when it was little more than a nostalgic ideology that conformed not at all to political realities. With Plato this fact is sometimes overlooked since he is such an uncompromising critic of existing Athenian politics, relegating democracy to the most degraded (unjust) form of state except for despotism. But Plato's criticism does not call into question the essential structure of the *polis* as a classical regime. He makes no fundamental distinction between state and society; indeed, he compares the state with the family and the rulers to familial authorities, a comparison, however, that his greatest student, Aristotle, will reject.[13] His ideally just state remains one premised upon class rule in which the politically dominant class forms the constitution of the state. What has been changed is that the ruling class of philosophers rule in the public interest since their class interest—the acquisition of justice—is now identical to the public interest, that is, to the maintenance of a just constitution.

Certainly there is no overlooking Aristotle's attachment to the *polis*; indeed he is its preeminent theorist. His major work, the *Politics*, is a paean to the political life of the city-state, as is his *The Athenian Constitution*, the only surviving part of a collection and analysis of over 150 *poleis*.[14] And he shares with Plato, however else he may disagree, the core vision of the classical state: a polity existing by nature, constitutionally structured on knowable principles of justice, and organized to promote the public interest and ethical development of its citizenry. So profoundly did Aristotle accept these basic assumptions that, in the *Nicomachean Ethics*, he insists that ethical issues are ultimately political issues, and that it is the major function of the state to create the conditions by which citizens become virtuous.[15]

That the *polis* exists by nature is self-evident for Aristotle, for the associational life of human beings demonstrates that they are not only social beings but political animals (*zoon politikan*) as well. In Aristotle's analysis, these associations are the family, the village, and finally the state. The family and village exist for mere life, according to Aristotle, by which he means essentially economic survival and social well being. The state, however, exists for the good (ethical) life, the life of the citizen. And experience demonstrates, he argues, that human beings, having sufficiently developed their basic familial and economic associations, inevitably form into political associations for the attainment of the good (just) life.[16]

There is, however, a deeper epistemological principle involved in this process of state formation for Aristotle that clearly distinguishes his analysis from Plato's. While empirically the family and village are prior to the state, metaphysically the state is prior to both in that it constitutes the teleological evolution of an *a priori* principle of *Immanent Form*, in Aristotle's terms, the *final form* of human associational life. Indeed, the form of the state for Aristotle is the constitution. The principle of justice is thus inherent within the constitutional evolution of the state itself, and in the actual participation of the citizens in the political life of the state, not, as in Plato, in a transcendent principle apart from the state. As such, Aristotle's entire attitude toward the actual life of the *polis* is radically different from Plato's. In his ideal state, and even in the *Laws*, his less than ideal, Plato attempts to eliminate politics entirely.[17] The good life for Plato is subordination to the rule of a small philosophic elite. For Aristotle, however, it is some form of participatory self-rule. The citizen in Plato's state is, in fact, little more than a subject; in Aristotle's he is truly a citizen.

Moreover, it is the form of citizen rule that determines the constitutional structure of the state for Aristotle, and since in his definition a citizen is one who both "rules and is ruled in turn," the constitution is simply an arrangement of political offices that determines who the ruling citizens will be.[18] In this, Aristotle attempts to balance the citizen's demand for a role in rulership with a recognition that those with the greatest political virtue, that is, those most capable of maintaining a just state and developing just citizens, should have the greatest role in the leadership of the state. At the most elementary level, then, constitutions can be classified by the number of those allowed to rule—one, few, or many, but when the issue of virtue (justice) is added, the classification becomes sixfold, for rule by one, few, or many can be just or unjust. The just constitutions in Aristotle's classification are monarchy, aristocracy, and polity; the corresponding unjust constitutions are tyranny, oligarchy, and democracy.[19]

What is ultimately fundamental in Aristotle's constitutional theory, however, is the prevailing class structure. This turns out to be, in fact, the determining factor in Aristotle's theory of the state, for the broad categorization of rule by one, few, or many is really a reflection of types of class rule. Rule by one or few is inevitably rule by the minority of wealthy; rule by the many is rule by the majority of poor. This view, of course, is premised upon the classical regime where the constitution is literally an organization of class domination within the structure of the state itself. An oligarchic constitution is one in which the offices of state are reserved for the wealthy, as a democratic constitution is one reserved for the poorer classes.[20] The issue for Aristotle, then, as for Plato, is not whether or not class rule as such is legitimate, but whether or not that rule is just or unjust, in the public interest or in self-serving class interest.

The problem is how to determine the ideally best constitution, and how to structure it in such a way that it does not degenerate into mere class domination. While Aristotle's ideal constitution is most likely aristocracy, he recognizes that in most circumstances the best possible constitution is polity, that is, rule by a lawful majority.[21] Few states can hope to find the leadership to create a genuine aristocracy, much less Plato's ideal of philosophic rulership that Aristotle concedes to be the hypothetically ideally best state, but a hopelessly unreal and impractical one.[22] Polity, however, is a realistic possibility for a number of *poleis* and, in some cases, it can be structured to approach aristocratic ideals.

What makes Aristotle's theory of polity particularly interesting is that polity is a "mixed constitution," a concept whose development and elaboration must be credited to Aristotle although the basic idea pre-dates him, and that was enormously influential in the thought of subsequent classical political thinkers. Polity is a form of state in which the principles of oligarchy and democracy are combined. Certain political offices are reserved for the wealthier classes, but the involvement of the common people in the affairs of state is also assured. In this way, the interests of the respective classes are not only politically represented, but they also mutually check each other, something that does not happen when one class alone dominates the state. This scheme will not, of course, work under all circumstances, any more than will any other constitutional arrangement, although it will work in more cases than any other just constitution. In particular, it will not work in those cases in which the divide between rich and poor is too wide. For this reason, Aristotle argues that polity requires a substantial middle class to mediate and temper the potential conflict between rich and poor.[23]

Aristotle's theory of the mixed constitution would prove to be enormously influential in later medieval political thought, but even more influential would be his assertion that man is by nature a political animal. Despite the fact that the mixed constitution, and indeed the *polis* organized in any constitutional form, was a class form of state, Aristotle did not view the state as nothing more than an extension of the social order. On the contrary, the state—appropriately structured—creates the conditions for a genuine political space in which the search for justice transcends mere class interests. Those, the citizens, who participate in this search are, therefore, realizing their potential as political beings, as something greater and more noble than as members of subordinate social organizations such as class or family. Indeed, Aristotle's critique of Plato is that his ideal state is simply the family writ large and, as such, negates the essential political character of the *polis*. When recovered in the later Middle Ages, the idea of man's inherently political nature and, therefore, of the natural character of the polity, would allow for the first time in centuries the development of political theory as a subject worthy of study in its own right, apart from existing social structures and religious beliefs.[24]

Yet, despite Aristotle's emphasis on the autonomy of the political domain, there is lacking in his theory of state any clear notion of an impersonal territorial sovereignty. This was true as well for Plato and indeed all Hellenic thinkers, and the reason is clear enough. In the first place, they did not conceive of their polity primarily from a territorial point of view, but as a political community constitutionally defined in terms of class relationships. That their *polis* was a territorial entity was obvious enough, but it was not the important element in a theory of the state.[25] And, more importantly, beyond a general notion of the dominant class as a sovereign authority, they had no conception of sovereignty in any modern sense of the term because, unlike the modern state, the Greek city-state did not exist as a structure of power separate from society, that is, from the class system.[26] A developed theory of state sovereignty requires a relatively autonomous state structure, not simply Aristotle's concept of politics as an autonomous domain, for the issue of ultimate authority to be raised to the forefront of theoretical concern. This condition did not exist in the classical regime. It did in incipient form, however, in the Roman state, both republic and empire.[27]

The primary source of Roman state theory was the republic that, like the Greek *polis*, began as a small city-state ruled by kings. Kingship was eliminated toward the end of the sixth century BCE and replaced by a republican constitution (*res publica*), which, in its classical Roman sense, meant a limited form of popular rule premised upon a concern for the common-weal (the English equivalent of republic is commonwealth). Initially, the republic was heavily weighted in favor of the patrician aristocracy, but by the third century BCE the constitution had developed into a "mixed" form of class participation and representation. The problem of class conflict that had plagued the Greek *polis* plagued the Roman state no less, and the republican constitution that eventually developed came about as an attempt to satisfy demands by the plebeian lower classes for a share in political power. This was not unlike the constitutional solution to class conflict recommended by Aristotle in his theory of the mixed constitution.

If the solution was similar to Aristotle's, the specific features of the mature republican constitution were, however, entirely novel. It was not the creation of a Salon or some such great lawgiver, but of the accretion of various political innovations in response to class conflict and demands for greater political power on the part of the plebeians. As such, it was a complex mélange of assemblies and magistracies, that is, of popular and executive bodies. Two consuls, elected annually, constituted the supreme executive and military power in the state, and upon leaving office, they and a multiplicity of subordinate magistrates entered the Senate with lifetime tenures. While the Senate's authority was formally advisory, it was in fact the most important deliberative body in the state. This was almost inevitably so, for the Senate comprised Rome's most politically experienced leadership, a leadership drawn initially almost entirely from the nobility. Nonetheless, from the middle of the fourth century BCE the evolution toward an increasingly democratized system accelerated. By the early third century, the republic was, if not a fully developed democracy in the formal constitutional sense, certainly a state premised upon popular sovereignty, for the ultimate law making authority now resided in the people as a whole.[28]

It was against this constitutional background that the greatest of the Roman political thinkers, and the primary theorist and defender of the Roman Republic, Marcus Tullius Cicero (106–143 BCE), must be understood. Cicero's theoretical concerns were a direct reflection of the actual state of political affairs that, by his time, had become a threat to the survival of the republic itself. The inability of the senatorial classes to rise above their narrow class interests, coupled with the expansion of Rome into a vast empire, was shifting the basis of authority from the Senate and other republican institutions to the military. Those, like Caesar, who commanded the army, increasingly commanded the state.

Like Aristotle's polity, Cicero's theory of the republican constitution, developed in his *Republic* (titled in honor of Plato's work of the same name), is premised upon the constitutional structuring of class interests.[29] While class constitutes the fundamental political problem in creating the just state, it also constitutes the solution. A correct ordering of class interests within the constitution can create a mutual checking of those interests such that the public interest ultimately prevails. Cicero, in short, is an advocate of the classical mixed constitution that he terms the composite state, a concept derived, not from Aristotle, but from the noted historian of the Roman Republic, Polybius (ca.200–118 BCE). A Romanized Greek, Polybius had drawn upon Greek political thought and applied it to the actual evolution of the Roman state, arguing that the greatness of Rome was due to its mixed constitution.[30]

The specifics of Cicero's constitutional analysis are also very much within the classical tradition and reminiscent of both Plato and Aristotle. Hence, Cicero argues that the simple forms of constitution, while possessing their own specific virtues, too easily degenerate into their unjust, that is, class dominated counterparts: monarchy into tyranny, aristocracy into oligarchy, and democracy into ochlocracy or mob rule. The composite state, on the other hand, combines the virtues of the simple forms yet, by the mutual checking of class interests, eliminates their defects. In short, it constitutes an ideally just form of state. Applied to the Roman Republic as it had historically evolved, Cicero argues that the consuls, Senate, and peoples assemblies constitute respectively the monarchical, aristocratic, and democratic parts of the constitution.[31] To be sure, Cicero insists upon a preponderant role for the Senate, recognizing the need for wise and experienced leadership, but given his famous definition of a republic as "the people's affair,[32] he equally insists upon the real inclusion of the democratic element in his ideal state.[33]

What is genuinely original, however, and fundamentally important in the subsequent development of Western theories of the state, is not Cicero's theory of the composite republican constitution as such. This, in itself, is hardly new, but follows the already well-developed classical ideal of the mixed constitution tending toward aristocratic dominance. What is new and important is the legal form in which Cicero casts his theory. Above all, the republic is a state for Cicero because it is founded on law, and it is the ideally just state because it conforms to the principles of law. The composite form of the constitution is thus crucial because it insures the rule of law, that law will reflect the public interest rather than the interest of a particular class.

To be sure, the Greek *polis* promulgated law, but the *polis* was not thought of primarily in legal terms, certainly not as a legal structure apart from society. Plato's ideal republic is devoid of law, and his best possible state is based upon law only as a less than ideal solution to political organization. Aristotle views law in a more favorable light, but it is the principle of philosophic reason embedded in law that interests him, not the law as such. The Romans were unique in this regard: For them the law constituted the essence of the state, and they thought of the state above all as a legal structure created to promulgate law. Cicero, himself a lawyer, thought of the state in precisely these terms and, in the final analysis, his ideal republic is just because it conforms to law.

There is, however, a component to Cicero's legal theory that modifies in a crucial way his reliance on Roman positive law, one that clearly illustrates his debt to classical Greek thinking. Cicero insists that the legitimacy of positive law is ultimately dependent upon its conformity to natural law, a concept first articulated by the Stoics of the Hellenistic period. In response to the decline of the *polis* and the emergence of the Macedonian and Roman empire states, the Stoics asserted the existence of a universal law of moral reason, the law of the *cosmopolis* that transcends the positive law of the *polis*. This idea of natural law proved to have a profound effect on subsequent theories of the state, as it did initially on Cicero, for it placed Roman positive law within a broader ethical framework. Hence, given the importance of law to Cicero and other Roman thinkers, the idea of natural law allowed their theories of state to be framed in those same ethical terms characteristic of the classical conception of the state. Without the idea of natural law, Roman state theories would have been in the final analysis little more than institutional justifications for existing legal practices.

Thus, for Cicero, the state and its laws are ultimately legitimate to the extent that they conform to the broad principles of natural law, principles that are embodied in the laws of his ideal republic. Justice, in short, is now conceived as a matter of law, and it is to be understood and promulgated by the wise statesman as law. It is for this reason that Cicero states in his *Laws* that the magistrate "is a speaking law, and the law a silent magistrate."[34] More than this, the very concept of the republic itself is to be understood from the point of view of law, for ultimately, Cicero argues that "those who share law must also share Justice; and those who share these are to be regarded as members of the same commonwealth."[35]

This idea that the state is above all a legal structure marks a major advance in Western theories of the state. The modern theory of the state is premised upon this view, and it owes much to the recovery of Roman law in the late medieval period. Most importantly, the modern theory of sovereignty, the essence of the modern state, may in part be traced back to Roman law sources as well, for in making law the basis of the state the Romans, unlike the classical Greeks, were able to articulate something approaching a concept of state sovereignty.[36] This was because a state conceived as a legal entity could be viewed as something distinct from society, a power standing above the broader social order.

In Cicero, for example, the *res publica* or commonwealth is understood to be a political community constituted by "common agreement about law and rights" (note again the emphasis on law as the basis of the polity), but such a community, he argues, must be organized into some stable constitutional structure ruled "by some deliberating authority."[37] This he terms *civitas* and, unlike the Greek *polis*, *civitas* comes reasonably close to our meaning of the term "state." This is because, like Cicero, we understand that the state is a legal-corporate entity that is distinct from the larger society and polity.

This distinction between state and society is, of course, purely conceptual, for it is impossible to conceive of a *res publica* existing apart from a *civitas*. If a republic is composed of those who agree on law and rights, the state (constitution) is the actual institutionalization of that agreement without which the republic could not endure. The distinction is, nonetheless, crucial in the later development of a theory of sovereignty, for conceiving the state as an entity apart from society allows for the conceptualization of political power as something abstract and impersonal, a clear advance over the Greek concept of the regime.

Moreover, the state is now understood to be not only something distinct from society, but from government as well. Thus, the sovereign power of the state remains for Cicero irrespective of the type of government, be it monarchy, oligarchy, democracy, or his ideal composite form. The form of government, or constitutional form of state if you prefer, has no bearing on the existence or extent of sovereignty, but only on the manner in which it is exercised. For the Greeks, such a notion was inconceivable since the classical regime did not clearly distinguish between state and government any more than it did between state and society.

Related to this distinction between state and government is the separation of personal power from political office, another crucial element in the theory of the modern state. The offices of state are now conceived as repositories of abstract and impersonal power such that the person holding office exercises the authority of that office, but does not personally own it or legitimately employ power beyond the constitutional limitations inherent in it. Hence, the Romans separated *imperium* (the sovereign power of the state) and *potestas* (the limited power of a minor official) from *magistratus* (the magistrate or official exercising *imperium* or *potestas*). The two consuls of the republic, for example, exercised *imperium*, but the *imperium* resided in the office of consul, not in the person holding the office. The Greeks were never able to make this distinction; their term *arche* conflates office with officeholder.[38]

Ultimately, the Roman theory of sovereignty, not fully developed until the period of empire, rests upon the idea of consent, as it does in the modern state as well as a formal theory of contract. This is the unmistakable meaning of Cicero's claim that the Republic is based upon an "agreement about law and rights."[39] Since, in a republic at least, the agreement must be between all of the citizens of the state, the inevitable conclusion to be derived is that ultimate power resides in the people. And the idea that sovereign power is derived from the people remained a constant in Roman political thought, not only in the republican era but throughout the period of empire as well. Hence, the later emperor's claim to *imperium* was understood to be the result of the *Lex Regia*, the supposed legal transfer of power from the people to the emperor, as its predecessor the *Leges Curiatae* had transferred power to the republican magistrates.[40]

At a much later time, this would come to be understood as the theory of "popular sovereignty," a theory that may fairly be said to constitute the core ideology of legitimation of the modern state. The Romans, however, never grasped the full implications of the theory, nor did the later medieval thinkers and canonists who drew upon the Roman law for their political understanding. Hence, the *Lex Regia*, which almost compels the modern mind to presume that power granted by the people is revocable, is, until the late medieval period, assumed to be alienable, that the sovereign power granted the emperor is held in perpetuity. As such, the incipient doctrine of popular sovereignty that legitimized the emperor's exercise of *imperium* became in fact little more than an ideological cover for monarchical absolutism.

These political ideas developed early in the republican era, and the theory of sovereignty in particular, were further developed throughout the period of empire. The concept of natural law (*ius naturale*) continued to form the ethical foundation of the civil law (*ius civile*) as well as the "law of all peoples" (*ius gentium*), a law unique to the Romans that encompassed those generally accepted legal principles common to all the different groups that made up the empire.[41] Each of these branches of law, and the great Roman legal theorists commentaries on them such as those of Gaius in the second century CE, were incorporated into the *Corpus Iuris Civilis* in the sixth century by the Eastern Emperor Justinian.[42] Justinian's "code," which was recovered in the West in the late eleventh century, led to the rapid growth of Roman law studies, first at the University of Bologna and, by the middle of the twelfth century, at universities throughout Western Europe where the study of Roman law had become a standard part of the curriculum.[43] It was in this way that Roman political thought, embedded in the Roman law itself, was passed on to the West and influenced both late medieval and early modern political theory.

Apart from the law, Roman political thought added little to the subsequent evolution of Western political theory. The Stoic contribution was, of course, profound: Its concept of natural law played a crucial role in the development of Western political thought including the evolution of early modern state theories, as did its idea of a fundamental human equality. But, with the partial exception of Stoicism, Hellenistic political thinking was on the whole apolitical if not downright antipolitical. The absorption of the Greek *polis* into the Macedonian Empire under Alexander the Great destroyed the autonomy of the small city-state and the relevance of those classical theories that were premised upon it. The subsequent division of Alexander's empire did not alter the situation; the divisions were themselves large empires that were for the most part governed by oriental potentates in a manner reminiscent of the archaic states of the Near East. It is hardly surprising, therefore, that Hellenistic thinkers, to the extent they thought about politics at all, thought about it in essentially negative terms and sought virtue not within the domain of political activity, as Aristotle had recommended, but inwardly, within the self alone.[44] Such a radically subjective undertaking required withdrawal from political affairs, not political engagement, hardly a condition conducive to theories of the state and politics.

Philosophically, these apolitical and subjective tendencies took various forms, reaching their zenith in later Roman Stoicism and in the neo-Platonism of such thinkers as Plotinus (CE 205–270).[45] It was in the domain of religious experience, however, that these tendencies took their most complete form, for the religious attitude was replacing the philosophical quest, a mark of how fundamentally inadequate classical thought was to the realities of empire. The concept of the ideally just state that had formed the basis of classical theorizing made less and less sense in an empire ruled by an absolute monarch and drifting toward military rule. The ideal, if it existed at all, was becoming a spiritualized concept and, ultimately, a religious dogma.

It is here, in religious thought that the final contribution of Rome is made to the development of state theory. The adoption of Christianity as the official state religion in the fourth century CE altered not only the course of Western history, but also the entire framework of political thinking on the state. While primitive Christianity exemplified the ultimate withdrawal from politics, more radically so than the spiritualized Hellenistic and neo-Platonic philosophies of the later empire, its acceptance as the religion of the empire compelled Christian thinkers to address the issue of the state. In this, the foundations of medieval political thought were laid.

Chapter Four

The Christian Republic

If contemporary political science is unique in developing stateless political theories against the background of a fully developed state system, medieval political thinking is notable for the opposite reason: It possessed the elements of a state theory without the existence of a state structure. These were derived initially from Roman sources and, later, from classical Greek sources as well. But political consciousness invariably reflects the existing form of polity, and when Greco-Roman concepts were employed to comprehend political realities now far removed from their original political context, particularly in conjunction with the futile attempt to recreate the Roman Empire in the West, their original meanings were inevitably distorted. Nonetheless, these concepts proved ultimately crucial in the early development of the theory of the modern state.

In political terms, what characterized the medieval period was not simply the absence of the state, but the existence of multiple centers of authority that were in a more or less continuous state of conflict over the scope and jurisdiction of their authority. In the most general sense, this conflict is best described as a conflict between *regnum* and *sacerdotium*, that is, between kingship and priesthood. While the conflict is often described as one between church and state, *regnum* and *sacerdotium* is a more accurate description of the medieval political situation. Apart from the fact that the state did not exist in the medieval period, a state–church conflict implies a conflict between distinct and separate political organizations, something not characteristic of the struggle between *regnum* and *sacerdotium*.[1] The conflict was between institutionally intertwined organizations over their respective role and authority in governing what eventually became known as the *Respublica Christiana*: a diversity of European peoples possessing a variety of legal and political structures but sharing a common religious faith.[2]

The significance of this conflict can be understood only from its historical origins in the Roman Empire of the fourth century. When Emperor Constantine recognized Christianity as a legitimate religion within the empire in 313 CE, and subsequently Theodosius the Great made it the official state religion in 393 CE, the advantages to the church were obvious. The disadvantages, however, were not as immediately apparent, for the emperor was not only the supreme secular ruler, but *Pontifex Maximus* (chief priest), as well. As a consequence, Constantine and future Christian emperors were directly involved in religious affairs. The emperor assembled church councils, settled ecclesiastical disputes, and was intimately involved in the articulation of religious doctrines and articles of faith. And herein lay the root of future conflicts between secular rulers and ecclesiastical leaders that was to characterize the entire medieval period.

It is important to bear in mind that this unity of kingship and priesthood was not unique to Rome but a fundamental characteristic of archaic and Hellenistic monarchies as well. It was quite natural, therefore, for the emperor of Rome to abrogate to himself priestly powers and, initially, given the authority the church gained in its alliance with the Roman state, this all worked well enough. It did not work in the longer run, however, because Christianity was not a state religion dedicated to the preservation of exist- ing political values and structures as were the pagan religions of Rome and earlier states. It was a profoundly otherworldly faith in a risen God, and its earthly agents were priests whose authority came from Christ through the apostle Peter. The "Petrine commission," based on the words of the Gospel of St. Matthew in which Christ founds his church on the leadership of Peter, and gives to him the "keys to the kingdom of heaven,"[3] precluded the claim of secular rulers to priestly authority.

The issue came to a head in the medieval period, and it was the church itself that lay the groundwork for a conflict that it ultimately would lose. With the final collapse of the Western Roman Empire in the fifth century as a result of the barbarian invasions, and its continuing isolation from the eastern branch that Constantine had created (the future Byzantine Empire), the church alone remained a viable political organization with roots in Roman civilization.[4] Hence, when it initiated its proselytizing mission in Western Europe, even before the empire's final disintegration, it inevitably attempted to spread this civilization, including its political ideals, to Germanic peoples whose political organization and understanding were at best at the level of chieftainship and in many ways not much beyond an extended tribalism. The Germanic (and Celtic) kings were enmeshed in kin- ship structures and their authority, even when hereditary, was essentially of a charismatic kind. They were war leaders, distributors of booty, and judges, and they ruled by their ability and charisma.[5]

From the perspective of a church that had come of age under an emperorship premised upon maintaining the faith, the Germanic concept of kingship was utterly inadequate. Hence, early on the church began to incul- cate Roman and biblical (Hebraic-Davidic) concepts of kingship among those Germanic leaders who had become Christianized. It taught that king- ship is a sacred office, that political authority is derived from God, and that the king rules by divine right.[6] As a consequence, the king should rule as God would have him, not as a barbarian war leader, but justly and for the common good, which meant, above all else, as defender of the faith.

The problem in Romanizing and christianizing Germanic kingship, while necessary to the church's mission and survival, was that it created a potential rival source of authority. Potentiality became actuality when on Christmas day 800 CE the pope crowned the Frankish king Charlemagne Emperor. The Carolingian Empire that Charlemagne ruled, which included a large area of Western Europe, was far in advance of the earlier Germanic tribal systems, but it was no Roman Empire, and the political consciousness of the ruling elite was far removed from the state consciousness of the old Roman elite. When Charlemagne died, his empire was divided among his sons as if it were their personal property rather than a state in the Roman sense.[7]

Nonetheless, what the church had created was a myth of a universal empire in the West that would come to shape the entire political landscape of the Middle Ages. The conflict between *regnum* and *sacerdotium* would last for centuries as a conflict between church and empire, ultimately between church and emerging territorial state, and it would take the form of a struggle between two monarchs, pope and emperor and later between pope and national monarchs, each of whom would at various times assert both kingly and priestly powers. Among the many paradoxes of the medieval political situation, surely the most notable is that this struggle was based upon a conception of kingly and imperial rule rooted in a political situation far removed from the realities of medieval life.

For Christian political thinkers, the dilemma was clear enough: how to recognize the divine origin of kingly authority and the legitimacy of the secular polity without conceding religious functions to the "state" and priestly authority to the king. The problem did not arise prior to Constantine, for so long as the state was hostile to the faith, the church could dispense with it as something worthy of theoretical or practical concern. Christ's injunction to "render unto Caesar the things which are Caesar's; and unto God the things that are God's,"[8] was sufficient for the faithful whose pilgrimage here on earth was soon to end and whose reward in the afterlife was no longer contingent, as both Plato and Cicero had asserted, upon service to the secular state.[9]

Once Christianity became the official religion of the Roman Empire, the primitive ideal could no longer be maintained. The church would have to come to terms with the state, and this required a rethinking of its inherently otherworldly and antipolitical assumptions. The problem was that both classical Greek and Roman political theory were inadequate to the purposes of thinking politically in Christian terms. Classical thought had neither provisions for a church structure apart from the state, nor an orientation that was spiritual and otherworldly. Initially, at least, an entirely new kind of state theory would be required.

St. Augustine (354–430 CE), the most important political thinker of the early church, produced the first comprehensive Christian theory of state, one that remained paradigmatic until the recovery of Aristotle in the thirteenth century. Developed most consistently in his monumental *City of God*, Augustine's state theory is thoroughly theocratic. Political authority is divinely ordained and, as such, absolute. There is no citizenship as the Greeks and Romans understood it, only subjectship. In conformity to the Pauline view that "there is no authority except from God,"[10] obedience is required in all circumstances save where the law requires violating the precepts of the faith, and even then passive disobedience alone is justified. And while Augustine concedes that a Christian king or emperor is the ideal, it is not a requirement for the legitimacy of the state. All political authority is divinely ordained, pagan no less than Christian. "The same God gave power . . . to Augustus and to Nero . . . and . . . the throne to Constantine the Christian, and also to Julian the Apostate"[11] St. Augustine emphasizes, and therefore all rule by the will of God.

Augustine quite literally turns the classical view on its head. In his analysis, the state is a conventional structure of power and law the purely coercive will of the monarch. The state exists because of the necessity of social order, not as the embodiment of moral virtue, as the classical unity of ethics and politics. For Augustine, virtue is now an otherworldly matter; it is reserved for those of the faithful who have been saved by the grace of God, those who belong to the "heavenly city," and its realization is to be had only within the church. Hence, it really makes no difference who the ruler is, Christian or pagan, since the constitution of the state is now irrelevant to the moral development of the subjects. Indeed, so irrelevant is it that Augustine asks, "as for this mortal life, which ends after a few days' course, what does it matter under whose rule a man lives, being so soon to die?."[12]

Needless to say, such a pessimistic view of the state is not one conducive to the development of a theory that holds out much promise for, in Aristotle's terms, the attainment of the "good life." But it is a view premised upon a radically different conception of human nature than that held by the classical thinkers. For Augustine, all human beings are by nature evil, born to original sin, and thereby manifest a continual propensity toward evil despite knowledge of natural and divine law. As a consequence, the state itself originates, not in Aristotle's natural evolution from forms of sociability to structures of political community, but in an agreement borne of necessity to impose a structure of power on a sinful humanity whose unlimited desires for the things of this world, the "earthly city," would otherwise reduce the human condition to what Thomas Hobbes would later term a perpetual "state of war."

It is certainly the case that Augustine accorded a higher status to the church than to the empire and secular authority because he accorded a higher spiritual end or purpose to the church. Some later thinkers even tended to identify the "city of God" with the church rather than as a metaphor for the "saved" as Augustine had intended. Nonetheless, Augustine legitimized the secular state in unquestionably theocratic and absolutist terms, and in this provided early Christianity with a workable, if deeply pessimistic, theory of the state. He did not, however, resolve the inherent problem of multiple authorities, indeed if anything he intensified it. Secular authority could, and did, employ Augustine to proclaim its divine right to rule in its subsequent struggles with the papacy.

What was required to transcend this impasse, of course, was some concept of sovereignty that would eliminate the dual claims to supreme political authority on the part of pope and emperor. And this is precisely the one political concept that the medieval mind could not comprehend, for both in terms of Roman concepts of kingship that the church itself had promulgated, as well as Augustinian theocratic justifications of secular and sacred rule, the claims to ultimate political authority were equally valid on both sides. While Augustine, of course, insisted upon the ultimate authority of the church in spiritual matters, something that was largely accepted by all during the medieval period, this did not resolve the issue. Indeed, it stood in the way of developing a fully explicit theory of sovereignty, for while the church repeatedly attempted to employ the superiority of spiritual ends as a claim to ultimate political authority, the actual development of a theory of sovereignty required, as we shall see, precisely the elimination of thinking in terms of final ends and theocratic rule.

But even apart from these theoretical difficulties, there was a very practical reason why the theory of sovereignty could not be developed during the medieval period. Following the collapse of the Carolingian Empire in the face of Viking invasions, and the consequent emergence of feudalism in much of Europe in the ninth century, most notably in France and subsequently in England as well, the state simply ceased to exist. Even on the assumption that Augustine's theocratic views could ultimately evolve into a fully developed theory of sovereignty under a powerful secular monarchy, feudalism clearly prevented such a possibility. The feudal monarch looked not at all like the absolute theocratic ruler posited in Augustinian and Roman sources, but as little more than one private bearer of power among others claiming equal authority within their own feudal domains.[13] And this was inevitable, for feudalism was premised upon a profound decentralization and privatization of social, economic, and political power in response to external crisis that could not effectively be responded to in any other way.[14]

The situation was further complicated by the fact that the church itself became thoroughly implicated in the feudal system.[15] Without a central authority to protect it, the church was required to engage in feudal contracts with various secular authorities to provide for defense of church lands and properties. Hence, the problem of dual authority persisted, but now in an increasingly complex web of feudal relationships that rendered the solution more remote than ever. And it was precisely these relationships that brought the issue to a head in the great controversy surrounding lay investiture (ecclesiastical appointment). The emperor since the time of Constantine had been directly involved in church affairs, and with the revival of the empire under Otto I (912–973), king of Germany, popes were made and unmade by succeeding German emperors. This power of ecclesiastical appointment of the pope and subordinate bishops by the emperor was paralleled at lower levels. Kings and powerful feudal lords had become accustomed to appointing their candidates to clerical office, from bishop to parish priest, within their own feudal domains. The result was a scandalous corruption of the church and, ultimately, under a resurgent papacy, the church responded. In

1075, Pope Gregory VII (1073–1085), through the authority of a church synod, abolished lay investiture.

The struggle that ensued between Gregory and then Emperor Henry IV over lay investiture laid bare the fundamental flaw in the continued existence of dual theocratic authorities within Christendom, for the dispute was not merely over a difference in policy, not even over long-standing feudal privileges, but over the claims of the emperor (and subordinate monarchs as well) to an autonomous theocratic authority within his own political sphere. Hence, Henry responded by rejecting not only Gregory's decision but, more seriously, the legitimacy of his papacy. Gregory in turn excommunicated Henry and relieved his subjects of fealty to him. Henry recanted, but a civil war in Germany resulted and a new king was enthroned. Henry was excommunicated again, but prevailed over his rival's claim to rule and gained the support of the German bishops who elected a rival pope claiming that Gregory's papacy was not legitimate. Henry then marched on Rome, installed his pope, and Gregory died in exile.

The conclusion to be drawn from the investiture dispute was clear enough: If the pope could depose the emperor, the emperor could depose the pope, and in either case the justification would be on the same theocratic grounds. Professor Hinsley has correctly summarized the situation by noting that the struggle was in reality between two popes, but it would be just as accurate to say that it was a struggle between two kings.[16] Both were monarchs, and both ruled theocratically. So long as this dual and equivalent structure of authority existed there was no final solution possible, either practically or theoretically. Henry's success was temporary, and ultimately the papacy would reassert itself. Hence, the resolution to the conflict over lay investiture ended in a compromise, the Concordat of Worms (1122), in which bishops were to be spiritually invested by the church in accordance with canon law, but the feudal temporalities that attached to the bishopric were to be granted as a feudal privilege through an act of homage to the emperor.[17]

The political implications of the compromise, of course, were obvious: Neither pope nor emperor was able to assert final and supreme authority within Christendom. And since the issue was now inescapably the issue of supreme authority, the compromise did not end the conflict. That the papacy ultimately triumphed over the empire (only to lose to the emerging territorial state) is, for our purposes, not the important fact. What is important is that the ensuing debate between pope and emperor laid the theoretical basis for the later development of the early modern state. And in this debate, both papacy and empire drew upon theoretical resources that went back, not only to the early church in the West, but to the Roman Empire itself.

For its part, the church early on came to recognize the potential danger to its status posed by the existence of an autonomous empire, however much it desired that the empire exist. As a consequence, Pope Gelasius I (492–496) attempted to delimit the scope of imperial power by asserting the superiority of priesthood to kingship. Of the two powers, Gelasius maintained, the spiritual is higher in dignity and importance than the secular and thus possesses greater authority. Later, in the eleventh century, this Gelasian dualism would be expressed in the famous allegory of the two swords, derived from the Gospel of Luke (Luke 22:38), in which the respective powers, material and spiritual, were distinguished. While the idea of two swords legitimized the authority of both *regnum* and *sacerdotium* (while maintaining the superior status of the spiritual, as did Gelasius's initial dualism)[18] it proved to be enormously ambiguous, and subsequent popes and emperors interpreted it in light of their own political interests.[19] Emperors employed it to assert independence from papal meddling in their affairs as the material sword rightfully belonged to them, while the papacy continued to assert that the superiority of sacred over temporal authority, even claiming that the material sword had been given to secular authority by the church.[20]

It is important to stress that the ambiguity of the Gelasian and subsequently two swords doctrines was not merely a failure of theoretical precision, not even primarily that, but a reflection of the inherent difficulty in integrating two theocratic rulers within the same Christian Republic. The Emperor was *rex sacerdotus*, king and priest, as the pope was priest and king. As such, religious and secular affairs could not be kept separate. The ambiguity was simply the inevitable manifestation of this fact, as the later investiture dispute was a stark illumination of it. It was, in short, the result of the absence of a supreme authority within Christendom and, consequently, of the inability to formulate a clear and consistent theory of sovereignty.

The problem was that the struggle over supreme authority was quite impossible to resolve so long as the debate revolved around the issue of higher ends or purposes. Secular rulers could and did concede a higher status to the *sacerdotium* and to the spiritual life it embodied, but it did not then follow that the pope had a claim to final authority over secular rulership. This was all the more the case given that secular rulers, territorial monarchs as well as the emperor, claimed theocratic authority even during the early feudal period when kingship was at its weakest. This certainly was the position of Otto I when he asserted his control of the papacy, and it remained the position of the rising national monarchies after the papacy had defeated the empire and laid its claims to universal monarchy over all of Christendom.

In theoretical terms, the way out of the impasse would require thinking of the political community from some other perspective than the teleology of higher ends and purposes. This is precisely what occurred at the end of the Middle Ages, most notably in the political thought of Marsilius of Padua, but until the actual political situation changed such thinking was beyond the capacity of medieval thinkers. Until the Christian Republic of dual theocratic rulership began to disintegrate with the rise of the national-territorial kingdoms, the long struggle between pope and emperor would continue to be framed in the theoretical language of ultimate ends.

This does not mean, however, that within this broad ideological context important theoretical advances were not made. Granted that the issue of supreme authority within Christendom could not be theoretically resolved in terms acceptable to all sides, the claim to such authority still required settling upon its locus and extent. Even if it could be demonstrated that the church ought to be politically superior to the empire and subordinate temporal authority, as the late medieval popes were asserting, where does this authority reside, and what, if any, are its limits? Does it inhere in the papacy, the College of Cardinals, or in the body of the faithful as a whole, and is it absolute or limited, alienable or inalienable? In fact, it was in response to these issues that the real medieval contribution to the theory of the early modern state was first articulated, for debates over church governance were carried into debates over secular governance as well, inevitably so given that *regnum* and *sacerdotium*, sacred authority and secular, were deeply intertwined institutions. It is for this reason that issues of medieval church governance become important in understanding the theoretical evolution of the early modern state.

It was the full recovery and development of Roman law in the twelfth century that provided the theoretical insights required to deal with these issues, as the subsequent recovery of Aristotle in the late twelfth and thirteenth centuries made pushing beyond the domain of legal thought to that of a pure political theory possible. It was, in fact, the combining of these two classical traditions, legal and theoretical, while incapable of producing a fully explicit theory of the state within the context of medieval political realities, that made possible such theoretical innovation at the close of the Middle Ages.

The recovery of Roman law, that is, of the entire *Corpus Iuris Civilis* (*The Body of the Civil Law*) of the Eastern Emperor Justinian (527–565 BCE), came to the medieval world first, however, and its importance cannot be overstated.[21] What prevented the West from having full access to this work earlier than the twelfth century was its isolation from the Eastern Empire and its concomitant disintegration into feudal localism. But once recovered, the *Corpus Iuris Civilis* soon became the center of a thriving intellectual life, first at the University of Bologna, then elsewhere throughout Europe.[22]

It is important to recall that Roman law had evolved within both a republican and, subsequently, imperial state structure, the latter premised upon a clearly defined legal conception of sovereignty. As such, it tended to confirm, initially at least, the emperor's assertion of sovereign authority (*imperium*), but because of its republican origins it did so on the basis of an incipient doctrine of popular sovereignty embedded in the *Lex Regia*, what came to be interpreted as an irrevocable legal grant of sovereign authority from the Roman people.[23] When the center of power shifted to the papacy, it adopted these Roman law principles of sovereignty. Not only was the pope's authority asserted to be equivalent to the emperor's in its theocratic assumption of divine origin, but also the fundamental legal principle inherent in the Roman conception of sovereignty, "*quod principi placuit legis habet vigorem*"[24]—"what has pleased the prince has the force of law." This claim to supreme law making authority, the fundamental premise of any theory of sovereignty, was encapsulated in the papacy's claim to a *plentitudo potestatis* (fullness of power).[25]

There was, however, another principle of Roman law, "*quod omnes tangit, ab omnibus comprobetur*"—"what touches all should be approved by all."[26] This initially was simply a rule of private corporation law, but canon lawyers extended it in the early thirteenth century to mean that acts of the pope, or subordinate ecclesiastical rulers, required the approval of a church council.[27] Setting aside for the moment who would constitute such a council, it is clear that the Roman concept of what in effect had become a doctrine of ruler sovereignty (the emperor was not only the source of law but above the law and, as such, not bound by it) would somehow have to be made compatible with a potential doctrine of popular sovereignty also embedded in Roman law.[28] Much of the debate within the church following the resurgence of the papacy revolved around precisely this issue: Is the locus of supreme authority the pope, a council, or some combination of both?, and the various answers that emerged would later influence thinking on the legitimate locus of sovereign authority within the early modern state.

It was primarily canon lawyers, under the influence of these new Roman legal conceptions, who provided the major impetus of theoretical innovation in this regard, and here another crucial development in legal theory occurred in the mid-twelfth century: the publication of the *Concordantia Discordantium Canonum* (The Reconciliation of Differing Canons).[29] Gratian, a monk and scholar at Bologna where Roman law was first studied in the West, produced this great collection of church law based on papal edicts or "decretals" and known simply as the Decretum. It is likely if not certain that the inspiration for Gratian's work was the *Corpus Iuris Civilis*; but it is certain that the *Decretum* was influenced by Roman law and incorporated some of its concepts, including that of the *ius naturale* (natural law).[30] And, just as the *Corpus Iuris Civilis* produced a whole scholarship of civilian commentators or glossaters, the *Decretum* soon produced an equivalent group of canonists known as the decretists, and later, after further papal edicts of the thirteenth and fourteenth centuries were collated into the *Books of Decretals*, the decretalists.

It was not only the idea of natural law that the canonists derived from the Romans however, but, as importantly, the private law of corporations, a unique invention of Roman jurisprudence that was almost as revolutionary in political thought as the subsequent recovery of Aristotle. The corporation (*universitas*) constituted a fictitious legal person representing a group of people not as individuals but as an organic or "corporate" whole. As such, and despite its basis in private law, the corporation offered entirely new ways of thinking about the locus of authority within the church and, by extension, in any body politic.[31]

Indeed, the very notion of a body politic was alien to medieval thinkers until the later Middle Ages when organic analogies began to be applied to the polity, most notably in the *Policraticus* of John of Salisbury (*ca*.1115/1120–1180), the most important of the pre-Aristotelian thinkers of his era. As a loyal ecclesiastic, John defends the papal claims to supremacy within Christendom, but he does so with a new awareness of the organic basis of the political order. Indeed, the church provided an ideal model of a *universitas* or corporate entity, for it had come to be conceived as the "mystical body of Christ," not merely as a *societas* of individual faithful. Thus, while John defends monarchy as the ideal form of government, the traditional medieval view, he at the same time understands the monarch to "bear the public person." That is, he understands the monarch to be an officer of the political community such that his acts represent the *universitas* or corporate community, not merely his own personal will.[32]

But this was not the only conclusion to be derived from the organic-corporate model, for canonists of the later twelfth and thirteenth centuries not only began to give a firmer legal basis to the corporate view than had John, they began as well to grant a greater autonomy to the *universitas*. Applied to church organization, this could mean, in its most radical formulation, that the pope is subordinate to the church as a whole (i.e., to a representative church council). More typically, it meant that the pope's theocratic authority must be exercised with the assent of the council.[33] Whatever formulation was developed, however, it is clear that the corporate-organic model of the body politic, whether applied to the church or to the secular realm (or to the relationship between the two) opened entirely new vistas of political thought heretofore limited by the prevailing Augustinian theocratic perspective. And, as we have noted, the canonists' purely church centered theories of governance would soon be carried over to debates about the locus and extent of secular authority within the emerging state.

One crucial example of these expanded political debates revolves around the issue of representation. The pure theocratic model requires no concept of representation since the pope or king rules by "divine right," but a corporate model clearly does. Again, canon lawyers, through the vehicle of church law, took the theoretical lead. They developed a principle of representation that gave to the representative *plena potestas* (full power) or *plena actoritas* (full authority) to make decisions binding on the corporate body as a whole.[34] This was not yet a fully developed democratic theory of representation, of course, since the representative body was understood to constitute an elite of the more knowledgeable and judicious members of the community (the *maior et sanior pars* or "greater and sounder part").[35] It nonetheless constituted a great advance in political thought that ultimately influenced subsequent thinking on representative institutions in the secular realm as well. Indeed, the link between canon and Roman law, that is, between ecclesiastical and secular political thought, had become pervasive.[36]

Moreover, this concept of representation was premised upon an as yet undeveloped but potentially revolutionary theory of consent. Given a corporate view, the representative body ultimately represents the polity as a corporate whole. This is logically inescapable, but it follows almost as logically then that the representative body exists only by the consent of the body politic. Carried to its logical conclusion, as it ultimately would be, the concept of consent would utterly delegitimize the theocratic basis of the pope's, and emperor's, claims to supreme rulership since the members of the body politic would now constitute the source of authority rather than God. It could lead to a radically democratic (republican) concept of the polity that the canonists wished to avoid. This, of course, assuming that the original authority of the people is inalienable, an obvious and easy assumption for us, but one that required a reinterpretation of the *Lex Regia* of Roman law that had supposedly transferred authority irrevocably from the Roman people to the emperor and, by extension in canonist legal theory, to the pope.[37] Such a reinterpretation began to be made as early as the twelfth century by civilian glossators, a reinterpretation the more easily made given the ancient Germanic tradition of community consent to legislative innovation.[38] And the ultimate impact of this reasoning would be upon neither pope nor emperor, but upon the monarchs of those rising territorial kingdoms that would soon render the *Respublica Christiana* utterly obsolete.

But herein also lay the fundamental limitation of political thinking in the early stages of the High Middle Ages: It was not only derived almost entirely from legal sources, but from legal sources that were far removed from the political realities of late medieval life. This was not only because law provided the only mode of political thinking available to men who had, apart from the narrow confines of Augustine's theocratic views, little else available, but also because all law promulgated by theocratic authority, and this included Roman as well as canon law, was considered sacred.[39] It is not surprising, therefore, that in a polity ideologically devoted to the sacred, whether in *regnum* or *sacerdotium*, that law understood to be itself sacred should constitute the essential source of political knowledge.

The genuine uniqueness of this mode of political thinking, as professor Ullmann has observed, is that it constitutes a reversal of the relationship between law and ideology characteristic of both classical and modern political thought.[40] We, no less than the ancient Greeks, understand the law to be a reflection of the underlying ideology or theory of legitimation: Laws protecting property, for example, are derived from an ideological or theoretical justification of property rights. To the medieval mind, however, it was the other way around. Property rights were derived from the law, not the law from an ideology of property rights. Even so abstract a principle as natural law, which could stand on its own as a foundational ethics, was extracted from the *Corpus Iuris Civilis* and derived its authority as much from that fact as from any purely theoretical justification.

It is not surprising, then, despite its limitations, and however odd it appears to the modern mind, that until the recovery of Aristotle the issue of supreme authority, its locus and extent, was approached primarily through the vehicle of law. In this, the High Middle Ages is reminiscent of ancient Rome: Its political theory was largely derived from legal principles, the reverse order of both classical Greek and modern political thought. At the same time, the difference between the two must not be overlooked. In Rome, the law was framed within a state structure; in the Middle Ages it was applied in the absence of a state and to institutions unknown in the ancient world. Distortions of the original meanings of legal and political terminology were inevitable.

Despite, therefore, the extraordinary creativity of both canonists and civilians in extracting such crucial concepts as body politic, consent, and representation from ancient and sacred law, the purely legal approach was too confining for the development of a comprehensive science of politics. Not only did the law set boundaries on the extent to which the secular could be conceived apart from the sacred, it also restricted political speculation to legal principles that could not adequately encompass the full range of theoretical issues. This is to say, in effect, that political theory, that is, theory conceived as an autonomous discipline not subordinated to law or religious injunctions, cannot exist apart from the state.[41] And it was the classical Greeks who, against the background of their small city-states, first developed an autonomous political theory and who, in the thirteenth century, provided medieval thinkers with the basic outlines of a pure theory of politics.

The key thinker in this regard was Aristotle. The recovery of his works in the late twelfth century, and most notably the recovery of the *Politics* (and *Ethics*) in the early thirteenth century, revolutionized medieval political thought. And certainly the most revolutionary idea was Aristotle's claim that the state (*polis*) is natural, that man is therefore a political animal. More than this, Aristotle asserted that the *polis* constituted the highest end of human sociability, and that it was therefore in political activity that the "good life" was to be obtained—the good life understood in typically Greek terms to be the ethically just life. Such reasoning, of course, ran counter to the entire medieval way of thinking about the political order. It clearly ran counter to the Augustinian ideology that undergird the theocratic assumptions of the church, indeed of temporal authority as well, and carried to its logical conclusion, as it ultimately would be, it constituted a justification for a purely secular form of polity and a strictly worldly form of political theorizing.

It is not surprising, therefore, that the church's reception of Aristotle was not initially enthusiastic, and in the longer run its first instincts would prove to be not entirely misplaced. Indeed, the threat of a purely secular Aristotelianism remained a constant concern of the church, as its ongoing condemnation of Averroism indicated.[42] So powerful and liberating were the political concepts introduced by Aristotle, however, that they could not be suppressed.[43] What was required from the church's perspective, therefore, and more generally from the perspective of all theocratic authorities of the late medieval period, was the incorporation of Aristotle into a broader Christian framework, no easy task given Aristotle's radically secular, pagan, and state centered views.

St. Thomas Aquinas (1225–1274), more than any other thinker before or after, accomplished this objective so well in light of the ideological constraints imposed by the church and other theocratic authorities that his philosophical works soon became the orthodox position. And the reason for Thomas's success is not difficult to discern. He was able to resolve the fundamental problem raised by Aristotelian philosophy: The apparent incompatibility between the natural world and the supernatural. Indeed, the fulcrum of the entire Thomistic system, political theory included, rested upon his resolution of this problem.[44]

In its essentials, Thomas asserts that the divine source of human reason establishes the fundamental unity of natural and supernatural goods. Aristotle was correct in positing reason as the defining characteristic of the species and in recognizing that reason ethically legitimizes the natural goods of this world. But reason legitimizes the natural because reason and nature are God given, part of a larger rational order, not because either stand on their own as the sole and final source of human value. For Thomas, the domain of the supernatural constitutes this final source, and while it is higher than the natural world and unaided reason, it cannot be incompatible with either since both the natural and supernatural are simply different aspects of the same divine order. Reason, therefore, cannot contradict faith, nor philosophy theology.[45] Indeed, properly used, philosophic reason must of necessity lead one to faith, and in his monumental work of scholastic dialectic, the *Summa Theologica*, Thomas employs both to demonstrate the consonance of human knowledge and divine purpose.[46]

This reasoning Thomas applied to the political domain no less than to the other areas of human existence. Hence, following Aristotle's *Politics*, Thomas asserts that the state is natural and that citizenship (not mere theocratic subjectship) is indeed a good and a means to moral improvement, both individually and socially. As a consequence, the constitutional structure of the polity becomes once again important for, in line with classical analysis, it determines the level of citizen participation and the corresponding form of political justice. *On Kingship* is Thomas's major work in this regard, and follows the general format of Aristotle's constitutional classification, although not entirely his methodology or conclusions.[47] For Thomas, monarchy is the ideally best polity, not only for purely political reasons, but because it reflects God's monarchical rule of the universe, an idea that would have been utterly alien to Aristotle.[48]

It is clear from this analysis that the political community, a natural good apprehended through human reason, is embedded in a larger supernatural order. Hence, as reason points to the necessity of justice within the political community, it is led to recognize the supernatural source of all justice that constitutes our final and complete end as human beings. This same perspective Thomas applies to his theory of law which, following Aristotle, he defines as a rule of moral reason not, as in Augustine, merely a mechanism of coercive control.[49] Hence, in the *Summa* where the theory is most consistently developed, human or positive law is subordinated to natural law (moral reason), but natural law is now understood to be rooted in the eternal law of God that regulates both the physical and moral order of the universe.[50] In Thomas's words, the natural law is the "participation of the eternal law in the rational creature."[51]

It is important to note that this reasoning maintains that concept of final ends by which the church had defended the superiority of the *sacerdotium*. This was, of course, crucial to the church's acceptance of the Thomistic synthesis of Christian faith and Aristotelian philosophy. What Thomas had changed in theoretical terms was not the traditionally asserted superiority of the *sacerdotium*, but the possibility of thinking about *regnum* in its own terms as a natural good without calling into question the ultimate superiority of the church and the supernatural good that it proclaimed to be its proper domain. In this, Thomas finally liberated medieval thought from Augustine's metaphor of the two cities that relegated the temporal order to the realm of sin and corruption.[52]

The problem was that the Thomistic synthesis was, in political terms, inherently unstable. It required the continued existence and viability of the *Respublica Christiana*, that is, of a single society divided not only between *regnum (imperium)* and *sacerdotium*, each led by theocratic rulers claiming similar political prerogatives but, by Thomas's time, new national-territorial polities as well. These were led by increasingly powerful monarchs who by the late thirteenth century were proclaiming "*rex in regno suo est imperator*"—"the king is emperor in his own kingdom."[53] The conflict between pope and emperor that had been there from Charlemagne on, indeed from the time of Constantine, was now widening to include other authorities that ultimately would prove to be much more dangerous to the pretensions of pope and emperor than either were to the other.

The new threat was not initially recognized, of course, because it constituted a novel form of political organization not yet reflected in political consciousness. Hence, following the investiture dispute, the struggle between pope and emperor soon renewed, the Concordat of Worms having resolved nothing in terms of the real underlying issues. By the thirteenth century, however, the papacy had essentially triumphed over the empire and, particularly from the reign of Pope Innocent III (1198–1216), began to assert a universal theocratic authority over all of Christendom. The assertion was ultimately futile, of course, for the papacy had triumphed over an institution that, in real political terms, was already moribund. Indeed, with the emergence of the new territorial states, the polity that it claimed authority over, the ancient *Respublica Christiana*, was itself moribund. The problem was in fact much more profound, for if the Christian Republic was now being rendered obsolete by the rise of the territorial state, the papacy would be rendered politically obsolete as well.

This analysis, of course, has all the clarity of hindsight. What seems obvious now was not at all obvious to the protagonists in the struggle. And when the conflict over supreme authority shifted from empire to emerging territorial state, it seemed initially to be no more than a continuance of the same conflict that had divided papacy and empire, a view that would ultimately be supplanted by new theoretical insights that recognized the distinctiveness of the territorial state and, correspondingly, the demise of the Christian Republic.[54] In this, St. Thomas's political theory would play a profound role, for it validated the legitimacy of the emerging state. It did not grant it complete autonomy, however, nor recognize that it had rendered the Christian Republic obsolete. He could not go that far, but others soon would.

The key event in this political and theoretical transformation was the conflict between Pope Boniface VIII (1294–1303) and Philip IV (Philip the Fair, 1285–1314) of France, the first of the new territorial states to emerge in the thirteenth century.[55] The immediate issue that sparked the confrontation was over the right of the French (and English) monarchies to tax clergy, something the papacy was not willing to concede. After a period of political struggle between the contending parties, Boniface issued the Bull *Unam Sanctam* (1302) that asserted an unqualified authority of the church (papacy) over both temporal and spiritual matters, over both *regnum* and *sacerdotium*. And the justification was based on the by now traditional doctrine of the "two swords," a doctrine so inherently ambiguous that it had been used to assert both temporal independence from priestly authority to the subordination of secular rulers to the papacy. There was no ambiguity in Boniface's interpretation, however, his Bull asserting unequivocally "one sword ought to be under the other and the temporal authority subject to the spiritual power."[56]

Clearly, the immediate issue of taxation, like the earlier conflict over lay investiture, was not really the fundamental issue at stake. The underlying problem had been there from the beginning of papal and imperial relationships and had now widened to include the rising territorial state: Where did final authority lie? And if it was still not possible to resolve the issue in theoretical terms, that did not prevent Philip from asserting his independence from papal control as vigorously as had the emperors before him. More so, in fact, for *Unam Sanctam*, which challenged that independence in the most radical fashion, precipitated an equally radical response, the consequences of which marked the beginning of the end of papal involvement in temporal affairs. More than this, it rekindled the issues of the legitimate locus and extent of papal authority within the church, issues that would ultimately transcend the church and shape the theoretical debates about the emerging territorial state itself.

The actual events are complex and cover an extensive period of time, but the general facts are sufficient for our purposes. Boniface was arrested by Philip's forces, released, and died soon after. Two years later, a French pope was elected and took up residence in Avignon. The Avignon papacy, which lasted for some seventy years, became a pawn of the French monarchy and a scandal to the faithful. The papacy was finally returned to Rome in 1377 by Pope Gregory XI, but he died soon thereafter and the College of Cardinals, with the connivance of the French monarchy, rescinded their first choice of an Italian pope and elected a second French pope who took up residence again at Avignon while the Italian pope remained in Rome.

Thus began the Great Schism, a scandal of the first order, not only within the church, but also within the whole of Christendom. It clearly posed a threat to the very existence of a Christian commonwealth, that is, to the whole edifice of medieval political thought and organization. It also required that the issue be settled by a general council of the church, and this carried with it the dangerous possibility that a more "democratic" conception of church governance might emerge; that the body of the faithful or their representatives constituted the supreme authority within the church rather than a monarchical pope. The decretalists had already developed such notions, and while their position had been essentially conservative, their initial speculations were available now for more radical interpretations.

Aristotle, of course, was key to this process of radicalization, for his political thought was not only compatible with the more progressive thinking of the decretalists (and civilians), it allowed for much greater theoretical speculation than possible from a purely legal perspective. It is no surprise, therefore, that by the mid-thirteenth century Aristotle had become the paradigmatic thinker.[57] Those who were to carry forward the theoretical battle against the pretensions of the papacy did so largely in Aristotelian terms, the most important of them emerging even before the Great Schism. Of these, three stand out as uniquely important: John of Paris (1250/1254–1306), Dante Alighieri (1265–1321), and, most notably, Marsilius of Padua (1275/1280–1342).

Both John and Dante proposed resolutions to the issue of the source of supreme authority within Christendom that, for different reasons, proved ultimately inadequate. John, a thinker in the Thomistic tradition, is perhaps the most conservative in his thinking, but as an apologist for Philip IV in his struggle with Pope Boniface VIII he is important theoretically in marking the beginning of the separation of *regnum* and *sacerdotium*. In this, John was the first to defend the legitimacy of a national-territorial state rather than that of the empire against the jurisdictional claims of the papacy. Nonetheless, John ultimately defends dual authority within Christendom, stripping the papacy of its claims over temporal power but maintaining its autonomy alongside that of temporal rulership.[58] In place of the Thomistic system of limited secular autonomy within a unified hierarchy of *regnum* and *sacerdotium*, John advocates, with certain exceptions, a separation of the two swords within the Christian Commonwealth.[59] Clearly this did not resolve the fundamental issue of supreme authority that was the source of the difficulty to begin with. Dante recognizes more clearly the need for one central authority, but posits the empire, an increasingly irrelevant political entity, as the supreme political unit.[60]

Nonetheless, both thinkers provide arguments that would prove crucial to the later development of more secularized and ultimately state centered political theories. In this, they must be seen as progressive thinkers who, as Aristotelians, were willing to push well beyond the theoretical limitations of canon and Roman law. Even Dante, who has often been viewed by later scholars as theoretically retrograde in his defense of the empire, is in fact progressive in many of the specific arguments he makes against the heirocratic (papal and ecclesiastical supremacists) defenders of the papacy.[61] And in this, both John and Dante focus on the key theoretical claim of the heirocrats: that the higher spiritual ends it represents legitimizes the political supremacy of the papacy. For very similar reasons both reject this claim, and both assert a principle that would prove to be profoundly important in the later development of the theory of the modern state, that the origins of political authority determine its legitimacy rather than its purpose or end.[62]

De potestate regia et papali (*On Royal and Papal Power*), John's major work in political theory written as a defense of the French cause against Boniface VIII, directly confronts, and rejects, the "higher ends" argument of the heirocrats. For John, "all ecclesiastical jurisdiction is spiritual,"[63] not temporal. This is not to deny the superiority of this jurisdiction, but it does not follow that the supremacy of ends legitimizes the supremacy of political authority. In a mundane but telling example, John asks, "What man would argue that because a teacher . . . or moral tutor guides . . . to a nobler end . . . than . . . (a) . . . doctor whose concern is with the lesser end of physical health, the physician should be subject to the teacher in the preparation of his medicines?"[64] Most importantly, however, is John's appeal to historical origins, for it is clear that royal authority preceded priesthood (i.e., true Christian priesthood) and therefore cannot be said to derive from priestly authority.[65] Hence, John argues, "In temporal matters the temporal power is greater than the spiritual, and in these matters is in no way subject to the spiritual since it is not derived from it. Both take their origin immediately from one supreme power, namely God."[66]

John equally rejects related claims to the superiority of pope and *sacerdotium*. The two swords doctrine appealed to by Boniface in *Unam Sanctam* is repudiated by John as biblical allegory that, as allegory, cannot be taken to prove anything about the real world of political authority.[67] This argument was, in fact, a major advance in medieval political thought, and reflects the influence of Aristotelian rationalism, for the rejection of biblically based allegorical thinking was the first step toward a fully rational and ultimately secular political theory. This does not mean that biblical exegesis did not remain important in the theoretical debates of the High Middle Ages, however, as John's interpretation of the Petrine commission demonstrates, an interpretation that further strips the papacy of its pretensions to authority over temporal rulership. According to John, a correct reading of the biblical text demonstrates that Christ gave "the spiritual alone to Peter, leaving the corporal to Caesar, who received it directly from God."[68]

If John's dualism theoretically freed temporal authority from papal rule, the issue of the locus and extent of political authority within both *regnum* and *sacerdotium* still remained. Hence, while John concedes that the pope's spiritual authority is God-given, and in this sphere alone the Petrine commission applies, it does not follow that the pope is an absolute monarch. He in fact represents the corporate body of the whole church, and it is that body, either as a general council or, as John seems to prefer, the College of Cardinals, that ultimately ought to prevail.[69] These ideas, clearly derived from the earlier canonists, and coupled with Aristotelian concepts, are employed by John to advocate a form of limited papal monarchy tempered with a kind of "popular sovereignty."[70] Under certain circumstances, then, the pope could be deposed by some representative church assembly such as a general council, precisely the issue in the Great Schism and the subsequent Conciliar movement.

It should be added that John applies to secular monarchy this same reasoning. Royal authority of any kind is God-given, but—another idea developed by canonists as well as civilians—through the people, and it is ultimately dependent on popular consent for its legitimacy.[71] Unlike the church, however, which John believes requires a single leader, temporal rulership need not be monarchical, as Aristotle had shown.[72] To be sure, to men of John's time the issue of church organization and its relation to temporal authority was primary. To men of later times the legitimacy of the new territorial monarchies would be primary, and then these ideas about church authority and governance would be imported into the resulting secular controversies surrounding the modern state.

While Dante is a defender of an increasingly irrelevant empire in his major political work *Monarchia*, he nonetheless makes important arguments in defense of the autonomy of temporal rule that are not unlike those advanced by John, including rejecting allegorical forms of thinking. Most importantly, however, is his shift from "higher ends" to "origins" as the legitimizing factor in the political autonomy of temporal authority, and here he advances a particularly interesting argument against the more conservative decretal-ists. They make the logical mistake of deriving a justification of papal supremacy from church traditions that postdate the church's foundation.[73] In effect, they engage in a tautology: Papal decrees are used to legitimize papal decrees. As Dante argues, "that the authority of the Church is not the cause of imperial authority is proved in this way: a thing cannot be the cause of the power of something else if that something else is fully functional when the first thing does not exist or exerts no influence; but the Empire had all its authority at a time when the Church did not exist or had no influence; therefore the Church is not the cause of the empire's power"[74]

While Dante advocates a world empire autonomous from papal interfer-ence, he does not suggest that the church is to be subordinated to the dictates of the emperor or secular rulership. This idea would come soon enough, its full development only when an explicit theory of sovereignty was articulated in the early modern period, a concept as alien to Dante as to other medieval theorists. Nonetheless, the complete autonomy of the empire and its supremacy in political affairs was only possible with the now com-plete separation of *regnum-imperium* and *sacerdotium*, that is, with the effective end of the *Respublica Christiana*.[75] This, as we have noted, was already occurring in fact, not as Dante imagined, with a resurgent empire, but with the emerging territorial and national state. What was required was a thinker who could conceive of the emerging political order in these new terms.

Marsilius of Padua came closer than any other late medieval thinker to doing just this. Unquestionably the most important and innovative political thinker of the late medieval period who in his *Defensor Pacis (Defender of Peace)* bridges the gap between the medieval and modern periods, Marsilius combines as it were the forward looking aspects of both John of Paris and Dante. But he goes considerably beyond both of these thinkers, so much so that it is at times difficult to avoid reading him as a modern theorist. He is not, although there is much in Marsilius that is a harbinger of modern theoretical developments, and there is little question that his theoretical contributions foreshadow the final demise of the Christian Republic.

What is most important in Marsilius's analysis, as in John's and Dante's, is his rejection of any notion that the higher end of the spiritual domain carries with it legitimate claims by the papacy to political control over all of Christendom. But Marsilius's argument goes much further than either of these thinkers could—or would. With Marsilius, the church is made utterly subordinate to the temporal authority of the emerging state. It is not simply this conclusion that distinguishes Marsilius as the most radical thinker of his age, however, but the entirely innovative way in which he arrives at it. He is an Aristotelian, of course, and as such still premodern in his thinking. But he is a thoroughly secular Aristotelian, an Averroist, who employs Aristotle in an entirely new way.

For Marsilius, the emerging territorial state is legitimized not on the basis of its final cause, but its efficient cause.[76] Since the final cause constituted the ultimate purpose or end of something for Aristotle, it was this that defined for him, and subsequently for medieval thinkers from St. Thomas on, the essential legitimacy of the state. The final cause of the state is the "good" (ethically rational) life and, as such, constitutes the highest end of human activity in this world. The problem for progressive medieval thinkers was that this world was transcended by a higher spiritual reality that the heirocrats claimed legitimized papal supremacy even over temporal authority, a claim that had reached its fullest expression in Boniface's Bull *Unam Sanctum*. And while late medieval thinkers such as John of Paris and Dante had managed to show that the higher end represented by the church does not logically translate into political supremacy, the continued use of the Aristotelian teleology of final causes simply made it more difficult to legitimize the temporal order in its own terms, fully autonomous from the ecclesiastical hierarchy.

In legitimizing the state in terms of its efficient cause, the difficulty was once and for all removed. In Aristotle, the efficient cause of a thing is that which directly gives rise to its existence, its immediate cause of being. In the case of temporal authority, and for Marsilius that meant the rising territorial state (*civitas* or *regnum* in his words), the efficient cause was government which, through the imposition of coercive law, maintained that peace necessary for a stable polity and, hence, human existence.[77] Understood in these terms, it followed for Marsilius that peace could not exist with multiple governments exercising coercive power, a truism for the citizen of the modern state perhaps, but not so immediately obvious to those who had lived for centuries under multiple authorities.[78] The claims of the papacy to a *plentitudo potestatis*, that is, to political-coercive authority over temporal rulers, therefore, could not be maintained irrespective of final causes or higher ends.

The genuinely radical nature of Marsilius's analysis becomes even more apparent in his attendant theory of law. Law (*Lex*) is now legitimized not on the basis of its correspondence to some ethical standard beyond itself (divine and natural law), or because it was promulgated by theocratic authority and as such is sacred (Roman and canon law), but because it is capable of coercing obedience.[79] Law, therefore, is now defined as will (coercive power), rather than as a rule of moral reason.[80] This means, and Marsilius is quite explicit about this, that even "unjust" laws retain their character as law; they remain legitimate irrespective of their ethical propriety.[81] And while this might seem to resemble St. Augustine's theory of law, and indeed of the state, there is a fundamental difference between the two. St. Augustine premises his views upon humankind's sinfulness; Marsilius upon a purely secular consideration of the efficient cause of the state.

The consequence of this reasoning was the unreserved subordination of the church, that is, the papacy, to the authority of the emerging territorial state. Since law is now defined simply as political will and coercive power, the church has no role whatsoever in temporal affairs, for the emerging state alone possesses coercive authority. The life of the spirit remains a higher end and the final cause of human existence to be sure, but it does not confer coercive authority on the pope and the ecclesiastical establishment. Their authority remains purely spiritual which, Marsilius argues, as had John of Paris earlier, was the intent of the Petrine commission, for "Christ gave to St. Peter or any other apostle no power other than that of binding men to and loosing them from sins."[82] Indeed, so radically does Marsilius strip the papacy of any claim to coercive jurisdiction over temporal authority that even spiritual matters, when they become issues of law, are assigned to the state. Punishment of heretics, for example, "belongs only to the ruler by authority of the human legislator, and not to any priest or bishop, even though it is divine law which is sinned against."[83]

In legitimizing temporal authority on the basis of Aristotle's efficient cause rather than final cause, and concomitantly law on the basis of coercive will rather than moral reason, Marsilius had finally laid the theoretical basis for the claims of the emerging territorial state to supreme political power. This would in itself constitute a radical innovation in late medieval political thought, but Marsilius is equally as radical in his conception of the locus of supreme authority, a conception that further enhances the claims of the state. For Marsilius, all authority inheres in the people as a whole. As such, it exists by consent, a doctrine he applies to both *regnum* and *sacerdotium*. The people, either as a whole body of citizens or as a whole body of believers, must consent to any rulership over them, a consent that now, unlike the ancient Roman *Lex Regia*, is revocable.[84]

In short, Marsilius advocates a republican form of government in both church and emerging state. To be sure, he does not expect the whole people to actually govern, anymore than would be expected in a modern democracy, but simply to retain final authority, an idea that would later be known as the doctrine of popular sovereignty. In the state, the people as a whole, or the "weightier part" thereof (*pars valentior*), constitute the human legislator that elects the government. While the government rules, it does so only with the consent of the human legislator which, in Marsilius' analysis, is the efficient cause of government (while government is the efficient cause of civil order, the human legislator is in reality the efficient cause of all parts of the state and, as such, of law itself).[85] The same model pertains in the church, except here the legislator is the whole body of the faithful or the weightier part that elect a general council. The council designates and deposes the administrative officials (priests and bishops including the pope) and has full and final authority on all matters of dogma and the appropriate governance of the church. The only difference between this and the state model is that God rather than the faithful legislator is the efficient cause of the church, but in terms of republican governance, the two are equivalent.

While it would be an error to read into Marsilius at this early stage of transformation to the modern world a modern theory of democratic governance, it would not be amiss to recognize how far in that direction he does go. The implicit theory of popular sovereignty, for example, while not new—the decretalists had already developed it—is taken to more radical conclusions than heretofore by Marsilius. The people are now the sole source of authority, temporal and spiritual, and their consent to governance in both church and state is revocable. While Marsilius does not deny the ultimate divine source of political authority, like the decretalists he argues that God speaks through the people.[86] It is true that he legitimizes the authority of the "weightier part" of the whole people, but he believes that the weightier part is to include most citizens, for in his view the average person is quite capable of political responsibility and is a surer guarantee of the effectiveness and legitimacy of the law.[87] The weightier part is in fact simply an affirmation of the principle of majority rule, and while Marsilius recognizes the legitimacy of various forms of government, including monarchy, he advocates an elective system of choosing the ruler or rulers.

Still, Marsilius's republicanism is not yet fully modern. This is certainly apparent in regard to the extent of the state's authority, for, in effect, Marsilius had transferred to the people the *plentitudo potestatis* heretofore claimed by the papacy, and the papal "fullness of power" became no less absolute when exercised by the people.[88] It is in part for this reason that Marsilius has been interpreted by some to be a defender of absolutism despite the republican thrust of his arguments.[89] It must be remembered, however, that the modern theory of rights would not be articulated for some time, and that for late medieval thinkers such as Marsilius the locus of authority was much the greater issue than its extent. Moreover, Marsilius holds to the later medieval view that "the people" constitute a corporate whole, a *universitas*, not merely a *societas* of individuals possessing inherent rights. The right of the community, therefore, is not immediately translatable into the rights of the individual against the state.[90]

What in the final analysis is missing in Marsilius's political thought, of course, is what is missing in all of medieval political thought: an explicit theory of sovereignty. Yet even here, as with so much else in his thinking, he is forward looking, laying the groundwork for its later development. The legitimation of a unified polity ruled for all practical purposes by temporal authority is, of course, the key factor in this regard. So too is his concept of law as "state law" legitimized in coercive terms, a concept that will later constitute the essential character of the modern theory of sovereignty. Moreover, Marsilius distinguishes the emerging state from government, recognizing that the form of government is irrelevant to the existence of the state.[91] The human legislator remains the supreme authority regardless of the form of government. And the most important distinction, that between state and society, is also to be found in Marsilius, although not yet in the clear and unambiguous manner required for a full scale theory of the sovereign and impersonal state. As we shall see, such a distinction would require that the community be visualized not as a *universitas*, a corporate whole (a "mystical body of the commonwealty"),[92] but as a collection of individuals who, as individuals, consent to a sovereign authority. There is in this a certain paradox, to be sure, for it was the development of corporatist-organicist models that first led to a more public concept of the polity, yet in the longer term these models would be rejected in the development of the modern consent-contract theory of the state.

That Marsilius goes further than his predecessors in making the crucial distinctions is unquestionable, however. The harbingers of the modern theory of sovereignty and the impersonal state are clearly there. In this, Marsilius was reflecting a more general trend in late medieval thought that was beginning to conceive of political terms in more impersonal ways. We note a shift from the feudal conception of political power as private property (lordship or *dominium*) to a more public conception, one in which the king (or pope) ruled over a corporate "body politic," not merely over a personal possession. In this, the ruler himself begins to be conceived not simply as a person with power but as the embodiment of a more abstract public power that transcends his person. The "kings two bodies" (the body natural and the body politic) as it was conceived in the postmedieval period, and the title of a famous book on the subject, had its roots in medieval thought.[93] Even the symbolism of power begins to shift to accommodate the emerging notion of the king as a public person. The Crown, once merely the symbol of personal power, becomes increasingly an abstraction standing for the public authority embodied in the ruler.[94] More generally, the entire concept of jurisdiction (*jurisdictio*), which initially referred to the claims of various rulers within *regnum* and *sacerdotium* to personal power, became increasingly a claim to impersonal authority over some public domain.[95]

All of these ideas and tendencies played a role in the Conciliar movement that arose as a result of the Great Schism. The existence of multiple popes (there was for a short period even three claimants to the chair of St. Peter) demanded resolution by a general council of the church. But the very existence of such a council raised the persistent issue of the locus of supreme authority within the church: Does it inhere in the papacy, or in the council? In one obvious sense, the very fact that a church council had to determine which pope was legitimate implied the superiority of the council. But most of the Conciliarists did not wish to go that far, certainly not as far as Marsilius, and the two great councils that did meet, the Council of Constance (1414–1418) and the Council of Basle (1431–1449), settled for a more limited interpretation of the council's authority.

The history of the Conciliar movement is a subject in itself, and cannot be given full justice here. Suffice it to say that the Conciliar thinkers were treading on ground already well worn, extending and modifying arguments that had been put forward long before the crisis they now confronted, from the canonists through Aristotle and Marsilius. That they were unable to make the final break from medieval political assumptions, and the ideal of a Christian Republic that was in reality already moribund, should not be surprising. To expect of men then to grasp fully the emerging political realities would be as unfair, and as futile, as to expect political thinkers today to possess such political understanding. The entire history of Western political thought confirms that political consciousness is an imperfect reflection of the existing form of polity, and that political theory, and the comprehension of new political realities, progresses slowly at best.

In immediate terms, it made little difference. The Conciliar movement failed and the papacy retained its claims to monarchical absolutism within the church, although its assertion of temporal supremacy was increasingly challenged by the monarchs of the emerging territorial states. In the longer term, however, the influence of the Conciliarists was profound, both in their failures and in their successes. Their failure to reform the church was a direct cause of the Reformation, a movement that was crucial in the early formation of the modern state. And their success in articulating the already well-developed theories of consent, representation, and public conceptions of political authority gave rise to theories of governance that would subsequently shape the structure of the early state.

Indeed, it was these theories that constitute the real contribution of the High Middle Ages to the concept of the modern state, not any explicit theory of sovereignty. The Conciliarists, and the entire corpus of Roman law, canon law, and Aristotelian political philosophy from which they derived their ideas, provided later thinkers with models of government structure that pre-dated the modern theory of sovereignty. The Middle Ages paradoxically bequeathed to the modern world a concept of the structure of the modern state before it had any real idea of the state as such.

Chapter Five

The Making of Leviathan

Ultimately, the theoretical innovations of the High Middle Ages cannot be understood simply in the terms of the specific issues that gave rise to them. For medieval thinkers what was important were the immediate problems they confronted: the relationship between *regnum* and *sacerdotium*, the supremacy of pope or emperor, or territorial monarch, and the locus of authority within the church or temporal polity. These issues, however, and the theoretical responses to them, were reflections of the much deeper social and political changes occurring within medieval society. In a host of ways new local political structures were emerging that influenced the development of late medieval thought. Concepts of consent may have been formally drawn from Roman law sources, but they were already inherent in the feudal contract itself, and fully developed at the end of the Middle Ages. Corporation theory, while also derived from Roman law, reflected at a deeper level the growing organicism of society beginning to articulate itself into guilds and other corporate structures. Most importantly, however, was the deterioration of feudalism and the corresponding growth of towns that were to play a crucial role in the emergence of the modern state. In this, a common historical pattern was repeated, for both the archaic and classical states were cities that became states.

The medieval town, as a general rule, stood outside of the feudal system of personalistic political relationships. It therefore developed its own governing system that emphasized the autonomy of the town from outside control. In some cases, towns became states onto themselves, most notably in Italy and Germany in the fourteenth and fifteenth centuries. The great Hanseatic League of German towns for a period of time rivaled the growing national monarchies. Most importantly for the theory of the modern state was the development of "republican" conceptions of government, particularly in the Italian city-states.[1] These ideas were given real life in the city, and thus confirmed the ideals of a more open and democratic view of governance that had been expressed from the twelfth century on. As such, they came to play a role in the subsequent evolution of the theory of the modern state, although not immediately.

Most importantly, the late medieval towns spawned a new class system that would come to constitute the sociological basis of the modern state. The old feudal forms of stratification became hardened into legally defined estates, and new classes begin to emerge, the most important of which was the "third estate" or urban bourgeoisie.[2] The interests of this class lay in a growing monied economy of trade, banking, and industry that undergirds the modern state, not in the economic and political structure of feudalism. The bourgeoisie's role in supporting the emerging territorial state varied, of course, depending on circumstances. In France and England, they were crucial supporters of the monarch's attempt to create a territorial and national state. In Italy and Germany, they supported the autonomy of the city-state.[3] But, in the long run, the bourgeoisie would become the dominant class of the modern national and territorial state, and the intellectual bearers of those democratic and republican ideals that had first arisen in the late medieval world but failed for wont of a political system capable of expressing them in real terms.

Given the importance of the modern city-state in the transition from the medieval to the modern world, it is understandable why an Italian Renaissance thinker from a small city-state should produce the first clearly recognizable modern theory of politics. Ideas reflecting the experience of any one of the multiplicities of political forms that emerged from the medieval milieu were easily transferred to others however.[4] This was certainly the case with Machiavelli (1469–1527) who may be said to have laid the metaphysical cornerstone of the theory of the modern state, if not its essential foundations, a task that would finally and definitively be accomplished by Thomas Hobbes later in the next century.

Machiavelli's focus was entirely upon pragmatic and amoral considerations about the nature of rulership, whether in a monarchical or a republican system. The former is developed in his most famous work, *The Prince*, the latter in his *Discourses*, but in either case Machiavelli argues that successful political leadership requires the raw ability to acquire and maintain power, which includes violence, deception, and chicanery.[5] Thus, when he asserts in *The Prince* that "a prince who wants to keep his authority must learn how not to be good,"[6] we recognize immediately that this rule of *realpolitik*, stated as a purely practical and empirical fact of successful rulership, thrusts us into a moral universe utterly alien to classical and medieval political thought. In theoretical terms, it spelled the final end of the classical theory of the state premised upon a "unity of ethics and politics" and the late medieval concept of a unified Christendom organized around the concept of "higher ends." Machiavelli provides us with the first glimpse of the new science of politics that would ultimately define the modern state—a purely secular science of a purely secular institution.

What makes Machiavelli uniquely interesting in the development of the theory of the modern state, however, is that he is the first to employ the term "state" (*lo stato*) in something like its modern meaning. The term *lo stato* was derived from the Latin word *status*, which simply meant, as it still does, "condition." Thus, in the High Middle Ages the *status regis* initially referred to the personal condition of the king, his wealth for example, but it began to be used in a more public sense during the later thirteenth century to refer to the king's authority within his territory.[7] In this, the evolution of the term followed the general pattern of other medieval terms of a proto-political character in acquiring a more impersonal meaning. With Machiavelli, however, *status* or *lo stato* is employed to describe a territorial polity that appears to be completely impersonal, that is, that exists apart from the person of the ruler.

In our own era in which new terms come and go with extraordinary rapidity, and no less so than in the social sciences, we are accustomed to accord them little importance. There are times, however, in which a new word or a novel usage creates the possibility of genuinely innovative theoretical insights. This is so because in replacing the traditional nomenclature the theorist is freed from the paradigmatic assumptions inherent in the older terminology. Such was the case with Machiavelli's use of "state," for the commonly accepted terms for temporal authority such as *polis*, *civitas*, and *regnum-imperium* were classical in origin and feudal in content. They could not be used without implying the very political formation that the modern state was in the process of abolishing. The "state," in Machiavelli's usage, carried no such implications, and alerted the theorist to the emergence of a new form of polity.[8]

But to what extent did Machiavelli himself fully understand the new and emerging meaning of "state"? To be sure, he seems to use the word in a distinctly modern sense, but how cognizant is he of his own modernity? Does *lo stato* in his mind refer entirely to an impersonal entity, or does it still imply a more personalistic concept of polity characteristic of the classical regime of the ancient *polis*, or of more traditional concepts of personal forms of rulership?[9] The question is no mere excursion into historical trivia, for it involves the fundamental issue of when did "state consciousness" first appear. What is certain is that the necessary preconditions for its appearance, the existence of the state, were already in place, if only in rudimentary form.[10] It is less certain that its conscious reflection in theoretical terms was yet fully manifest.

It certainly was not yet reflected in any explicit theory of sovereignty, for the modern theory of sovereignty could be articulated fully and explicitly only with the emergence of a large and centralized territorial polity. Such was occurring in Machiavelli's lifetime, though not in Italy as he so ardently hoped. In France, England, and Spain, however, this process of territorializing and centralizing was already far along and fully consolidated by the sixteenth century. And, as in the archaic states of the ancient Near East, it was accomplished in its initial stages by monarchs asserting absolute power premised upon a theocratic ideology of legitimation. In a sense, this process appears retrograde in that it obviated the late medieval development of concepts of consent, but these ideas would eventually emerge again in new guise. What was required in the first instance, however, was the centralization of political authority within unambiguous territorial lines, and this required the kind of power only an absolute theocratic monarchy could impose.

The age of absolutism in the development of the modern Western state stretches from the Renaissance through the eighteenth century and, in some cases, beyond. The primary requirement for the existence of the absolutist state, as for every state before or since, was the ability to extract taxes from the always unwilling subjects. Apart from the lack of a monied economy, feudal monarchies were largely incapable of even assuring services in kind. Absolute monarchs were more successful in this regard, and early on began to establish centralized bureaucracies to collect taxes and, more generally, to assert centralized power throughout the state's territory. The second requirement, very much dependent upon the first, and also absent in the feudal system, was the eventual establishment of standing armies, for the early absolutist states were above all war states. The reason for this may lie in part in the nature of the territorial state itself, but the age of absolutism corresponded to the Reformation and Counter-Reformation and thus the emerging states became embroiled in the religious wars that devastated much of Europe in the sixteenth and seventeenth centuries.

Paradoxically, the bourgeoisie initially supported the absolutist states, particularly in France and England, because the process of centralization they engendered created that common economic and legal system required for a viable system of manufacturing and trade. Hence, in the early stages of its development the bourgeoisie supported mercantilism, the corresponding economic structure of absolutism and another key source of its centralizing power. And the formalization of a common legal system, even if promulgated by absolute monarchs, was just as crucial to the economic interests of the third estate, for it aided in the elimination of the particularistic feudal barriers to a system of national trade and economic development.[11] More than this, it ultimately laid the basis for thinking of the state as a supreme legal structure, the necessary precondition for a formal theory of impersonal sovereignty.

That the interests of the growing third estate would eventually come into conflict with the absolutist state was, in historical hindsight, entirely predictable. Its long-term interests were capitalist and republican, not mercantilist and monarchical, and it could hardly be expected to continue supporting a state whose purpose was the maintenance of an increasingly parasitic noble class.[12] For this reason, it was inevitable that the bourgeoisie would eventually have gone into opposition to absolute monarchy and the social and economic system it supported. The principal cause of its eventual opposition, however, dramatically shaped the entire nature of political discourse from the sixteenth century down to the French Revolution and even into the nineteenth century. This, of course, was the Reformation and Counter-Reformation, and it was in the debates surrounding this great religious divide that the theory of the modern state was given its defining form.

In its early stages, the Reformation aided the process of state formation by legitimizing the emerging absolute monarchs' break from church and papacy. This process, of course, was already underway in the late medieval period, clearly evident in thinkers such as Marsilius of Padua. The Reformation was its consummation. But the Reformation also encouraged state formation by intensifying the centralization of political power. In legitimizing the spiritual authority of the monarch within his territorial domain, matters of faith now became a source of political control. Monarchs could determine the faith of their subjects. Political control was further enhanced by the views of the early Reformation divines who returned to an "Augustinian" concept of authority. Luther not only justified the existence of secular political authority but advocated a strict policy of nonresistance to it. So too did Calvin (1509–1564), certainly the most important early Reformation thinker, for he possessed a clearer notion of the state than Luther. He understood the church to be bounded by the territorial state, not, as in the medieval *Respublica Christiana*, a transnational and transcultural entity.[13]

While the religious sincerity of the early Reformation thinkers cannot be doubted, there is no question of the political value the Reformation presented to the centralizing monarchs of the emerging national states. It vastly enhanced their power, and in justifying the divorce from Rome and the absolute authority of the monarch within his territory, it laid the basis for a theory of both external and internal sovereignty. Paradoxically, perhaps, the Counter-Reformation had much the same effect, for while Catholic monarchs retained their allegiance to Rome, at least in the formal sense, they became in effect the spiritual leaders within their territories. The ensuing struggle between Protestant and Catholic Europe further enhanced the power of the new national and absolutist monarchies.

From the perspective of the modern state, therefore, the Reformation is best understood as a political struggle in the guise of a religious movement. Theology was political ideology, for the issues of the source and extent of monarchical power had now to be framed within the confines of religious debate. In this, the Reformation period was similar to the later Middle Ages, but with one very crucial difference: The state now constituted the dominant form of polity, not church, empire, or fiefdom. Hence, religious issues became state issues, and the political crisis that ensued produced radically new forms of political thinking.

In retrospect, the crisis was inevitable. Given that the monarch now had the authority to impose articles of faith, resistance on the part of those subscribing to other faiths was predictable, although the early reformers largely failed to grasp the inherent logic of this development. Thus, doctrines of resistance began to appear as political authority increasingly repressed discordant religious persuasions. The Calvinist John Knox (1505–1572) is the most notable thinker in this regard, advocating the right of resistance against any authority that did not support the "true religion."[14] The other side of this, of course, was the duty to suppress any religion that was not "true." This logic, in various forms, became increasingly common in Catholic as well as Protestant countries and inevitably raised fundamental issues of the legitimate extent of political authority.

What is particularly noteworthy about the early theories of resistance, however, was that they all assumed that resistance was legitimate only if initiated by lower magistrates or corporate entities with legal or quasi-legal standing such as estates, not by individuals. This was true for Luther once the issue of resistance could no longer be avoided, as it was for Calvin and other Protestant leaders. Despite a theology that emphasized the direct relationship of the individual to God without the intermediary of a priesthood, they could not yet conceive of that same relationship of the individual to the state. This was, in major part, because they did not yet possess a clear concept of the state. Despite the growth of absolute monarchy, political authority still retained medieval connotations that it was legal and corporate in nature. By the middle of the sixteenth century, however, doctrines of resistance finally began to justify individual resistance. This constituted a genuinely revolutionary doctrine against "heretical" political authority, but, more importantly in the longer term, it led to purely political theories of individual rights premised upon a clearer conception of the impersonal sovereign state.[15]

Compounding the crisis, intensified by these increasingly revolutionary if still in part medieval doctrines of resistance, was its international character. Catholic and Protestant principalities in Germany (Germany was not yet a state) became embroiled in conflict that soon engaged most of the European powers. The result was the Thirty Years War (1618–1648), a devastating conflict that had profound social and political consequences. Spanish dominance came to an end and France emerged as the preponderant European power. Other European powers emerged as distinct territorial states and, in the case of England and the United Provinces, the development of constitutional forms of government began to evolve in contrast to French absolutism. Germany, however, was ruined. Its association with the empire had, as in Italy, kept it from developing into a unified state, and the war not only intensified its fragmentation but utterly destroyed the entire infrastructure of civil and political life. Like Italy, but at much greater cost, it would not become a state until late in the nineteenth century.

In terms of the development of the modern state, however, the most important consequence of the Thirty Years War was its conclusion in the Treaty of Westphalia (1648). This marks, if you will, the formal recognition of the modern European state system. Religious controversy would continue, but the treaty recognized the legitimacy of varying religious confessions within territorial boundaries. This rendered the medieval church and empire essentially irrelevant in real political terms, although the empire remained as a nominal overarching organization of the multiplicity of statelets that comprised it. Territorial sovereignty was now officially recognized. The modern state, in short, was now understood to be the legitimate form of polity in the modern world.[16]

Indeed, it is at this time, in fact during the Thirty Years War, that the theory of the modern state finally emerges in clear form, for now the essential elements of the modern state were in place. Sovereignty is now understood to exist territorially, and the individual is increasingly seen to exist apart from the corporate communities to which he belongs. It is on the basis of these emerging factors that the theory of the modern state, that is, the modern theory of sovereignty, will be constructed. But sovereignty had now to be conceived both in its external as well as internal manifestation. Our primary concern is with the internal aspect of sovereignty: How is the state legitimized within a given territory, and what is the relation of the individual to it? The external aspect, however, the relationship of one sovereign power to another, cannot be entirely ignored. Not only does it have a bearing on internal concepts of sovereignty, but it is also implicated in the later development of the state's ideology of legitimation.

Surely the most important early thinker in this regard is Hugo Grotius (1583–1645), traditionally considered the "father" of international law. His most famous work, *De Jure Belli ac Pacis* (*The Rights of War and Peace*), written during the Thirty Years War, unequivocally recognizes the emerging territorial state system. As the title of the book indicates, Grotius also recognizes the inevitability of conflict between sovereign states and the necessity, therefore, of establishing those "rights," that is, those ethical rules that ought to govern their behavior in war no less than in peace. These rules, according to Grotius, are to be found in natural law.

The concept of natural law was in itself, of course, nothing new. Indeed it constituted the dominant ethical theory of the later Middle Ages, particularly in the thinking of St. Thomas and his followers. What was new was its application to relations between states, to what may now legitimately be termed international relations, something that did not exist in Thomas's day. But just as the Thomistic tradition had shown the compatibility between civil (human) and natural law, Grotius demonstrates the same relationship between the customary practices of nations and natural law. These customary practices were understood in terms of the ancient Roman *ius gentium*, initially conceived as laws regulating relations between different peoples of the Roman Empire now applied to relations between different territorial states. And while this form of reasoning pre-dated Grotius, most notably in the Spanish Jesuit Francisco Suarez (1548–1617), Grotius went much further than others in recognizing the legitimacy of state sovereignty.[17]

What is of particular importance in Grotius's thinking is the increasingly secular interpretation of natural law. He defines natural law in conventional form as a "dictate of right reason," but he disengages it from the larger teleological system characteristic of Thomas and the medieval tradition. It now exists, as it originally did in the Stoics, as an autonomous rule of moral reason whose ethical claims according to Grotius "cannot be changed even by God himself."[18] The consequence of this initial secularization coupled with the pragmatic rules of the *ius gentium* was to produce a purely secular theory of positive international law.[19] But applied to internal sovereignty, it would produce a purely secular theory of the state as well.

Indeed, this process of secularization continued after Grotius, and found its "complete" expression in the work of Samuel Pufendorf (1632–1694). In his *On the Law of Nature and Nations* and, more succinctly, in *On the Duty of Man and Citizen According to Natural Law*, a purely secular theory of natural law is applied both to states and the interstate system. For

Pufendorf, as for Grotius before him, natural law is derived from the innate drive of humankind for security. Since security requires social cooperation, the rules of natural law become those that contribute to the maintenance of the social order (*socialitas*). And while this conclusion may seem to accord with the medieval view, it is a conclusion derived ultimately from utility, not from teleological thinking or Christian precepts. Although Pufendorf concedes that the precepts of natural law "have a clear utility," he maintains "they get the force of law only upon the presuppositions that God exists and rules all things by his providence."[20] It would eventually become clear, however, that the principle of utility would work just as well without God and, ultimately, without reference to natural law at all.

The problem is all the more apparent when Pufendorf denies that natural law is inherent within the human mind, but are rather only rules of moral reason logically derived from grasping the necessity of social order. These rules ultimately are those imposed by the sovereign authority through positive law, because the propensity of human nature to violate these rules requires the exercise of real power to actualize them in real terms. This "imposition theory" constitutes the modern school of natural law, and Pufendorf its most notable exponent.[21] Carried to its logical conclusion, as it already had been by Thomas Hobbes, the imposition theory easily leads to the conclusion that positive law alone, derived from a pure principle of utility, establishes the ethical basis of the state. And while Pufendorf denies that he is Hobbesian, the logic of his theory of natural law would inevitably lead in Hobbesian directions and, ultimately, to the abolition of the entire natural law tradition.

This, however, is to get ahead of ourselves. Pufendorf reflects the now formalized reality of the modern state and state system consummated in the Treaty of Westphalia. There is, as a consequence, a much clearer sense of the inherent nature of a system of centralized sovereignty. Indeed, the term sovereignty is now used in its modern sense, as an impersonal entity distinct from both ruler and ruled. This clarity of understanding, however, did not occur all at once. Indeed, it began even before the Thirty Years War, in the work of Jean Bodin (1529/1530–1596). Arguably, Bodin provides the first modern concept of sovereignty, although it would not be until Thomas Hobbes that the concept is given its enduring form.

Bodin was a prolific writer, but his truly important work for the development of a modern theory of sovereignty is the *Six livres de la Republique* (*Six Books of a Commonwealth*). The *Republic* was written against the background of the St. Bartholomew's day massacre (1572) in which thousands of French Calvinists, the Huguenots, were slaughtered with the acquiescence of King Charles IX. This event was simply the most horrific manifestation of years of religious struggle between Catholics and Protestants within France. Despite the influence of the *Politiques*, moderates who wished to see a political compromise on religious issues, the intensity of religious belief made compromise exceedingly difficult, although this is what occurred eventually. For Bodin, as for Hobbes later, the solution ultimately required a centralized authority whose supremacy over all other entities within the territorial state—feudal, religious, or political—was unquestioned. The solution, in short, was sovereignty, a concept that was simply incapable of being articulated clearly in the medieval period.

The immediate theoretical difficulty in the development of a modern theory of sovereignty was the prevailing legitimizing ideology of absolute monarchy: the "divine right of kings." The ideological premises of the divine right theory were simple enough. The king rules by a right granted by God and his authority is absolute and hereditary, not limited by any constitutional constraints imposed by the people or their agents. As such, the king is like a father who exercises paternal power over his subjects. For their part, the subjects owe the king a purely passive obedience. They are not citizens who possess inherent rights against arbitrary authority, but mere subjects, objects of the king's will. This was not understood to mean that the king could rightfully claim to violate natural law or Christian precepts of justice, but there was no legitimate claim to a right of resistance should he do so.

It was its very simplicity that made the divine right of kings such a popular doctrine, at least for those whose religious profession accorded with the king's.[22] Those who were of a different religious persuasion were inevitably drawn to different conclusions, but the doctrine was not easily rejected. Its correspondence to centuries of medieval concepts of kingship, particularly when coupled with Augustinian notions of political authority, made it almost a cultural fact of existence in the early modern period.[23] Yet, the doctrine was in fact modern, emerging first in France and given explicit theoretical form by James I of England in his *Trew Law of Free Monarchies* (1598).[24] It emerged as the legitimizing ideology of early modern absolutism, but its link to the medieval past surely constituted a major source of its influence.

From the point of view of state formation, the theory of divine right was entirely adequate to legitimizing the centralizing processes initiated by absolute monarchs. As a modern theory of sovereignty however, it was entirely inadequate. Indeed, it was not a theory of sovereignty at all, but merely an assertion of the divine source of the king's absolute authority.[25] There was in this no notion of an impersonal state separate from ruler and ruled, of a perpetual source of central authority that transcends the particular person of the ruler. Nor, obviously, was there a recognition of the secularity of political power, as something distinct from a religious ideology of legitimation. The Reformation had broken the medieval unity of *regnum* and *sacerdotium* as an institutional fact, but clearly not as an ideological basis of rulership.

What was required in the first instance for a modern concept of sovereignty was what had always been required but impossible to attain in the medieval period: the disentanglement of religious concepts from political theory. Machiavelli had accomplished this objective boldly and clearly, but failed to couple it with an explicit theory of sovereignty, and years of religious strife had obscured the possibility of developing a purely secular concept of the sovereign state. But that fact itself contained the solution to the problem, for increasingly it became apparent to serious thinkers that the Reformation had produced a crisis that could not be resolved within the confines of religious ideology. It was no longer a matter of attempting to unite a multiplicity of secular authorities with one universal church, something that had proven impossible, but of uniting a multiplicity of territorial states with a plurality of religious professions. The Treaty of Westphalia had formally accomplished this, but its theoretical basis had already been developed by Jean Bodin.

Bodin initially had supported a constitutionalist position, but in the aftermath of the St. Bartholomew's day massacre he came to recognize, in his *Republic*, the unequivocal necessity of absolutism.[26] In this, he essentially adopted the position of the *Politiques* as a supporter of royal authority over the claims of resistance from all religious persuasions, Protestant or Catholic.[27] He did so, however, with a now clear definition of sovereignty as "the absolute and perpetual power of a commonwealth."[28] By absolute, Bodin meant that the sovereign authority, whether embodied in a monarchical, aristocratic, or democratic government, could not be bound by any law, not even its own. Indeed, Bodin understood that legislative authority constitutes the essence of sovereignty and that any limitations upon it would render sovereignty meaningless. By perpetual, Bodin meant that the temporality of government does not impinge upon the inalienability of sovereign authority for, in a statement reminiscent of the concept of the "king's two bodies," Bodin notes that "the king never dies . . . and . . . as soon as one is deceased the nearest male of his stock is seized of the kingdom and in possession thereof before he is crowned."[29] Bodin preferred monarchy to other forms of government as most compatible with the maintenance of sovereignty, but the perpetuity of sovereign authority remains regardless of the form of government.

Clearly Bodin provided the outline of the modern theory of sovereignty, that is, one in which the sovereign authority is beginning to be understood as in some sense impersonal. To be sure, the state (commonwealth) in Bodin is directly represented by government (the ruler), but it also exists apart from government in some manner as well, for it is not the personal ownership (*dominium*) of the king (or of the nobles or citizenry) as in feudal monarchy, but a perpetual public power that the king exercises. This distinction between office and office holder had been a crucial concept within the Christian tradition from the beginning of course, but in Bodin it is now understood as a necessary distinction in the maintenance of sovereignty. And the separation of the state from society is even clearer in Bodin's analysis, for the sovereign authority now exists as an entity above and superior to all corporate bodies that had heretofore claimed political recognition. Bodin denies that sovereignty exists by consent, either by individuals or, as was more commonly thought at the time, by corporate entities such as assemblies of estates that had been developing since medieval times but that, with the rise of absolute monarchies, had been increasingly subordinated to royal authority. For Bodin, a theory of consent would imply mutual obligations between subject and sovereign and, hence, limitations on the authority of the sovereign, an implication that would be obviated in later contract theories.[30]

But Bodin provides only an outline of a theory of the sovereign state, for he is not always as clear in these distinctions as would later be the case. Most notable is his confusion between a particular form of government and the concept of sovereignty. Since sovereignty is indivisible for Bodin, another of its fundamental and logically derivative characteristics, he concludes that the classical mixed form of government is incompatible with its continued existence. For Bodin, a mixed constitution would mean that sovereignty is divided between the different components of government, and a divided sovereignty by definition could not work. For this reason he concluded that only the three simple forms of government (monarchy, aristocracy, and democracy) were true forms, that is, the only forms compatible with the maintenance of sovereignty.[31] With our modern concept of the impersonal state we now understand, of course, that the structure of government is irrelevant.[32] What matters is whether or not, however and by whomever laws are constructed, that they are capable of enforcement. Thus, Bodin's confusion means that the crucial distinction between government and state is not yet fully articulated, nor, as a consequence, is the state conceived as fully impersonal. Hence, Bodin espouses a concept of ruler sovereignty rather than a clear notion of state sovereignty.[33]

There are other confusions, or at least ambiguities in Bodin's theory of sovereignty, most notably his assertion that while the sovereign authority is absolute it is yet limited by natural and divine law (natural law here refers to its medieval usage, not to the more secularized theories of Grotius, Pufendorf, and Hobbes). It is generally conceded, however, that Bodin is simply asserting that the ruler ought to be bound by normally accepted ethical rules, not that those rules establish a right of resistance to sovereign authority when they are violated.[34]

Ultimately, Bodin's theory of sovereignty was coupled with the "divine right of kings" to produce an extraordinarily powerful defense of mature monarchical absolutism.[35] A now clear concept of the locus and supremacy of sovereign authority was anointed with the Reformation belief that all political authority comes from God, something Bodin himself had never disputed. Nonetheless, Bodin's theory did not require divine sanction; it constituted a purely logical articulation of the inherent locus and nature of sovereign authority, not a religious legitimation of it. What was inevitably to occur, therefore, was the final stripping of religion from the theory of sovereignty. This would take the form of a rejection of the "divine right of kings" for a purely secular concept of sovereignty derived from the theory of contract, a theory that Bodin had rejected. Indeed, it would be the theory of contract that finally, and unequivocally, produced the political philosophy of the modern state.

The theory of contract, of course, had ancient origins. The Sophists of the fifth century BCE employed an uncomplicated version of it, and in both Plato's and Cicero's *Republic* it is presented, then rejected, as a possible explanation for the creation of the state. And as a general concept, though not as a formal theory, the idea of contract was an integral part of feudal relations and impacted upon late medieval political thinking on the nature of consent. As a serious theoretical explanation for the existence and legitimacy of the state, however, it is modern. Following Bodin, it began to appear in a variety of Protestant thinkers as a means to justify resistance to tyrannical authority.

Most famous is the *Vindiciae Contra Tyrannos*, published shortly after Bodin's defense of absolutism in the *Republic*. The *Vindiciae*, however, propounded a theory of contract that was in part still premised upon religious assumptions.[36] Later, in the seventeenth century, Johannes Althusius (1557–1638), a German thinker influenced by the structure of a now irrelevant empire, developed a secular version of the contract in his *Politica Methodice Digesta* (*Systematic Analysis of Politics*) that, contrary to Bodin, legitimized popular sovereignty. Yet, even the more secularized versions of early contract theory were premised upon the view that the contract was made by corporate groups within society, and that resistance to tyranny could only come from those magistrates and political leaders representing them.[37] The modern or mature theory of contract, first articulated by Thomas Hobbes (1588–1679), would not only provide a relentlessly secular interpretation of the contract, but would base it upon the consent of individuals rather than corporate groups. This was the essential step in the fully developed modern theory of sovereignty and the state.

The mature theory of contract is in its essentials both simple and elegant. The theory is premised upon the notion that political authority is created by consent. This is in itself hardly a revolutionary idea, of course. Conciliar thinkers and others had developed it in the later Middle Ages, as Protestant theorists of resistance did subsequently. Its potential power as both an explanatory and legitimizing concept, however, especially when framed as a theory of contract, deserves particular note. There is, in fact, a strong empirical basis to the notion of consent that no other foundational political idea possesses, for a political system that fails to meet people's fundamental needs cannot last whatever the legitimizing ideology may be, whether "divine right" or even a belief in a Pharonic god king. At some level, no polity can exist without at least the tacit consent of its subjects or citizens.

The difficulty in any theory of consent, however, is in determining precisely what people have consented to. Under normal circumstances people will naturally tend to assume that existing political structures and usages conform to what they in fact desire. For this reason, political theory in the High Middle Ages and early modern period tended to legitimize customary law and monarchical forms of government. Even Bodin's advocacy of absolutism carried with it a defense of custom and traditionally accepted natural law limitations on the exercise of power. But usage and custom are not a valid basis for determining the nature of consent, for they may not, in fact, conform to what people would choose were they not already biased in their choice. Conversely, advocating resistance premised upon a theory of consent, as the more radical Protestant sects were doing, did not necessarily constitute a valid position either. That some people were unhappy with the religious persuasions of their king was clear enough, but that did not mean, given the alternatives of political disorder and civil war, that they would not have consented to existing arrangements.

The theory of contract was an attempt to resolve these problems, to determine what people would have consented to if their inherently conservative biases or revolutionary passions were rendered inoperative. The theory simply proposed that the act of consent be viewed as a formal contractual act made out of a pre-social and pre-political (hence pre-ideological) situation, a "state of nature." Since neither society nor polity could exist in such a condition, it would by definition be a condition of absolute liberty and, what would subsequently prove problematical for theories of the modern state, absolute equality. The contract and state of nature were understood by all contract theorists to be purely hypothetical, of course, since no people has ever lived in a state of nature, nor has any society been created through a formal agreement. These constituted a kind of "thought experiment" to determine what people would actually consent to were they imagined to be in a condition in which human nature alone is revealed, unaffected by existing social and political distinctions and ideological persuasions.

That the theory of contract constitutes the foundation myth of the modern state is clear. All historically existing states have been legitimized on the basis of some foundation myth or other, whether the act of foundation is by sacred lineages, pagan Gods, the Judeo-Christian God of divine right, or, as in the theory of contract, by the consent of the people. And, as with all foundation myths, what is at issue is the source and extent of ultimate authority, which is simply the issue of origins now posited in hypothetical terms. As we have seen, when the question of ultimate authority arose between papacy and territorial monarch in the late medieval period, thinkers such as Marsilius and John of Paris began to appeal to origins, asserting the primacy of temporal authority in secular affairs on the basis that royal authority had pre-dated priestly authority. And while in the theory of contract the question of origins is resolved by reference to a purely hypothetical condition rather than to any historical circumstances, the source and extent of ultimate authority, that is, sovereignty, remain the fundamental issues, their resolution depending upon how one interprets the imaginary act of contracting.

Hobbes's theory of contract is the most important of the mature theories because it is the first to finally, and without ambiguity, articulate the modern theory of state sovereignty. This is accomplished in several of his works, but most clearly, and famously, in his *Leviathan: Or the Matter, Forme and Power of a Commonwealth Ecclesiastical and Civil* (1651). And it is clear that Hobbes himself recognizes the revolutionary character of his theoretical insights, that they constitute a radical rejection of the entire corpus of classical and medieval political thought. He dismisses those who "value . . . the authority of an Aristotle, a Cicero, or a Thomas, or any other doctor whatsoever" as fools who put their faith in men rather than right reason.[38] By right reason Hobbes meant science, a coupling of mathematical methods with the insights of the new materialist physics of Galileo. In this, Hobbes extended the purely secular approach to political thinking first developed by Machiavelli, but at a now much more sophisticated level.

As with all mature contract theorists, Hobbes derives his theory of sovereignty from an initial analysis of the state of nature that he character-izes as a "state of war" pitting "every man against every man."[39] This con-dition, according Hobbes, is the result of a human nature that is inherently power seeking, a conclusion he derives from both a "Galilean" analysis of the ceaseless force of our innate drives, and from a brutally honest appraisal of his own (and others) motivations.[40] Given that the conditions of natural equality prevent any one from gaining the upper hand (the stronger will be destroyed by temporary alliances of the weaker), and that unrestrained lib-erty impels us to continuously seek power, the state of nature is inherently a state of ceaseless conflict. In Hobbes's famous characterization it is a condi-tion in which there is "no society; and which is worst of all, continual fear, and danger of violent death; and the life of man, solitary, poor, nasty, brutish, and short."[41]

The issue of "why contract" out of the state of nature is, therefore, not at all problematical for Hobbes. The real issue is not "why do we consent to the formation of the state?"—clearly we have no choice—but "what are the terms of the contract?" Hobbes's answer is as unequivocal as it was, and is, controversial. The contract (covenant) is made "of every man with every man, in such manner, as if every man should say to every man, *I authorize and give up my right of governing myself, to this man, or to this assembly of men, on this condition, that thou give up thy right to him, and authorize all his actions in like manner.* This done, the multitude so united in one person, is called a COMMONWEALTH, in Latin CIVITAS"[42] (today it is called the state, a term that Hobbes uses elsewhere, but here continues to use the more traditional terminology despite his very untraditional analysis). This trans-fer of the right of self-governance, in short, is total and hence irrevocable, which means in effect that the terms of the contract are that all power is given to the person or persons who now represent the wills of all the con-tractors, that is, of each individual in society. The individual who had heretofore possessed total power and right now has neither other than that granted by the person or persons who govern. It is the modern version of the ancient Roman *Lex Regia.*

The controversy that arises is the seemingly contradictory idea that insatiable power seekers would ever be willing to alienate all of their power to any person or persons. Indeed, it is precisely this apparent difficulty that lies behind the subsequent Lockean version of the contract and the entire liberal tradition of state analysis that would follow down to our own day.

For Hobbes, however, the logic of his position was inescapable. Any attempt to retain powers and rights (in Hobbes's analysis the two are identical) would leave individuals free to resist political authority, which would mean a return to the state of nature (war) or, more precisely, would mean that the state of nature had never been left. Clearly, for Hobbes, those Reformation thinkers who were advocating resistance were not only wrong, they were politically dangerous, a fact empirically vindicated in the Thirty Years War and, in Hobbes's time, the English Civil War that formed the background to his political thinking.

It is now clear why Hobbes's analysis constitutes the first unquestionably modern theory of state sovereignty. Note that while the transfer of power is to one man or assembly of men, that is, to government, the real import of the transfer is that it turns the multitude of *individuals* (not corporate groups) into one person, into a public entity. And, states Hobbes "he that carrieth this person is called SOVEREIGN, and said to have *sovereign power*; and every one besides, his SUBJECT."[43] In other words, the government exercises ("carries") the sovereign power of the state; it is not itself the state. This distinction, of course, is crucial to the theory of the modern state and overcomes Bodin's confusion of the indivisibility of sovereignty and the mixed form of government. Although Hobbes prefers monarchy for pragmatic reasons, it now makes no difference what the form of government is, mixed or otherwise, for the government is entirely distinct from the state.

Society is also clearly distinguished from the state in Hobbes's analysis, another crucial element in the modern theory of state sovereignty, for no society exists, or can exist in his view, prior to the creation of the state. There is no preexisting class system out of which the state is created and legitimized, as in the case of the classical regime or later medieval theories of the emerging state. The state creates society, and remains a sovereign entity above society and beyond the claims of any social grouping for political authority apart from the state. In Hobbes the state is finally and clearly conceived as separate from both ruler and ruled; it is entirely impersonal.[44]

Hobbes's theory of contract, therefore, is the modern theory of state sovereignty; not ruler sovereignty, nor yet the even more modern concept of popular sovereignty developed subsequently by Locke and Rousseau. There is in this somewhat of a historical puzzle since the idea of popular sovereignty had actually been developed earlier than state sovereignty by the late Conciliar thinkers and, later, by such thinkers as Althusius.[45] The demise of the medieval concepts of popular sovereignty, however, was inevitable with the collapse of the Conciliar movement and the rise of monarchical absolutism. Hobbes's theory of state sovereignty legitimized monarchical absolutism, and more powerfully than earlier doctrines of ruler sovereignty that were under increasing attack. As such, Hobbes provided a theoretical comprehension of the absolutist state that best conformed to the actual facts of the political situation.

The problem for Hobbes's contemporaries, however, was that his theory denied to all factions the justification for asserting the primacy of deeply held beliefs against the dictates of sovereign authority. For those who resisted royal absolutism and were beginning to articulate concepts of popular sovereignty and doctrines of resistance, most notably the Puritans in England, Hobbes's theory of state sovereignty was obviously anathema. Hobbes's had put sovereignty, more absolute and indivisible than Bodin's, beyond the power of any group to control or limit. What was maddening to the Puritans, however, was that Hobbes had made this the result of consent, the very thing that would seemingly lead to a doctrine of popular sovereignty and a right of resistance. For the Royalists, on the other hand, Hobbes's legitimation of monarchical absolutism (or any form of absolute sovereign authority) had actually delegitimized it. The prevailing justification for absolutism was divine right, a concept of ruler sovereignty premised upon religious assumptions. The coupling of Bodin's more sophisticated theory of sovereignty with the concept of divine right strengthened it, but did not alter its essential character. Hobbes's theory of state sovereignty, however, utterly rejected the idea that the king rules by anything other than power granted by consent. Such a radically secular theory seemed destined to destroy the very basis of absolute authority it ostensibly legitimized, as indeed it ultimately did.

The most troublesome problem in the longer term, however, one that had particular relevance to the emerging middle class, was that the transfer of unlimited, absolute, and inalienable power to the state appeared to be contrary to any possibility of individual liberty, religious or otherwise. This, however, is not what Hobbes himself concluded. He argues that the sovereign authority cannot and need not interfere in all aspects of life. People should be free to "buy, and sell, and otherwise contract with one another; to choose . . . their own trade, and institute their children as they themselves think fit; and the like."[46] This was a crucial point, for the rising bourgeoisie, soon to become the dominant social class undergirding the modern state, was not willing to concede control of the economy and everyday life to the state. Civil society, as it was to become known, must be free from sovereign authority.

Hobbes clearly provided that legal stability that had initially drawn the support of the new middle class for the emerging absolute monarchs. His assertion that sovereign absolutism and economic freedom are compatible was the necessary addition to the requirement of legal order, but despite this the early support of the bourgeoisie for absolutism had increasingly shifted to a demand for liberty premised initially upon Reformation doctrines of resistance. Indeed, in Hobbes's England, the Puritan revolutionaries, led by the new middle classes, were beginning to develop a purely secular and political concept of individual rights. In the long run, therefore, the bourgeoisie would adopt the Lockean theory of popular sovereignty rather than Hobbes's theory of state sovereignty.

This question of rights, however, involved a more profound issue: Precisely what ethical rules apply in the exercise of Hobbes's sovereign authority? Does its absolute and indivisible character release it from any constraint whatsoever beyond that which is self-imposed? In Bodin's theory the sovereign would ideally, if not legally, be constrained by natural law. In Hobbes's, the issue is more problematical. He does in fact employ the doctrine of natural law, something that would be impossible to ignore in the seventeenth and eighteenth centuries, but he defines natural law as little more than rules of self-interest or prudence, the most fundamental of which is "to seek peace and follow it."[47] Indeed, for Hobbes, natural laws "are not properly laws, but qualities that dispose men to peace and obedience."[48] Natural law imposes no ethical constraints beyond this for, as Hobbes insists "covenants, without the sword, are but words, and of no strength to secure a man at all."[49] In brief, natural law is meaningless apart from the imposition of positive law, that is, without the sovereign state. This, of course, is the modern theory of natural law that would be more fully articulated by Pufendorf. And the essential characteristic of this theory is that self-interest and utility constitute the real basis of the state, not natural law or some equivalent ethical standard apart from the state itself.

At a much profounder level than in either Marsilius or Machiavelli, Hobbes's theory of contract spelled the end of the classical and late medieval view that the state is to be understood from the perspective of final ends. As he notes, "there is no . . . *finus ultimus*, utmost arm, nor *summum bonum*, greatest good, as is spoken of in the books of the old moral philosophers."[50] The issue, then, is no longer "what is the ethical purpose, *telos*, or goal of the state?", but "what are the means by which the state maintains social and political order?" As Max Weber would later insist, "Ultimately, one can define the modern state sociologically only in terms of the specific *means* peculiar to it, as to every political association, namely the use of physical force."[51] Not ends, but means, in short, utilitarian considerations of power and self-interest define the modern state and the theory of sovereignty that legitimizes it.

It was in response to this radically new theory of the state that the modern doctrine of popular, and limited, sovereignty was articulated, most notably by John Locke (1632–1704). And while this involved perhaps more a modification of Hobbesian assumptions than an outright rejection of them, Locke's theory of contract nonetheless was crucial in laying the essential foundations of the contemporary liberal-democratic and constitutional theory of the state. That theory, developed most consistently in his *Second Treatise on Civil Government* was, like his less relevant *First Treatise*, a response to Sir Rober Filmer's defense of divine right monarchy in his *Patriarcha*. In its essentials, Locke's critique of Filmer is that since all political power is based upon consent, not upon divine right and patriarchy as Filmer claims, no rational being would agree to submit to absolute monarchy.[52] This critique, however, was obviously directed at Hobbes more than at Filmer, and Locke will insist that the theory of contract cannot logically justify Hobbes's absolute state sovereignty anymore than it can justify Filmer's absolute ruler sovereignty.

The difficulty in Locke's argument is that it is not entirely consistent in its description of the hypothetical state of nature and, as a consequence, in the clarity of its theory of contract. Initially, and contrary to Hobbes, Locke defines the state of nature as a condition of peace and harmony because "the *State of Nature* has a Law of Nature to govern it, which obliges every one: and Reason, which is that Law, teaches all Mankind . . . that being all equal and independent, no one ought to harm another in his Life, Health, Liberty, or Possessions."[53] (Locke appears to employ the concept of natural law here in its medieval sense, although elsewhere he defines it in a more modern form.[54]) Subsequently, however, Locke provides a quite different picture of the state of nature, arguing that the greater part of humankind are "no strict Observers of Equity and Justice," and that as a consequence the rights of the individual are "very uncertain, and constantly exposed to the Invasion of others."[55] This is essentially the Hobbesian view, and its apparent inconsistency with Locke's initial account of the state of nature has drawn much attention from Lockean scholars.[56]

Despite the inconsistency, there seems little doubt that for Locke no less than Hobbes the contractual act is impelled by motives of fear and insecurity, and most specifically for Locke by the insecurity of property. Hence, Locke argues that "the great and *chief end* therefore, of Men's uniting into Commonwealths, and putting themselves under Government, *is the Preservation of their Property*."[57] Locke defines property broadly such that the inalienability of the right to life (by definition inalienable, even for Hobbes, since no rational creature would consent to part with it) is extended to estate and personal liberty as well. As such, these rights exist by nature, not convention, and, contrary to Hobbes can neither be created nor destroyed by government. The purpose of government, therefore, can only be the preservation of people's inalienable property rights, their "Lives, Liberties, and Estates,"[58] and it is this and this alone that constitutes the purpose of the contract.

Locke's theory of natural rights is key to his concept of popular and limited sovereignty. That sovereignty must not only be derived from the people but remain with them is logically imperative for Locke since any final authority above the people would constitute a danger to fundamental property rights. This ultimately was the problem with Hobbes's theory of sovereignty: It posited all rights, including property (both liberty and estate) as ultimately state derived. Hobbes's assurance that the sovereign authority need not interfere in the private domain and economic life was not a sufficient guarantee of the preservation of property or any other right, at least not for the increasingly powerful and propertied middle classes.

But just as logically imperative was the idea that sovereignty must be limited, for the assertion of inalienable rights precluded any notion of absolute sovereign authority, popular or otherwise, over any individual. And it is here that Locke's more pacific view of the state of nature plays a crucial role, for it obviates Hobbes's objection that anything less than absolute sovereign authority will inevitably lead to the initial condition of civil war and anarchy. If human beings can know, and follow, natural law principles, then civilization is possible without absolutism. The problem remains, nonetheless, that this view is inconsistent with the more Hobbesian elements of Locke's theory.

The real difficulty, however, was that the doctrine of popular sovereignty did not in itself solve what would become the defining problem for Locke and, indeed, for the entire liberal tradition since: how to ensure that government protects rather than violates rights. To be sure, Locke's separation of civil society (the private domain of individual property rights) from the state constituted a part of the solution, as did his insistence that government is not created by contract but established merely as a trustee of those rights.[59] This separation of state from both society and government is, of course, the defining characteristic of the modern state and, in Locke, is crucial to ensuring the protection of basic rights. It was not sufficient, however. What was required was the creation of constitutional mechanisms to prevent government from potentially violating rather than protecting rights.

Surely one of Locke's major contributions to Western political thought, and subsequently that of the derivative liberal tradition, is his constitutional theory. Yet, while Locke's constitutionalism is premised upon the modern theory of contract, it owes much to the medieval past. Indeed, he was greatly influenced by the sixteenth-century Anglican theorist Richard Hooker (1554?–1600) who, in his *The Laws of Ecclesiastical Polity*, returned to a medieval and Thomistic conception of both church and secular government in response to the more radical Puritan's claims to a right of resistance.

As we noted in the previous chapter, the great paradox of medieval thought is that it elaborated in theory and practice much of the structure of modern state forms of government without ever articulating a theory of the state and sovereignty as such. In Hooker's analysis, these included parliamentary limitations on the power of the monarch—a key feature of Locke's thought—premised upon a corporatist-consent (not modern contract) view of community rights characteristic of late medieval thought.[60] And, indeed, in England more so than anywhere else in Europe, with some possible exceptions such as the Netherlands and Switzerland, parliamentary and representative institutions such as estate assemblies had developed out of the medieval milieu to a high degree and by Locke's time had become the basis of resistance to the king and his claim to divine right absolutism.[61]

Nonetheless, it must be stressed that the theoretical assumptions behind Locke's thought and his underlying political philosophy were quite different from Hooker's. Locke's theory of popular sovereignty is derived from a modern rather than medieval concept of contract. As in Hobbes, the contractors are individuals possessing fundamental rights, not corporations holding these rights in trust. It is therefore the rights of the individual *qua* individual that are to be constitutionally protected. Among those protections Locke recommends in the *Second Treatise* are a periodically elected legislature, majority rule, and the "separation of powers" (a concept subsequently to influence the thinking of Montesquieu in his *The Spirit of the Laws*, and through that work the American founders). And while the separation of powers corresponds more closely to presidential systems such as the United States than to parliamentary systems characteristic of Locke's England or contemporary British government, the fundamental principle that power should not be concentrated in any one branch of government remains a fundamental constitutional concept in all modern liberal-democratic states.[62]

Clearly, however, the democratic principle itself, the periodic election of legislative representatives, is the key limitation on the power of government for Locke. A government dependent upon the popular will is less likely to violate people's rights. What is problematical, however, and remains so in the contemporary state, is that democracy poses a potential threat to the underlying class structure of the state. Locke's theory of contract of necessity presupposes an initial equality of all contractors, but the right to property in an increasingly commercial society must of equal necessity lead to inequality. Those electors in subordinate class positions, should they appeal to the initial equality (i.e., their fundamental humanity), potentially threaten the stability of the class system and, hence, the legitimacy of the state.

The obvious, but ultimately unsatisfactory solution, was to limit the franchise to the propertied classes. This, as Locke intended, is precisely what happened, and property qualifications for voting lasted well into the nineteenth century and even beyond in all the major liberal-democratic states, in this country and in Europe. The problem was that the logic of the Lockean contract made it theoretically difficult to assert equal rights on the one hand yet limit the means to protect those rights on the other. That this difficulty was recognized early on is clear; the Leveller faction within the parliamentary army under Oliver Cromwell articulated a demand for a still limited manhood suffrage in the famous Putney debates. Locke, influenced by the Levellers, was hardly unaware of the issue.[63] But in the seventeenth century, the limitation of the franchise remained less controversial than it would become later with the emergence of an increasingly large and politically radical working class and, later still, with the rise of the suffragette movement. Ultimately, universal suffrage would prevail as the only legitimate form of franchise in the modern liberal-democratic state. That class inequality has now been coupled with universal suffrage creates inherent tensions within the modern state, and constitutes for some analysts a potential "legitimation crisis."[64]

The last of the major contract theorists Jean-Jacques Rousseau (1712–1778) did however confront this issue of social class more explicitly in his theory of the state than his predecessors. To be sure, both Hobbes and Locke acknowledged the issue, but only to justify for different reasons the existence of a class system given the initial condition of equality in the hypothetical state of nature. Rousseau goes further, attempting to legitimize a particular form of class structure within his ideal state that is consonant with the initial condition.

What makes Rousseau's theory so particularly interesting is that it comes closest to describing the modern state in its theoretical essence while entirely misjudging what it would of necessity become in empirical fact. Indeed, some have even interpreted it as essentially a critique of the large and increasingly impersonal territorial state.[65] For this reason it is best to understand Rousseau's theory as a modern version of the classical theory of the ideal state, as an attempt to found the ethical basis of the ideal as a means to judge the inadequacies of the real, rather than as a representation of any existing or potentially existing state. It is, however, modern, radically so in fact. The underlying epistemological basis of Rousseau's ideal state shares nothing in common with classical or medieval views even though the goal of establishing an ethical foundation to the state is common to both.

Rousseau's theory of contract clearly is framed as a response to both Hobbes's and Locke's analysis. For Rousseau, each had illuminated one of the foundational principles of the modern state while ignoring the other. Hobbes had correctly understood that sovereignty must be absolute, but failed to see that individual liberty must be just as unqualified. Locke had understood that liberty must be secured, but had wrongly limited the sovereign authority in the name of individual rights and, in any case, had rendered popular sovereignty inoperative by putting the legislative authority in the hands of representatives rather than the people as a whole. What Rousseau proposes to do is to combine Hobbes's absolutism with Locke's doctrine of popular sovereignty and individual liberty, but in a way that transcends the inadequacies of each. He frames this project in the form of a question: "Where shall we find a form of association which will defend and protect with the whole common force the person and the property of each associate, and by which every person, while uniting himself with all, shall obey only himself and remain as free as before?"[66]

The Social Contract is in effect an extended answer to this question. Rousseau claims that his theory of contract resolves the contradiction between absolute sovereignty on the one hand and absolute individual liberty on the other. In his version of the contractual act the citizen is at once utterly obligated to the state yet remains completely free. In political terms, this is equivalent to "squaring the circle," to making the state the source of two apparently contrary qualities. Yet without this unity of obligation and freedom Rousseau believed the state could neither survive nor be considered ethically legitimate. No social order can sustain itself without a total commitment to its necessity, and this means for Rousseau an unquestioning obedience to the law of the sovereign. In this, he agrees with Hobbes, though not for the same reasons. Yet, without an equally extensive freedom the state cannot be legitimized, for legitimacy can be granted only by those who freely give it. Needless to say, the emerging modern states of Europe were in Rousseau's view entirely illegitimate since divine right monarchy precluded freedom, and Lockean forms of liberty, where they existed, were at best limited and incomplete.

The answer to the puzzle that Rousseau presents is to be found in his analysis of the state of nature. Unlike his predecessors, both of whom posit a preexisting human nature, Rousseau insists that prior to the formation of the state human beings, while unconditionally free and equal, are little more than irrational animals. They are without language, lacking in all sociability (apart from brief mating liaisons, Rousseau's "natural man" is even more isolated than Hobbes's), and devoid of ethical purpose.[67] They are motivated by self-interest, although of a benign kind, and apart from a natural capacity to pity another's suffering have no traits of civilization whatsoever.[68]

The difficulty with this analysis is that the contractual act requires rational calculation on the part of the contractors, something Rousseau's natural man is incapable of. Moreover, there needs be some inconvenience in the state of nature to impel the creation of political society, and this is never clearly specified by Rousseau.[69] The problem is that the logic of contract theory is simply not adequate to Rousseau's purposes. A different theoretical model would have served him better, and the theory of contract, so crucially important in the early development of the legitimizing ideology of the modern state, was in fact soon to be discarded by political thinkers.

These difficulties aside, in Rousseau's analysis the state is neither the result of rational calculation, as in Hobbes, nor rational calculation combined with ethical principles such as natural law and right, as in Locke, but rather is the cause of rationality and ethical knowledge. In Rousseau's words, "The passing from the state of nature to the civil state produces in man a very remarkable change, by substituting justice for instinct in his conduct, and giving to his actions a moral character which they lacked before."[70] Hobbes and Locke had gotten it backwards. They assumed a preexisting human nature that explained and legitimized the formation of the state, but it was the state itself that produced the behavior mistakenly assumed to be innate. In Rousseau's terms, they "spoke about savage man and they described civil man."[71]

The implications of this critique of earlier contract theorists are profound. If it is the state itself that makes humans social and ethical beings, then one cannot legitimize the state by reading back into the state of nature some notion of an innate human nature. This is all the more the case if the state is not organized appropriately, a condition Rousseau believed to be true of all modern European states. It was this, not the state as such, that produced not only the power seeking behavior upon which Hobbes erected his theory of the state, but the Lockean doctrine of natural law meant to hold this behavior in check. And for Rousseau the basis of this inappropriate organization could be traced to one fundamental cause: class inequality.[72]

The seemingly obvious solution to the problem would be the creation of a classless society and, indeed, some have read into Rousseau's *Second Discourse* something approaching this kind of pre-Marxian Marxism. But for Marx, and quite in line with all modern anthropological evidence, a classless society is inherently a stateless society, and this Rousseau rejects. As we have seen, in his view a stateless society is by definition not a human one. Yet, if the state is necessary, and if social class is inherently the sociological basis of the state, how then can natural equality, and therefore liberty, be made compatible with its civil counterpart?[73]

The greater part of *The Social Contract* is essentially an attempt to resolve these issues, to demonstrate that in the appropriate class organization of state and society the essence of natural equality can be maintained and thereby liberty in which "every person . . . shall obey only himself and remain as free as before." What Rousseau proposes in this regard, then, is not the elimination of social class, but its modification such that "no citizen should be sufficiently opulent to be able to purchase another, and none so poor as to be forced to sell himself."[74] Under these conditions liberty is maintained since no one's free agency is subordinated to another's class interests. To be sure, this is not identical to the absolute equality of the natural condition, but it accomplishes the same objective of maintaining liberty, or at least Rousseau believes it does.[75]

From a Lockean, and certainly from a subsequent classical liberal perspective, limiting the possession of property would constitute a violation of one's natural rights. For Rousseau, however, all (civil) rights are conventional, created in the act of contracting. And while Rousseau concedes that property is "the most sacred of conventions," he is simply affirming the obvious that in every state property of some kind—hence social class—has always existed. Its legitimacy therefore resides in the fact of its pervasiveness in state systems, not in any metaphysical category transcending the state such as natural law-right.[76] Hence, while it would violate sacred convention to eliminate private property entirely, it would not be a violation of convention to limit its possession. In Rousseau's view, extreme acquisitiveness is a sign of a decadent social and political order, not the true basis of consent as both Hobbes and Locke had mistakenly believed.

The profounder implications of Rousseau's conventionalism transcend the issue of property rights, however. They go to the core of Western state theory, for the traditional view had been that conventions cannot validate ethical principles, and that conventions alone, therefore, cannot legitimate the state. Historically the state had always been legitimized upon some notion of an absolutized ethical standard, whether the classical concept of form, the medieval notion of natural law, or the modern doctrine of divine right. Even when a more strictly secular theory of the state began to emerge with Machiavelli, few thinkers, even Hobbes, were willing to eliminate at least the language of a priori ethical standards, if not the substance. What Rousseau argues in *The Social Contract* is that while ethical standards are conventional, created by consent alone, where state and society are appropriately organized they nonetheless are as valid and obligatory as ethical standards supposedly derived a priori from nature or from God. This is a radical assertion given the history of Western ethical and political thought, and it could be sustained only by a radical interpretation of the terms of the contract by which these conventions were created, that is, by a radically new concept of sovereignty that Rousseau terms the "general will."

The general will is Rousseau's great and enduring contribution, not only to state theory, but to Western political thought generally. It is the general will, a purely conventionalist theory of the state and sovereignty, that unites freedom and obligation, Locke and Hobbes. As the term itself indicates, the general will is the political will of the entire community, and this can be created only in an act of contracting in which each individual turns over all of their rights and powers, not to one man or assembly of men as in Hobbes, nor in effect to a representative legislature as in Locke, but to each other. In this way legislative authority remains perpetually in the hands of the citizens as a whole such that the citizen "shall obey only himself and remain as free as before." And, setting aside the practicality of such a scheme for the moment, the logic of Rousseau's position is unassailable. Given his extreme conventionalism and therefore the necessity of the sovereign authority to create a moral obligation in law (for there is no *a priori* moral standard apart from law), obedience to law can be considered free only so long as the citizens have made the law themselves.

For Rousseau, then, freedom depends upon a concept of popular sovereignty much more radical than Locke's, yet as absolute as Hobbes's theory of state sovereignty. Indeed, Rousseau in effect conflates the two concepts of sovereignty into one. "The public person," says Rousseau "is . . . called 'State' when it is passive, 'Sovereign' when in activity."[77] Correspondingly, individuals are called " 'citizens,' as participating in the sovereign authority, and . . .'subjects,' because they are subjected to the law of the state."[78] Given that most are subjects most of the time, state sovereignty thus remains the fundamental reality even in Rousseau. This suggests that even a radically democratized sovereign authority does not obviate the reality of state sovereignty, that this is the truth of the modern state despite appeals to the will of the people.

Nonetheless, Rousseau would insist that so long as the law of the impersonal state reflects the general will, obedience to law remains an act of freedom, that obligation and liberty in his ideal state are one. The obvious difficulty, however, is that the legislative assembly of the whole people, no less than Locke's representative assembly, must in practical terms work upon the principle of majority rule. How then can it be asserted that the citizen who must obey laws to which he has not agreed is free?

Rousseau's answer is as ingenious as it is problematical. Given that the general will is general (i.e., an expression of the will of all public spirited citizens), it is always morally correct in the sense that it always attempts to articulate the public interest.[79] This, at least, so long as the general will remains general, that is, has not become perverted by the emergence of particular wills contrary to the public good as Rousseau believes to be the case in all existing European states. In a properly constructed state Rousseau argues that citizens will always seek the general will rather than their private (class) interests and, as a consequence, the dissenters will freely give their obedience to the law since as citizens their primary motive is to the public good, that is, to the continued existence of the general will. What matters to the minority is that the majority has sought the public interest, not that unanimity has been attained. In those rare cases where there is resistance to sovereign authority, Rousseau admits that the recalcitrant citizen must be coerced into obedience. But, he insists in a statement that remains as controversial now as when it was first articulated, "this . . . only forces him to be free."[80]

It is this statement, more than any other, that has led some to conclude that Rousseau is an exponent of totalitarianism, but this is not Rousseau's logic or intent. Rousseau's concept of liberty is classical or positive, though articulated on a modern conventionalist basis, in which freedom is understood to be conformity to some moral end or purpose. This is contrary to the Hobbesian–Lockean and derivative classical liberal position that conceives freedom in strictly negative terms, as simply the absence of law prohibiting some action, the moral intent of the action or lack thereof being entirely irrelevant. Force and freedom in this view can never be conflated. If liberty is defined in positive terms, however, then any action contrary to the moral purpose of the state cannot be considered freedom, and force to compel obedience cannot be considered contrary to freedom but, in fact, its realization. That this reasoning will not satisfy those within the liberal individualistic tradition goes without saying, but Rousseau is simply attempting to construct a concept of freedom that is rooted in a broader ethical framework, not glorify force in the name of freedom.

Indeed, the real issue for Rousseau is not how to legitimize coercion in his ideal state, but how to insure that it will rarely if ever be necessary. The answer lies in maintaining the purity of the general will, of guaranteeing that it will reflect the public interest rather than deteriorating into the private interests of the citizens. To this end, Rousseau advocates a number of measures (not all to be found in *The Social Contract*) both political and socioeconomic. The political measures have largely to do with the structure of the state, the most important of which is to insure the autonomy of the general will. Many of Rousseau's proposals in this regard are fairly obvious. Most importantly, the legislative body of all citizens must meet regularly, although not frequently since its primary purpose, Rousseau argues, is to confirm the existing government and constitutional structure. What is crucially important to Rousseau, however, is that the general will not be confused with, or subverted by, government. Like Locke, Rousseau insists that government is not created by a contractual act but is instituted only to carry out the dictates of the general will. In this, Rousseau clearly maintains the modern distinction between state and government, so much so that the principles upon which each is premised are entirely different.[81] The state must be democratic; the government may take a number of forms. For Rousseau the ideal is an elective aristocracy.[82]

As to the social and economic measures recommended, they essentially aim at eliminating the profusion and intensity of private concerns that, in

Rousseau's mind, characterize the modern European state. These would include an agrarian economy, simplicity of manners, and the like, ideals that would endear Rousseau to the later Romantics but ones that hardly conformed to the reality of the size and scale of the emerging territorial state. Most importantly, however, is preventing the emergence of extreme class divisions. This, as we have noted, is the paramount factor in maintaining the general will, that is, the legitimacy of the state, for a society divided by extremes of wealth and poverty, of property and its absence, will inevitably pervert the general will, transforming it from a body seeking the public good to one rent by class conflict. It is for this reason that Rousseau's economic theory, developed most consistently in his *Discourse on Political Economy*, is premised not upon the endless accumulation of wealth as in the Lockean-liberal tradition, but upon its limitation through state regulation.[83]

The problem in this analysis, and indeed the problem inherent in all modern contract theory, is that whether property is defined as natural or conventional, the class inequalities that result contradict the original condition of equality. That Rousseau limits these in his ideal state is true enough, but this does not ultimately resolve the issue. There is, of course, an obvious way out of these theoretical difficulties: Drop the theory of contract and erect a theory of the state that does not require an initial condition of equality. This, as we have noted, was the method of every political thinker until the mature theory of contract, but it was an approach employed by some early modern theorists as well.

Most notable is *The Commonwealth of Oceana* by James Harrington (1611–1677), a quasi-utopian work advocating a republican system of government. In the seventeenth century, republican ideals competed, unsuccessfully, with contractual theories opposing absolute monarchy, Harrington's utopia being theoretically the most important of these. Its importance, however, at least for the contemporary reader, is not so much the specifics of his republicanism, but its recognition that the distribution of property determines the structure of the state. It was Harrington's conclusion that a viable republican system requires a balance of classes and a predominant middle class (the yeomen in Harrington's time) as anchor to the entire system.[84]

Clearly Harrington pursued a tradition of political thinking that was not only classical-Aristotelian, but that hearkened back to Machiavelli and Renaissance republicanism as well.[85] Just as clearly it constituted a rejection of Hobbes's contractual and rational-legal theory of the state that ignored class as the determining factor in state formation. But it also looked forward to such thinkers as, Burke, Tocqueville, Hegel, and others who, despite their differing political ideals, all recognized the class basis of the state and premised their political thinking upon it. And they, the sociological theorists of the state if we may so term them, were entirely correct in this.[86] Why, then, did this tradition of political thought not become the basis of the legitimizing ideology of the modern state? It was not simply Harrington's republicanism that failed in this regard, but any theoretical legitimation of the state based on social class.

The answer should by now be readily apparent. The state had become increasingly centralized by the absolute monarchs of Western Europe and this had required the subordination of heretofore autonomous groups: towns, guilds, feudatory domains of one sort or another, inferior magistrates, and, most importantly, the system of estates. The mature contract theorists, beginning with Hobbes, had legitimized this process of state centralization even when, in the case of Locke and Rousseau, it was in opposition to absolute monarchy. But the legitimation was premised precisely on recognizing the state as an impersonal sovereign authority superior to any other group within its territory, including social classes. This in turn required that political authority be derived from individuals rather than from traditional corporate groupings such as estates, and this could be accomplished only by assuming an individual equality of rights in the foundation (contract) of the state.

The problem, of course, was that none of this altered the fact of class stratification, as the mature contract thinkers were well aware. But here the key element in the abstract-impersonal state, the separation of state and society, provided the way out of the dilemma so to speak. With the partial exception of Rousseau whose radically democratic conception of sovereignty required regulation of the class system, the contract theorists simply relegated class issues to the private domain of civil society and, in the case of Locke, offered only private solutions. In this way, the ideology of legitimation of the modern state became premised upon a denial of what the state inherently is: the political organization of a class stratified society.

The consequences of this, in effect, depoliticization of class issues was soon to produce quite contrary results. The last two centuries would be characterized by the emergence of class politics both radical and liberal, and demands for the extension of the franchise were invariably extended to demands for social and economic reform requiring state intervention. The difficulty was, and remains, how to integrate—or rather reintegrate— a political structure legitimized in impersonal and egalitarian terms with a social and economic order organized on quite different premises. Political theory invariably reflected this dilemma. The classical liberal tradition, the outlines of which are to be found in Hobbes and Locke though not fully developed until the early nineteenth century, would require rethinking. Clearly, some notion of an ethical responsibility beyond the purely economic individualism of civil society would have to be introduced into the equation. This, however, would require reinvigorating the concept of an ethical community standing between the now autonomous individual and the centralized state.

This brings us back to Rousseau. On the one hand, as a modern contract theorist, Rousseau perpetuated the concept of the centralized state and individualism (it is the individual who contracts and who possesses a share in sovereign authority), but he also insisted on the necessity of an ethical community as the moral—though conventional—basis of the state. The latter is encapsulated in his concept of the general will, a concept that would have implications far exceeding, and probably contrary to, what Rousseau could have imagined or wished. It had a profound influence on later thinkers, Hegel most notably, who while jettisoning Rousseau's epistemology and methodology affirmed the state as above all an ethical community. Yet it also became the basis for the most powerful and ultimately destructive state ideology of the modern world, nationalism, the glorification of a bogus ethical community premised upon the "general will" of the nation.

Chapter Six

The Metaphysical Theory of the State

> The state is the actuality of the ethical Idea. It is ethical mind *qua* the substantial will manifest and revealed to itself, knowing and thinking itself, accomplishing what it knows and in so far as it knows it. The state exists immediately in custom, mediately in individual self-consciousness, knowledge, and activity, while self-consciousness in virtue of its sentiment towards the state finds in the state, as its essence and the end and product of its activity, its substantive freedom.[1]

So begins Georg Wilhelm Friedrich Hegel's analysis of the modern state in his *Grundlinien der Philosophie des Rechts* (*Philosophy of Right*), his major contribution to modern state theory. Given the complex language that Hegel (1770–1831) employs, and the idealist metaphysics that undergirds it, it is perhaps not surprising that he is not widely read. Yet, it is simply impossible to study the theoretical history of the state and leave Hegel out of account, both because he provides a legitimizing ideology of the modern state that has had a great influence on later liberal thinkers, and because he advances an analysis of its actual structure and function that is far ahead of his time.

Hegel's idealism was a response to the "transcendental idealism" of Immanuel Kant (1724–1804) who, in turn, was attempting to resolve the profoundly disturbing issues raised by David Hume (1711–1776). Hume had asserted that reason was capable of positing neither the existence of any absolute moral truth,[2] nor even the reality of concepts employed to understand the empirical world (the most famous example is Hume's argument that cause and effect, while concepts required to describe the empirical world, are themselves not empirically verifiable).[3] The rejection of any a priori moral order had, of course, been developing for some time, and in Hume's political thought resulted in a strictly utilitarian legitimation of the state.[4] This involved a rejection of the theory of contract, and of the ancient tradition of natural law and natural right.

Kant's response to Hume was to argue in his most celebrated work, the *Critique of Pure Reason*, that theoretical reason (empirical science), properly understood, is capable of factual knowledge, although not knowledge of empirical "things in themselves."[5] He insisted also on the reality of ethical categories in his the *Critique of Practical Reason* and other works of moral philosophy. Here Kant attempts to demonstrate the autonomy of the moral will such that reason is required to obey certain ethical obligations imposed by the will: the famous "categorical imperative," the essence of which is to treat others from the point of view of ends, never means.[6] This, of course, is reminiscent of the ancient natural law tradition, although the underlying metaphysical and epistemological premises are not entirely the same.[7] Nonetheless, the political conclusions drawn by Kant, contrary to Hume, are similar to the natural law theory in that ethical judgments apart from mere utility can be made about the appropriate form of state. In Kant, this leads to a defense of republican forms of government and, in vehement opposition to Hobbes, to an absolute prohibition against war.[8]

While initially it had seemed that Kant's transcendental idealism had saved both theoretical and practical reason from Hume's critique, subsequent thinkers began to have doubts. The domain of practical reason did not seem adequately integrated with that of theoretical reason; that human nature somehow seemed divided into two parts corresponding to the distinction between fact and value.[9] Of the various solutions to these difficulties, it was Hegel's that ultimately proved most influential.

Hegel managed to transcend these dichotomies by unifying them in a higher synthesis or unity. This, of course, is the terribly misunderstood dialectic developed in its formal aspects in his *Logic*.[10] Essentially, Hegel argues that the form and content of thought, subject and object, facts and values—in brief, the entire phenomenal world and our actions within it—constitute a unified whole in a ceaseless state of contradiction and transformation. How we comprehend our empirical and moral existence, therefore, is shaped by the actual circumstances—cultural, historical, and political—in which we are immersed and, conversely, our comprehension shapes the reality that is shaping us. We thus comprehend not through stasis, but through transformations of our social and political reality that we ourselves bring about, though unwittingly for the most part, a kind of unconscious *praxis*. As such, the world, both empirically and morally, is not something out there that is either not comprehensible, as in Hume, or divided into distinct realms of theoretical and practical knowing, as in Kant, but knowable precisely because it is embedded and interconnected in our very existence as natural and ethical beings.

The difficulty, if left at this, is that the dialectic would seemingly relativize (historicize) both empirical and ethical knowledge since philosophy, science, and ethics could comprehend only that which has been given historically through the various dialectical transformations. What was needed was an absolutized metaphysical grounding for the dialectic. This Hegel provides with his concept of the *absolute Idea*. The absolute Idea constitutes the ultimate rational organization of the universe that, in Hegel's analysis, the dialectic is progressively unfolding to human consciousness. While every historically given form of consciousness, theoretical or practical, has thus been limited in that it only imperfectly comprehended reality, consciousness has also approached reality ever more closely over time. Once consciousness becomes fully aware of reality, of the unchanging rational basis to existence (being comprehended through dialectical becoming), the dichotomies introduced by Kant are overcome. Consciousness now knows itself to be the true reality because it recognizes its own reality as the universal rationality of all things.[11]

Such a metaphysical understanding would not be possible, of course, unless history had already reached its end stage. This Hegel of necessity presumes, and concludes that his philosophical system constitutes, so to speak, the "end of history." Minerva's owl, to paraphrase Hegel's famous statement in the "Preface" to the *Philosophy of Right*, had taken its final flight. What this meant ultimately for Hegel is that the potentiality of human freedom had now, for the first time, been attained, for only now was it possible for the will to be in conformity with absolute rational principles of ethical behavior.[12] Kant had argued correctly, in line with the primary ethical tradition of Western thought, that freedom can only be defined as the exercise of the rationally moral will, but the will could not be fully rational until it grasped the absolute Idea in its fullness. The dialectic of history had resolved the Kantian dichotomies, as Hegel's philosophy now comprehended this process in a grand retrospective of historical evolution.

Now, one need go no further to understand why Hegel's influence on contemporary social science has been nonexistent. His idealist metaphysics is seemingly incompatible with the materialism and empiricism of the social sciences. It is important to stress, however, that Hegel's idealism—he terms "absolute idealism" in contradistinction to Kant's "transcendental idealism"—is premised not upon vague ideal abstractions but upon the historically given expression of those abstractions in concrete-objective form.[13] It was for this reason that he rejected subjective forms of idealism and the romanticism of the post-French revolutionary period.[14] A purely personal ethical and spiritual life divorced from the historically given institutions of social and political life is at best meaningless for Hegel. Indeed, this emphasis on objectification is key to understanding Hegel's theory of the modern state.

Hegel's historiography is premised, therefore, on tracing the evolution of human consciousness in the actual evolution of the historically given institutions of social and political life. This he details in his *Philosophy of History*, but summarizes sufficiently for our purposes in the *Philosophy of Right*. Broadly viewed, Hegel argues that earlier forms of civilization either had failed to develop those institutions necessary for consciousness to become autonomous—the "oriental realm" in Hegel's typology—or had only partially developed them such that consciousness could not perceive reality in its completeness. Those that had begun the process of liberating consciousness, the classical Greek philosophers, had nonetheless set in motion the movement of thought in history that would culminate in complete understanding of the unity of thought and institutional reality—in brief, of the absolute Idea.

The Greek realm was nonetheless wanting in Hegel's analysis. The citizen of the Greek city-state was totally immersed in the polity; his self-identity was one with it. The *polis*, which in other regards Hegel has the greatest admiration for, lacked the possibility of subjectivity, a key term in Hegel's political analysis. Freedom in its fullest sense, realized only in the modern state according to Hegel, requires that the subjective will of the individual be granted a wide latitude; that its willing of the universal not obscure its particularity. Seen in this light, the Roman realm had the opposite inadequacy for Hegel, for, in the age of empire, class conflict reduced the polity to "insatiable self-will."[15] It was the Roman Empire, on the other hand, that salvaged Christianity from obscurity, thus insuring its ultimate incorporation into the Western world.

The passing on of the Christian tradition belongs to the Germanic realm, in Hegel's historiography the last stage of human history before the emergence of the modern state. And what was crucial in this was that Christianity, and for Hegel the Protestant Reformation in particular, introduced subjectivity into world history by emphasizing the inner religious experience. But pure innerness is not sufficient for full human actualization and freedom for Hegel. This inner subjectivity rooted in otherworldliness needed to be connected to an outer this-worldly reality. The dialectic between the medieval church and empire provided this linkage according to Hegel, for while they struggled with each other for supremacy, they were premised upon the same idea: a unified Christian republic. As a consequence, Hegel argues, the outcome produced a situation in which "the realm of fact has discarded its barbarity and unrighteous caprice, while the realm of truth has abandoned the world of beyond and its arbitrary force, so that the true reconciliation which discloses the state as the image and actuality of reason has become objective."[16] This is the meaning of Hegel's statement in the opening quotation of this chapter that "the state is the actuality of the ethical Idea" in which self-consciousness finds "its substantive freedom."[17]

Now it must be admitted that for many Hegel's Euro-centrism will prove as problematical as his metaphysics. Yet, given that the key political institution of the modern world is the state, then Europe must of necessity constitute the focus of historical analysis, for the state in its modern sense is unquestionably a European institution. In this sense he is entirely correct in beginning with the classical and Christian worlds, for the entire history of Western state thought begins there. What ultimately is important at any rate, cultural prejudices aside, is what he saw historically objectified in his own time, an entirely new form of polity that had been formally recognized in 1648 in the Treaty of Westphalia and that, following the great French revolution of 1789, was increasingly evolving into its modern form.

The French Revolution had enormous importance for Hegel, for it not only spelled the end of the ancien régime in France, but under Napoleon, in much of the rest of Europe. Most importantly, the revolution had been carried out by the third estate, the emerging bourgeoisie, which came to assert its political legitimacy and to wrest the power of the state from the control of the nobility. For Hegel, this was the crucial fact, for he understood that the sociological foundations of the modern state of necessity would be constituted by a new class system premised upon the dominance of the bourgeoisie. As importantly, he understood that the mode of political thinking characteristic of this new class was utterly inadequate to a genuine philosophy of the modern state.

This new mode of thinking involved two interrelated ideologies, liberalism and nationalism, both products of the French Revolution and both constituting the core worldview of the newly empowered bourgeoisie. Liberalism, in its early or classical formulation was an economic as well as political doctrine, both derivative from John Locke. Locke's political theory legitimized the impersonal state on the basis of the protection of rights, but rights defined in economic terms as property. In Adam Smith, Ricardo, Malthus, and other classical economists (and to some extent even earlier in the work of the French *physiocrats*) these rights were elaborated into a comprehensive doctrine of laissez-faire capitalism. The classical liberal doctrine of the negative or minimalist state followed inevitably from these economic premises. The state was crucial to the functioning of a capitalist market, but its functions, particularly in the economic sphere, were to be limited almost to the point of nonexistence.

The political doctrine of liberalism underwent a more profound modification in the works of Jeremy Bentham (1748–1832) and the utilitarians. In his primary work on utilitarianism, *An Introduction to the Principles of Morals and Legislation*, Bentham discarded the entire philosophical basis of the liberal doctrine in Locke and his followers—natural right and the theory of contract—for the principle of utility in which rights, as well as all other ethical categories, were legitimized on the basis of their capacity to produce pleasure or minimize pain.[18] When applied to the community as a whole, that is, to the political domain, the function of the state becomes, in Bentham's famous formulation, to insure "the greatest happiness of the greatest number."[19] And while this might seem to justify an interventionist theory of the state (as in fact initially it did for Bentham), in fact the early utilitarians were powerful advocates of the laissez-faire system and the negative state, asserting that the free market was the surest guarantee of the greatest happiness principle.

All that was required for a fully developed utilitarian theory of the state was to base its constitutional structure upon these same utilitarian principles. This was accomplished primarily by James Mill (1773–1836), Bentham's most famous follower, who in his *An Essay on Government* advocated the essentials of the classical liberal constitutional ideal. These included protection of fundamental rights, limited government, and representative democracy as the surest guarantee of the "greatest happiness of the greatest number."[20] In effect, Bentham and his followers had combined Locke's incipient liberalism with Hobbes's hedonistic psychology. When this political theory was combined with classical economics, as it was in a movement known as philosophical radicalism, the classical liberal theory of the state was complete.[21]

Classical liberalism became in essence the legitimizing ideology of the modern impersonal state, now increasingly democratic and capitalist, throughout the nineteenth and into the twentieth century. The difficulty, however, was that in real human terms this new science of politics was utterly lacking as an ideology of state legitimation. The principle of utility worked well enough as a justification of civil society, but for most people, and certainly for Hegel, the state's authority must rest on something more ethically substantive than this. In the early history of state formations some ultimate purpose—some final end—to the state's existence had always been posited, typically in a foundation myth of some kind or other. That the increasingly secular and utilitarian view of the state, evolving since the Renaissance if not perhaps from the later Middle Ages on, had culminated in a conception of the state founded on nothing more than individual self-interest and centralized power would subsequently raise legitimation issues to the forefront of theoretical concern. Hegel's theory of the state must be understood in light of these issues, as must the later development of modern liberalism that draws upon Hegel's critique of the classical doctrine.

What did provide a more human, if even less theoretically profound, basis of state legitimation was nationalism. Indeed, nationalism was initially an unthinking response to the French Revolution and its export rather than the application of any prior theoretical developments. This would come later, although nationalism never did attain a significant theoretical status. It certainly did not for Hegel, although one of the most serious yet common errors in interpreting Hegel's theory of the state is to read him as a German nationalist.[22] Hegel certainly accepted nationalism as a politically useful sentiment when linked to some actual territorial state; he clearly did not accept it as a valid legitimation of the state.[23]

Early liberals did, however, for it provided a semblance of community that softened the otherwise harsh reality of the market system and the growing class inequality of capitalist society. And initially it seemed compatible with, and even necessary to, the liberal ideology, for such nationalist principles as "self-determination" appeared to protect those key liberal rights that now defined the territorial state.[24] Indeed, nationalism was initially framed in cosmopolitan terms, a unity of humankind organized into sovereign territorial states premised upon a common set of rights and republican principles of government. Mazzini (1805–1872), the great Italian nationalist, is the most notable representative of this type of early nationalism.[25] Moreover, Nationalism was based on the notion of "the people" as the repository of political authority, an idea that had its roots in the liberal doctrine of popular sovereignty developed in its most radical form in Rousseau's concept of the general will.[26] While few early liberals supported such a radically democratic conception of the state as that proposed by Rousseau, it was unquestioned that the state's legitimacy did require popular consent whether conceived in utilitarian or contractual terms.

Ultimately, however, nationalism would prove incompatible with liberal ideals. With the increasing extension of the franchise, nationalism became democratized, deriving its theoretical justification from a radical interpretation of Rousseau's general will as the *volkgeist* or some other quasi-romanticized or spiritualized concept of "the people." The nation now came to stand, not merely for citizens within a given territory, but for those with common linguistic, cultural, and even racial characteristics to which individual rights were all too frequently subordinated.[27] And the principle of self-determination, once viewed as a defense of liberal ideals, now became a justification for the implementation within territorial boundaries of policies contrary to liberal principles, and ultimately, toward the end of the nineteenth century, for the imperial conquest of "inferior nations" on the part of European powers.

These facts, however, postdate Hegel. What was important to him at any rate, was not the ideology of liberal-nationalism as such, which he found woefully inadequate to a theory of the modern state, but the underlying economic and sociological conditions that had generated this ideology. In his view the modern state could not be understood apart from the increasingly industrialized and capitalist structure of society and the concomitant dominance of the modern bourgeoisie socially, economically, and politically. In brief, it could not be understood apart from civil society, a term that had its origins in the eighteenth century and that is employed by Hegel to describe the complex of legally recognized socioeconomic and class relations that undergird the modern state.[28] What makes Hegel's analysis unique, however, is that while it is premised upon the existence of civil society, it does not derive its model of state formation and legitimation from it. This, in fact, is what distinguishes Hegel's theory of the state from the liberal theory that, to Hegel's mind, confuses the state with civil society.

As with so much else in Hegel, however, it is not quite this simple and direct. Hegel's critique of liberalism for confusing state and civil society rests upon a more profound epistemological critique: its failure to grasp the difference between *reason* and *understanding*. Understanding for Hegel is the comprehension of phenomena that are presented to consciousness in their immediacy, as they are initially perceived in their specific manifestations or particularities. This is the domain of empirical science that understands the world by abstracting from it certain logical principles or laws of a descriptive and explanatory nature. These abstractions, however, refer only to the workings of the empirical world, in Hegel's terms to the mere content of what is given in sensation, and its limitation is that it fails to unite content with form, that is, the particular with the universal rational principle that is manifest as potentiality in all levels of existence: in nature, in history, and ultimately in human consciousness. While understanding thus points to the existence of form, it never comprehends it except, in Hegel's words, abstractly as an "abstract universal."

The other, philosophical mode of comprehension Hegel terms reason. Unlike understanding, reason does unite content with form such that the rational principle that is immanent within the particular is revealed to consciousness.[29] It is the dialectical evolution of the world in all its manifestations that exposes its rational potential for Hegel, for what is "real is rational" and is revealed precisely in this evolution. This means that thought can become something more than empty abstractions only when it is connected to the concrete expression of the underlying universal rationality of things. When, in reason, it is connected, it becomes for Hegel the concept (*Begriff*), thought which is expressed concretely, outwardly in human institutions and inwardly as the comprehension of the universal inherent in these institutions. In Hegel's terms, therefore, unlike the mere abstract universal posited by the understanding, reason reveals the "concrete universal."[30]

It was precisely this that liberalism, that is the classical doctrine with which Hegel was familiar, failed to comprehend, for its theory of the state was based upon understanding rather than reason. As such, it was premised upon the prevailing structure of socioeconomic and political institutions. It took at face value the existence of the territorial state, the modern theory of sovereignty that legitimized it, and the atomistic individualism of civil society upon which the contractual as well as the utilitarian concept of sovereignty was based. And it assumed that what now existed constituted a final and complete expression of human possibilities. Consequently, liberalism reflected a static, mechanistic, and linear rather than a dynamic, organic, and dialectical grasp of reality. The result was, when applied to the state, a purely abstract concept of political institutions.

This is most evidently seen in Hegel's critique of the liberal theory of rights. It is, Hegel argues "one of the commonest blunders of abstract thinking to make private rights and private welfare count as absolute in opposition to the universality of the state."[31] Abstract thinking, that is, understanding, is capable of going no further than what exists empirically, yet assumes that what exists at any given time is complete and inevitable. As such, it cannot go beyond the characterization of institutions, in this case rights, as entities that exist merely as abstract categories. I as an individual have rights, but the larger context in which these rights exist, most importantly the state, is ignored or rather is legitimized as a universal—but only as an abstract universal. And the same problem applies to duties, the other side of rights. I have a duty, an "ought," to respect other's rights, but the mere assertion of "an ought to do" is as abstract as the rights I am supposed to respect (it was for this reason that Hegel rejected the purely abstract character of Kant's categorical imperative).[32]

What is lacking in the liberal view according to Hegel is the recognition that rights, duties, or any other ethico-political category do not exist abstractly but concretely in the institutions of the state that alone give them reality. This reality is not simply that the state exists to protect rights or to enforce duties through coercive law. This is the classical liberal theory of the (negative) state that is based upon a purely abstract conception of these terms. Rather, the state exists to actualize these rights and duties, not just in the sense of objectifying them outwardly in the constitutional structure of the state, but inwardly in individual consciousness. And since the modern state in Hegel's analysis has finally objectified fully the conditions for a completely rational comprehension of rights and duties, it follows that for the first time in history, human freedom—the unity of individual will and political authority or, in Hegel's terms, of the particular will and the universal—is possible.[33]

This is the logic behind Hegel's claim that the modern state constitutes the highest form of freedom, a claim that has remained controversial because its meaning has not always been properly understood, or has been grossly misinterpreted in nationalistic terms. And note that Hegel's conception of freedom is radically different from that of the liberals of his day. Like the classical thinkers, Hegel has a positive concept of freedom in contradistinction to the liberal theory of negative liberty. To be free means to exercise one's liberty with some ethical end in view, and to know why that end is ethically imperative. And for freedom to exist in its fullest extent it is not sufficient that the ethical end be simply a matter of belief, religious or cultural, but that it be known by reason to be valid, something possible only where subjective reason is united with its objectification within the constitutional structure of the state.

It will be noted that this view of human freedom, premised though it is upon conformity to the authority of the state, does not abolish individual subjectivity. On the contrary, for the uniqueness of the modern state according to Hegel, and the very basis of its legitimation, rests upon the fact that it is premised upon subjectivity. The individual's will remains subjectively free because it wills that which is objectified in the state. The particular will is not subordinated to the universal will of the state, rather it is made real, or "universalized" in its particularity. This is crucial, for were subjectivity abolished the state would be little more than a coercive institution above and apart from the individual, and this would be true irrespective of the form of government, whether democratic or not. In Weber's famous definition, it would be simply a legitimation of violence, an institution premised upon force rather than upon the subjectively free will.

Indeed, this emphasis on the subjectively free will is key to Hegel's theory of the state. In this, Hegel is in fact expressing a view that had been developing since the High Middle Ages, in Marsilius for instance, but particularly in the modern period, that will constitutes the basis of state legitimation. The problem was that modern thought from Hobbes through the classical liberal tradition had defined will as desire or appetite and subordinated reason to it.[34] In Hobbes, for example, the will is defined as nothing more than "the last appetite in deliberating,"[35] a definition that in its essentials was adopted by the early utilitarians. Reason was thus made the servant of the appetitive will rather than, as in medieval thought, its moral master. It was reduced to mere self-interested calculation that, in political terms, led to a theory of consent or utility that posited the state as little more than a "necessary evil." The exception to this thinking, of course, was Rousseau (and later Kant) who posited will as the moral basis of the state, but Rousseau's general will is a purely conventional standard derived from contract, an idea that, for reasons that should be at least partly apparent by now, Hegel clearly rejects.

What ultimately made Hegel's treatment of will unique was that it ceased to conceive of will and reason as distinct. Indeed, Hegel conflates will with reason such that will becomes a moral category rather than a set of appetitive drives.[36] This not only overcomes the modern reduction of reason to self-interested calculation, but the medieval view as well that puts moral reason in incessant warfare with a will perverted by original sin. The latter is the basis for what Hegel termed the "unhappy consciousness" of the Christian psyche, that is, a consciousness divided against itself.[37] In Hegel, will is neither elevated above reason as in the modern view, nor subordinated to it as in the medieval view, but is subsumed within it.

Hegel's insistence, then, that the modern state is premised upon will rather than force is to say that the state constitutes by definition an ethical construct, an idea that runs counter to the entire tradition of thought from Marsilius on, and particularly since Hobbes, that had rejected the notion of the state, or any other construct, as a final end. What is crucial in Hegel's analysis, however, is that the ethical basis of the state is revealed only at the culmination of its development, an idea, setting metaphysical differences aside, reminiscent of Aristotle. This means for Hegel that a truly philosophic science of the state must not concern itself with the state's historical origins, whether they be conceived as divine right, or patriarchy, or contract, or some other myth of foundation, but with the existing state as it reveals its inherent rationality, that is, its ethical universality.[38]

At the same time, the modern state did evolve out of earlier and more basic social elements, "moments" in Hegel's terminology, that remain crucial to its existence. While these in themselves do not constitute the ethical universal, they are moments in its development. Thus ethical life (as opposed to the simple morality of abstract duty, of the "ought-to-be"),[39] which is only realized fully in the state, is first imperfectly realized in these subordinate social institutions. These, according to Hegel, are constituted by the first and second moments of ethical life: the family and civil society.

In the family, ethical life exists in its "immediacy" of love and mutual support. This, however, is still far removed from a rational comprehension of the ethical basis of life. Love of family is entirely an affair of the heart, not of reason or even of understanding.[40] Thus, while the family, whose chief function for Hegel is the care and education of children, is essential to the existence of the state, it is not in itself sufficient for its complete actualization.[41] The state, therefore, cannot simply be an extended family ruled patriarchically as was characteristic of the archaic states of the Middle East or, in Hegel's historiography, of the oriental world.

It is Hegel's analysis of civil society, the second moment of ethical life, which is most decisive in his theory of the modern state, however. The emergence of civil society reflected the actual changes that had been occurring in the formation of the modern state, the separation of the state from society and the economic system, and the increasing differentiation of functions characteristic of this process. This differentiation had abolished feudal constraints on economic activity and thereby emancipated individuals to pursue their economic interests. It had, in short, created a capitalist free market in which human selfishness is given free reign.

Most would conclude from this analysis that civil society is the very antithesis of ethical life rather than one moment in its development as Hegel maintains. Not only is civil society premised upon individual self-interest rather than ethical universality, but it comes about at the expense of the family, the first moment of ethical life, which is severely impacted by the competitive market. Yet, Hegel considers the development of civil society a great ethical advance because it expands the domain of subjectivity. The family is premised upon traditional values and patriarchal rule, and these preclude the full exercise of the subjective will. Civil society, by contrast, liberates the subjective will. Individual choice, particularly economic choice, now becomes possible.

A subjectively free will oriented only to selfish pursuits would not in and of itself, of course, constitute an ethical advance over familial relationships. What makes civil society an ethically progressive institution for Hegel is that it compels individuals to take account of other's needs as well their own. In Hegel's words, "in the course of the actual attainment of selfish ends . . . there is formed a system of complete interdependence, wherein the livelihood, happiness, and legal status of one man is interwoven with the livelihood, happiness, and rights of all."[42] The capitalist market, as a theoretical ideal at least, transmutes individual self-interest into a larger public interest. Purely selfish and individualistic motives are transformed into a system of interdependence, a "system of mutual needs" in Hegel's terms, premised upon the recognition of the legal basis of universal rights. One's claim to the right of property, for example, becomes valid only to the extent that one recognizes other's claims and accepts the legal duty to respect them.

This analysis, of course, is transparently similar to the economic theory of Adam Smith and, indeed, Hegel clearly follows Smith and the early classical economists in his concept of civil society.[43] What differentiates Hegel from the classical liberal's defense of emerging capitalism, however, is the political implications he derives from this new economic system. The liberal tradition from Hobbes on, and certainly from the early utilitarians, had been to posit a purely negative conception of the state in the name of *laissez-faire* individualism. The state in this view existed only to protect the rights of property and, as such, was to remain aloof from the purely private realm of civil society. Hence, the liberal theory of the state was in effect no more than a reflection, and justification, of civil society that Hegel concludes is merely "the external state, the state based on need, the state as the Understanding envisages it."[44]

Herein lay the essence of Hegel's critique of the liberal theory of the state. It was a theory that comprehended the state only in its external (empirical) manifestation as a legal protector of rights, as the mere offshoot of civil society. But rights and, correspondingly, duties in this view are purely abstract according to Hegel. That is, they are recognized as necessities inherent in the individualism of the market, not as ends in themselves, as the necessary condition for a fully rational freedom. This is why Hegel argues that the external state of civil society, the not yet fully actualized state of the concrete universal, is the state of understanding rather than of reason. The liberal theory of the state thus falls far short of the philosophical science of the state in which reason reveals the state as "the actuality of the ethical Idea."

It is precisely because liberalism confounds civil society with the state that Hegel rejects the early liberal theory of contract, the key legitimizing ideology of the emerging territorial state. Contract establishes a relationship between property holders in the private domain Hegel insists, not between the individual and the state. To employ contract as a basis of state legitimation is to confuse the state with civil society. It is, in Hegel's words, to "have transferred the characteristics of private property into a sphere of a quite different and higher nature."[45] It is for this same reason that Hegel rejects Rousseau's theory of the state despite the fact that he agrees in so many substantive ways with it. While the concept of the general will, for example, comes close in many ways to Hegel's conception of the state, it is a concept mistakenly derived from the theory of contract.[46]

Yet, this critique of the liberal theory of the state does not lead Hegel to divorce the state from civil society. On the contrary, for civil society is the second and crucial moment in the development of ethical life without which the state, as the final moment in this process, could not exist. The problem with the liberal view for Hegel was that on the one hand it utterly separated civil society from the state, yet on the other understood the state only from the perspective of civil society. At the same time, he criticizes those idealist theories that attempt to preserve the ethical purity of the state by disengaging it from both civil society and family, yet understand the state only from the perspective of an extended family. Hegel's critique of Plato, of whom he otherwise has the greatest admiration, is precisely that his ideal state is premised upon its separation from family and private property, of which the philosophic rulers were to have neither, yet is simply the family writ large. In this, Plato had abolished entirely the subjective will that, for Hegel, is the very basis of ethical life.[47]

What Hegel advocates, therefore, is a certain integration of civil society with the state, one that avoids its total separation from, or confusing with. This is to be accomplished by the incorporation of the class system within the constitutional structure of the state, an idea reminiscent of the classical regime, but now applied to the modern state. The question for Hegel, then, is not how to exclude the dominant economic class of civil society, the bourgeoisie, or how to give it absolute free reign, but how to incorporate it within the state such that the ethical Idea is realized. The answer, he argues, lies not directly within the state, but within civil society itself, which is already organized on a quasi-legal and political basis into class based interest groups or corporations. And, according to Hegel, "as the family was the first, so the Corporation is the second ethical root of the state, the one planted in civil society."[48]

Such interest groupings are, of course, characteristic of all advanced state societies with their developed division of labor. These, however, are not strictly speaking corporations since they are not typically the legal creations of the state, although they may or may not be subject to legal oversight. The corporations of which Hegel speaks, while arising naturally to aggregate and represent the various economic interests that arise in civil society, are quite specifically "under the surveillance of the public authority."[49] Moreover, as we shall see, they are actually incorporated into the governance of the state as representative bodies and, as such, must be constituted as real legal entities. Hence, while dedicated essentially to the protection of private property and the economic interests of the bourgeoisie, corporations also have a variety of public functions, not only political representation, but certain judicial and policing functions as well.[50]

In the broadest terms, however, the key function these corporations perform for Hegel is to mediate between the family and the state, a middle structure so to speak that facilitates the unification of the social and political order. Apart from representing particular interests in the political process, they act to civilize the otherwise aggressively competitive and individualistic nature of civil society. This they do by aggregating interests into a larger social context (a role played by political parties in modern liberal democracies),[51] and by providing a safe harbor for the individual, a kind of second family that blunts the harsh competitiveness of the market.[52] In short, they create an organic and social counterweight to the inherent atomization and isolation of civil society.

But if corporations mediate between civil society and the state, they also act as bulwarks against the arbitrary imposition of state authority without which the subjective will, hence freedom, could not exist.[53] Here Hegel is pursuing a line of reasoning to be found in thinkers such as Alexis de Tocqueville who were concerned that the lack of intermediate associations between a centralized state and an atomized society harbored despotic potentialities.[54] Tocqueville had recognized that the key paradox of the modern state, its centralization of all political authority coupled with an extreme individualism, constituted a serious threat to the very individualism that was to be protected. And, Tocqueville emphasized, it was the theory of popular sovereignty itself that would legitimize the despotic state, suppressing minorities in the name of the majority.[55] For this reason, and in fundamental agreement with Hegel's analysis, Tocqueville argued that what we would now term pluralism is absolutely crucial in a liberal democratic state.[56]

This, finally, brings us to Hegel's constitutional theory of the state as "the actuality of the ethical Idea," the final moment in ethical life. On the surface, Hegel's constitutional analysis follows the traditional tripartite distinction between branches of government: legislature, executive (which subsumes the judiciary), and crown as head of state. While the crown is symbolically the ultimate source of authority, in real political terms Hegel is advocating a limited constitutional monarchy.

What makes Hegel's treatment of these branches of government unique, however, is the idealist-organicist mode of analysis he applies to them. The legislature, in Hegel's words, has "the power to . . . establish the

universal" ... The executive ... "the power to subsume single cases and
the spheres of particularity under the universal ... and the crown ... the
power of subjectivity, as the will with the power of ultimate decision."[57]
This is clearly something more than the simple equation of "the legislature
makes the law, the executive enforces it, and the head of state symbolically
represents it." The law in Hegel constitutes an ethical universal, not a vote
of a mere majority of deputies representing nothing more than the dominant
interests in civil society. And while the executive must apply the law to particular cases, as in any modern liberal democratic state, it is bound by the
universal in Hegel, as is the crown itself, not merely by a positive law devoid
of ethical content.

It is Hegel's treatment of the crown that is most revealing of the underlying
metaphysics, however, for here subjectivity and will, the key terms in
Hegel's theory of the state, are given their most concrete expression. For
Hegel, the crown contains within itself the final determination of the acts
of the legislature and the executive, or, in Hegel's words, "the power of
the ... three moments of the whole"[58] (itself and the other two branches of
government). Acts of the legislature and executive are legitimized by the formal authorization of the crown. As such, the crown is the visible expression
of the subjective will, not in its incomplete form as given in civil society, but
in its state form as the actualization of the "ethical Idea." It is the state
made manifest; it is, in other words, the sovereign authority of the state
subjectively (and thus for Hegel objectively) revealed.[59]

Hegel emphasizes this same organic unity of constitutional structure in
his treatment of the liberal doctrine of the "separation of powers," a concept developed most notably by Montesquieu and of particular importance
to American constitutional theory. In the liberal view, the separation of
powers constituted a bulwark against tyranny by, in James Madison's
words, "pitting ambition against ambition," the political interests of one
branch of government against that of another such that no permanent
center of state power could sustain itself over time.[60] Although Hegel agrees
that the separation of powers is a guarantor of public freedom, he utterly
disagrees with the liberal understanding of it. In the liberal view, each
branch of government is merely negative and hostile to the other, as if each
existed separately and alone, while their inner unity—their relationship to
the universal end of the state—is ignored. This, again, Hegel argues, is characteristic of the abstract understanding, to possess only a one-sided view of
what is ultimately a many-sided dialectical unity of negative and positive.[61]

What is absolutely crucial to Hegel's organicist concept of the state, however, is that the branches of government are organized upon a class basis.
For Hegel, these include the business class or bourgeoisie, already organized
into the corporations of civil society, as well as the agricultural class of peas-
ants and landed aristocracy and the universal class of administrators drawn
largely from the bourgeoisie. While this simple tripartite system hardly
encompasses the complex division of labor of modern industrial society, it
does express the essential distinctions emerging in Hegel's time, and it

suffices to illuminate the class basis of his ideal state. It should be noted as well that these class distinctions correspond roughly to the three moments of ethical life—family, civil society, and the state—and consequently to increasing awareness of the ethical basis of the state.[62]

While the executive's powers and functions are those that would be characteristic of any modern state, it is important to note Hegel's insistence that it must be comprised of a highly trained and educated elite chosen by ability rather than birth. In this, Hegel is advocating a modern civil service that until Napoleon had hardly existed anywhere in Western Europe, and that was all but nonexistent in post-Napoleonic Germany except perhaps in nascent form in Prussia. Indeed, Hegel was far ahead of his time in this regard, so much so that, despite his idealist metaphysics, his civil service ideal has been compared with Max Weber's analysis of modern state bureaucracy as an ideal type of rational-legal authority.[63] At the same time, his idealism confers upon the civil service a role far exceeding that posited by Weber, that of embodying and expressing in its executive functions the ethical Idea embodied in the state. Since this ideal constitutes the universal for Hegel, he terms the class of rulers the "universal class." It is the one class that exists for the state and the state alone.[64] It is the modern state equivalent of Plato's philosophic rulers.

It is the legislature that most reveals the inner logic of Hegel's organic unity of class and state, however. While its constitutional form and function are straightforward enough—it is a bicameral law making body—its specific class organization is vaguely reminiscent of the British parliamentary system. The lower house is to be composed of representatives from the business class, the upper house from the landed nobility of the agricultural class. The former is to be an elective body; the latter a hereditary institution. This difference in representation is premised upon the difference in class consciousness. The business class is rooted in civil society in which the idea of freedom is inherent in the capitalist market and the system of property rights. Free election is thus the corresponding form of representation. The agricultural class reflects the traditional and largely unconscious values of the family and hereditary landed property. Hence, a traditional-hereditary form of representation is required in this case.[65]

These two classes, however, had already organized during the late medieval period as estates, that is, as legally recognized class assemblies. The legislature is thus the assembly of estates, the sole purpose of which is to bring "public affairs into existence."[66] Since the estates are by definition class based, this means that the articulation of public policy and its implementation into law will of necessity reflect differing class interests. This may be said to be true in any state, of course, but by making it explicit and building it into the structure of the state Hegel is able to show how constitutional mechanisms of mediation between classes can be created to transform class interest into public interest. In this, Hegel pursues a line of reasoning reminiscent of Aristotle and the classical theory of the mixed regime but, of course, applied now to the modern state.

Given this kind of social and political integration, it follows for Hegel that the liberal theory of representation is entirely misguided. Contrary to the liberal concept of "one man one vote," Hegel argues that election to the lower house of the legislature must be on a group or functional basis, for "the circles of association in civil society are already communities. To picture these communities as once more breaking up into a mere conglomeration of individuals as soon as they enter the field of politics . . . is *eo ipso* to hold civil and political life apart from one another and as it were to hang the latter in the air . . . ."[67] Direct suffrage, premised upon liberal individualism, is by definition to leave the state without any social (class) roots. It is to elevate a misguided view of civil society as nothing more than a collection of individuals as the final end of human endeavor and, in effect, to make the state so impersonal as to render it meaningless. And it is the corporation that here plays its final, crucial political role. The corporations of civil society are, for Hegel, the electoral bodies that choose the representatives to the lower house of the legislative assembly of estates. Hegel's organic state is thus a corporatist state.

It should not be thought, however, that Hegel carries this organic unity to illiberal conclusions. To be sure, he rejects the classical liberal theory of the state and its corresponding notion of rights, but it is the form of reasoning— or rather understanding—involved that he rejects, not the idea that people ought to have a wide range of individual freedoms. Indeed, the principle of subjectivity that characterizes the ethical basis of Hegel's ideal state requires as much. Thus, Hegel recognizes the necessity of freedom of both individual and public opinion, of a free press, of the separation of church and state and the sanctity of private morality (the legislature ought not to legislate in this domain Hegel argues), and, as we have seen, of a pluralistic society and a capitalist economy.[68] That Hegel has so often been misinterpreted as an advocate of an authoritarian and even totalitarian theorist of the state constitutes a regrettable misunderstanding of his political thought.

If the whole of Hegel's vision of the state is now put in view, it is apparent that modes of integration, or mediation in Hegel's terms, are crucial to the state's existence. At the apex of the state stands the crown as the subjective embodiment of the ethical Idea, and beneath the crown the government and class based estate assemblies are intertwined. Branches of government, while distinct, do not constitute merely a separation of powers but involve modes of integration as well, and the estates mediate between the state and civil society. Civil society, moreover, is itself a mediated structure of associations, and corporations are integrated into the governing structure of the state as both interest aggregating and electoral bodies. Finally, the family, the first moment of ethical life, is reflected in the state in the upper house of the legislature where traditional values that might otherwise be swept away by the competitive market of civil society are maintained. Most importantly, the family is reflected in the crown, which Hegel insists ought to be a hereditary position. In this, Hegel argues that "monarchy has been brought back to the patriarchal principle in which it had its historical origin, but its determinate character is how higher, because the monarch is the absolute apex of an organically developed state."[69]

It might almost be said that the whole of Hegel's philosophy of the modern state is comprehended in this analysis of the crown. Note that Hegel takes an institution whose origins precede the modern state and, in its evolution to a more advanced state form, recognizes in it the very essence of the modern state. In this, Hegel's method, like Aristotle's, is thoroughly teleological, for while the state is empirically the end product of earlier political events, as the final end of human ethical development it is prior to its historical antecedents. In Hegel's words, it "is not so much the result as the beginning."[70]

It now becomes possible to grasp Hegel's theory of sovereignty as it reveals itself in this "beginning," and clearly "reveal" is the appropriate term here, for Hegel discovers the meaning of sovereignty in its actual development within the structure of the state itself, not in deducing it from a hypothetical state of nature or from utilitarian premises. And while it is his concept of domestic sovereignty that will primarily concern us, Hegel's understanding of its international dimension is also uniquely his own. While, like other theorists of international relations from Grotius to Kant, he understands that states confront each other in a potentially hostile way, he also recognizes that the modern sovereign state could not exist apart from other sovereign states. This is so Hegel argues, because "a state is as little an actual individual without relations to other states as an individual is actually a person without *rapport* with other persons."[71]

What is so uniquely Hegelian in this view is its focus on the organic unity between elements within a system. In surely the most famous part of his *The Phenomenology of Mind*, the development of human consciousness, the self, is conceived as a dialectic between persons—master and servant—struggling for mastery over one another.[72] The self for Hegel, therefore, is a social construct; it exists only in its relation to others. In much the same way, Hegel sees the same process at work in relations between states. The real meaning of external sovereignty for Hegel is its capacity to create and legitimate the state within a system of mutual recognition without which the state, *qua* state, could not exist.

It is this analysis of external sovereignty, however, that leads Hegel to perhaps his most controversial views. Given that the system of international relations can exist only through the sovereign autonomy of each state, it follows for Hegel that interstate relations are inherently conflictual. Indeed, like Hobbes, who in every other regard he would reject, Hegel argues that all states are in a "state of nature," that national interest must therefore be the highest law, that treaties as a consequence constitute merely an abstract "ought" that cannot ultimately be enforced.[73] Warfare is thus inevitable and, most controversially Hegel argues, ethically good in that it binds the citizen to the state through sacrifice and courage.[74] Kant (who detested Hobbes's political conclusions) was therefore wrong in believing that perpetual peace could be created through a League of Nations.[75] Indeed, if

Hegel's analysis of external sovereignty is correct, a sovereign world "state" would not be a state at all, for there would be no mutual recognition of sovereign autonomy required for the state's existence.[76]

It is Hegel's theory of domestic sovereignty that is most important for our purposes, however, and given that sovereignty reveals itself as an organic unity of mediating institutions, it follows that sovereignty must be the organic unity of the state itself. Since this organic unity constitutes the "actuality of the ethical Idea," sovereignty is thus a metaphysically ideal category. In Hegel's words, "the idealism which constitutes sovereignty is the same characteristic as that in accordance with which so-called 'parts' of an animal organism are not parts but members, moments in an organic whole, whose isolation and independence spell disease."[77]

While Hegel clearly is propounding a theory of state sovereignty, it now means something quite different than it did for Hobbes and subsequent liberal thinkers, and not just in the metaphysical sense. The state for Hegel is neither strictly impersonal nor a mere corporate abstraction defining the role of government. It is a "living organism" reflecting the ethical order of the entire society. As such, state sovereignty does not mean for Hegel that the state is entirely apart from society, something standing abstractly between rulers and ruled, but an organic component of it. As such, the earlier dispute between theorists of state and popular sovereignty is transcended,[78] even more so than in Rousseau, for the mediating structures of Hegel's ideal polity, including functional forms of representation, subsumes the one in the other.[79]

It must be emphasized again, however, that Hegel's idealist concept of sovereignty is premised upon a class theory of the state, the integration of the class structures of civil society—the corporations and estates—into the constitutional system. In this, Hegel returns, albeit in a philosophically new way, to the traditional view of the state, from the classical through the medieval period, that prevailed until the modern theory of contract attempted to derive sovereignty from a classless state of nature, that is, from a hypothetical condition of abstract individualism and absolute equality. For Hegel, not only was this a misunderstanding of the nature of sovereignty and, therefore, of the state, it was sociological nonsense. All societies beyond the most primitive are class divided, and for Hegel civil inequality is necessarily a reflection of natural inequality.[80] Civil society, he argues, simply expands natural inequality into a "right of particularity" that "raises it to an inequality of skill and resources, and even to one of moral and intellectual attainment."[81]

That the state's legitimacy rests ultimately upon the class system, however, raises perhaps the most fundamental issue in Hegel's theory of the modern state. As Hegel himself recognizes, the selfsame class system that is required for the state's existence and legitimacy also produces extremes of poverty and wealth. For the wealthy, a culture of selfishness is produced that is contrary to the ethical purposes of the state. For the underclass, poverty leads to the same contrary consequences, for it exists not only in the narrow economic sense, but as moral and intellectual poverty as well.[82] The brutalizing conditions of early industrial capitalism were making all this inescapably clear.

These facts were not only troublesome in themselves, but raised the most difficult theoretical issues for Hegel. On the one hand, it would be impossible to eliminate class inequality since this would be contrary to nature and to the "right of particularity," to that subjectivity necessary for the existence of civil society and, hence, the state itself. In Hegel's words, "to oppose to this right a demand for equality is a folly of the Understanding which takes as real and rational its abstract equality and its 'ought to be.' "[83] On the other hand, if left completely unchecked, civil society would create such extremes of wealth and poverty that, even apart from the human toll, the state would cease to realize its ethical purpose. Hegel's ideal state is to be based on class integration, not class exploitation.

Hegel's attempted solution to the dilemma is what we would now term the welfare state. In Hegel's words, "The public authority takes the place of the family where the poor are concerned in respect not only of their immediate want but also of laziness of disposition, malignity, and the other vices which arise out of their plight and their sense of wrong."[84] Such thinking, needless to say, was far in advance of the times. It would not be until nearly the last quarter of the nineteenth century that liberal thinkers would begin to advocate a more positive concept of the state, and they would use Hegel as their theoretical guide. It was not until the later twentieth century, however, that Hegel's other key insight would begin to haunt the theoretical consciousness of state theorists—that the welfare state may be inadequate to the task of eliminating poverty or even of ameliorating its attendant consequences.

That Hegel doubts his own solution to class inequality and exploitation is clear enough. There is, to be sure, no difficulty in his maintaining that the state has a valid regulatory role in civil society, for Hegel never completely separates the two. The universal ethical principle of the state appears "in civil society as a factor immanent in it"[85] Hegel argues, and, as such, civil society cannot claim that complete autonomy from the state that the classical liberals advocated. The problem however, as he clearly recognizes, is that any state intervention sufficient to resolve class exploitation would destroy civil society and hence the state itself, yet anything less than this would fail to resolve the issue.[86] This pessimistic assessment of the situation would come to influence later Marxist thinkers as, indeed, would much of Hegel's analysis of the various ways that capitalism would be driven to resolve its own inner contradictions, including economic imperialism.[87] For Marxists, the solution to class exploitation would be much simpler: the destruction of civil society and the state. Such a solution was not available to Hegel, yet, as he himself recognized, his advocacy of a welfare state was not ultimately a solution either.

Such, then, is Hegel's theory of the modern state, a theory that stands in sharp contrast to the classical liberal view. Given that classical liberalism had become the ideology of legitimation of the modern state through most of the nineteenth century, this was no small accomplishment. Hegel's real importance, however, was his influence on subsequent theories of the modern state, most importantly on the modern liberal theory that, along with closely related social-democratic doctrines, has now become the essential legitimizing ideology of the modern state in most of Western Europe and the Anglo-American countries.

Hegel's influence on the liberal doctrine began in the later nineteenth century with a group of British thinkers collectively known as the Oxford Idealists. Under the leadership of T.H. Green (1836–1882), they followed in the great tradition of their classical liberal precursors, the Philosophical Radicals (early utilitarians) in attempting to reform British politics. The difference between the two, however, both in practical and theoretical terms, was enormous.

On the practical-political side, Green and his followers were primarily concerned with the unanticipated consequences of industrial capitalism and the negative state that supported it; in other words, on the precise conditions the early liberals had promoted. This shift in reformist policy was entirely understandable, for the problems Hegel had identified as endemic to civil society—poverty, class exploitation, and a culture of selfishness—had intensified many fold. Left unattended, the liberal state itself would be threatened, a fact evident in the rise of increasingly radical socialist and anarchist groups. The solution adopted was the positive or welfare state first suggested, with some serious reservations, by Hegel.

Theoretically, while the shift to a defense of the welfare state was derived from Hegel, Aristotle and Rousseau were employed as well. As such, the metaphysical and epistemological assumptions of classical liberalism—materialism and empiricism—were rejected for idealism and apriorism. Hence, in conformity with Hegel, Green argues in his key political work *Lectures on the Principles of Political Obligation* that the state constitutes a moral essence, that sovereignty is constituted in the ethical structure of the state itself, not something derived from contract or mere utility, and that the whole purpose of civil life is to bring about a moral (ethical in Hegel) progress that Green, like Hegel, defines as "the harmony of will and reason."[88] The values of the institutions of civil life, Green argues, "lies in their operation as giving reality to these capacities of will and reason, and enabling them to be really exercised."[89] The operative term here is "enable," for it requires an interventionist state to make moral progress—the harmony of will and reason—a reality as opposed to a mere abstract ideal. The problem with the negative state for Green is not that it is not premised upon values important to moral progress, but that it has produced a state of affairs that in reality prevent those values from being realized for increasingly large numbers of people, the working class poor in particular.

It needs to be stressed that Green was no less a liberal than his classical forbears. Individualism, property rights, liberty of expression, limited government and so on, equally constituted the core of his political values.

Indeed, these were to his mind the entire basis of moral progress, but the unity of reason and will meant for Green, as it did for Hegel, that these ideals exist in reality only to the extent that they are self-willed and self-actualized. This is the essence of human freedom no less for Green than for Hegel, and it meant that the state could not be conceived merely as an abstract-impersonal entity premised upon nothing more than the potential of force and coercion. The state is an organic extension of society, and its institutions must embody those fundamental values that are subjectively willed by the citizens as ethical beings. Hence, fundamental individual rights are as crucial to Green as to the early liberals, but for Green they must be based upon the state maintaining them in a way that enhances the moral development of all.

It follows, therefore, that rights for Green are not negative (or abstract in Hegel's terminology), but positive. They embody a moral purpose and can be made a reality only to the extent that the state insures their reality. Hence, in regard to property rights, Green notes that the mere existence of a property right in the abstract is useless to those, the working class, who have no property in reality. They "might as well, in respect of the ethical purposes which the possession of property should serve, be denied rights of property altogether."[90] The welfare or positive state thus came to replace the negative or minimalist state of classical liberalism, not as a repudiation of liberal values, but as their actualization. Hence, property was not to be eliminated, but the state was to have an obligation to create the conditions for its universal acquisition through forms of welfare, public education, and so on. The object was not to deny individualism or, in Hegel's terms, subjectivity, but to remove those obstacles that stood in the way of individual self-development. The object, in brief, was to make liberal individualism, from property acquisition to liberty of expression, really real.

Green and his followers were thus crucially important in the final development of the political theory of the modern state, in transforming the liberal theory of the negative state into a justification of the welfare state. To be sure, this process had begun earlier in the work of John Stuart Mill and the later utilitarians, but not upon Hegel's idealist basis. The adoption of Hegel's mode of analysis constituted a final break from the metaphysical and epistemological assumptions of the early liberal worldview. And the closely allied doctrine of social democracy, while its theoretical roots were different than those of modern liberalism, has replaced any notion of a revolutionary transformation of civil society into the same reformist advocacy of the welfare state as that promoted by modern liberals.[91]

But if the transformation of the liberal doctrine was inevitable, it was also problematical. To erect an idealist theory of sovereignty upon the foundations of a state that had developed theoretically on quite different premises, and in practice appeared to be merely epiphenomenal to civil society, was bound to be fraught with difficulties. Whatever the limitations of a materialist interpretation and justification of the negative state, there was no ambiguity in either the Lockean or utilitarian liberal traditions about the limitations of sovereign authority. Such is not necessarily the case in a theory of the positive state derived from idealist premises. In pursuing the Hegelianized interpretation of the state, some of Green's followers arrived at less than liberal conclusions.

Bernard Bosanquet (1848–1923), for example, in his *The Philosophical Theory of the State* was willing to subordinate the individual to the state in a more profound way than many liberals found acceptable.[92] Even liberals of Green's persuasion, such as L.T. Hobhouse (1864–1929), became alarmed at the possible illiberal conclusions to be derived from an idealist-organicist (as well as a Rousseauian) theory of the state, and in a book by the same title as this chapter he attacked Bosanquet's Hegelianized views.[93] In the United States, where the state had always been marginalized, these issues did not arise as dramatically. But here too, though at a later date, Hegel's idealist theory of the state came to inform liberal thought, most notably—if indirectly—in John Dewey (1859–1952),[94] and the appropriate level of state intervention, and the consequent fear of an increasingly centralized sovereign authority, have remained core issues ever since.

In the history of state theory, such theoretical difficulties often point to more substantive issues at their core. Such is the case with modern liberalism, for the potentially illiberal conclusions to be derived from an idealist inter-pretation of the state are really contingent upon the need for an increasingly interventionist state. If all that is required, in Green's words, is the removal of obstacles to individual self-development, then the issue remains purely theoretical. Hegel's idealist theory of the state, recall, is premised precisely upon individual subjectivity, not upon subordination to an absolutist sovereign authority. If civil society produces conditions that require increas-ing state involvement in economy and society, however, then the potential is there for a state that overwhelms the realms of subjectivity that both Hegel and Green insist must be maintained.

The problem is now compounded by a fact neither Hegel nor Green and the early modern liberals contemplated, that an interventionist state might generate an increasing demand for more state involvement on the part of clientele groups, and not just working class. Indeed, while some of the grossest forms of poverty may have been eliminated by the modern welfare state, demands for what have become in effect entitlements have increased dramatically. There is a real question as to the state's ability to continue to meet these demands, and whether or not it can maintain its legitimacy if it fails to do so.

What makes this issue particularly problematical is that the metaphysical and ethical underpinnings of modern liberalism that were forged by Hegel and Green are now little more than ephemeral memories. The modern state in contemporary political consciousness is hardly an ethical construct, much less the "actuality of the ethical Idea." Modern welfare state liberalism is now essentially a series of demands for more state intervention without a solid theoretical and ethical foundation to them, a fact that does not bode well for the legitimacy of the modern state in the long term. Pressured to provide more economic security than perhaps it can under its current constitutional structure, and increasingly devoid of an ethical purpose beyond utilitarian considerations, the state in crisis may not ultimately be able to sustain the support of its own citizens.

These issues, however, are crucially implicated in contemporary social science theories of the state and are best discussed in that context. What needs to be emphasized, however, is that Hegel was the first to frame these issues as issues of the modern state, not modern social science, and this because he understood in crucial ways the inherent character of the modern state however problematical his political thought, and his metaphysical assumptions, may have been in other regards.

Chapter Seven

The Sociology of the State

The state is the *"monopoly of the legitimate use of physical force* within a given territory."[1] So claims Max Weber (1864–1920) in what has become the generally accepted definition of the modern state in the social sciences. While seemingly a mere commonplace, it is, as we have seen, a definition resulting from centuries of institutional and ideological development. This book has focused on the ideological component of the modern state, its genesis and evolution, and it is a crucial feature of Weber's sociology that it includes the ideological dimension. The monopoly of physical force is the modern form of state power for Weber not merely as an institutional fact, but as an ideological fact, as a form of rule legitimized in a specific way.

As a modern social scientist, however, Weber's concern was not with legitimizing the modern state, a violation of his scientific ideal of "value neutrality," but of understanding it. That the state must lay claim to legitimacy is a fact for Weber, but it is not the domain of science to determine the ethical validity of the legitimation. Sociologically, Weber argues "The state cannot be defined in terms of its ends . . . . Ultimately one can define the modern state sociologically only in terms of the specific *means* peculiar to it, as to every political association, namely, the use of physical force."[2]

Herein lies the most historically notable feature of Weber's sociology of the modern state: It marks the final end of thinking of the state from the perspective of final ends. This constitutes the culmination of a process that began with Machiavelli (who greatly influenced Weber), perhaps with Marsilius, but now in the form of modern social science with its emphasis upon empirical analysis, methodological rigor, and value neutrality. These factors pre-dated Weber, of course, having their source in nineteenth century materialism and positivism that traces back beyond Comte to Bentham and the early utilitarians. And while Weber modifies these earlier methodological approaches in important ways, his sociology of the state remains a sociology of means, of the empirically verifiable forms of power or, in Weber's terms, of domination.

Clearly Weber's sociology constituted a thoroughgoing rejection of the Hegelian theory of the state, the dominant mode of state theorizing in nineteenth century Germany. Hegel's theory was precisely an attempt to reconstitute within an historical teleology the concept of final ends; Weber's to abolish it. Ultimately it was Weber's view that prevailed. No contemporary social scientist could possibly work from Hegelian premises, and even the still prevalent legitimizing ideology of modern liberalism has been essentially stripped of its Hegelian roots. The modern state is now not only sociologically conceived as a set of mere institutional means, its legitimizing ideology is premised upon only the vaguest notion of ethical ends. In this, the modern state constitutes the political aspect of Weber's famous summation of modernity as "the disenchantment of the world."

This transformation in the conceptualization of the state from an institution premised upon ethical idealism to one conceived purely from a materialist, empiricist, and ethically neutral perspective has remained the basis of all modern social science theories of the state. It was not, of course, Weber alone who rejected idealism for an uncompromising materialist theory of the state. So too did Emile Durkheim (1858–1917), Ferdinand Tonnies (1855–1936), Herbert Spencer (1820–1903), and numerous other less well-known sociological thinkers. While each of these possessed a unique understanding of the modern state, they all pursued similar lines of reasoning in delineating its sociological foundations. In general, the state was seen as emerging on the basis of increasing social differentiation variously expressed. For Durkheim the state reflected an increasing division of labor, in his terms from "mechanical" to "organic" forms of solidarity.[3] It did as well for Herbert Spencer who combined a concept of increasing social differentiation with Darwinian notions of evolution.[4] For Tonnies the state was the outcome of a shift from *Gemeinshaft* (community) to *Gesellschaft* (society), that is, from traditional and personal relationships to rational and contractual ones.[5]

The Spencerian concept of the state as the end product of an evolutionary process was paradigmatic for these other thinkers as well, an idea that is considered suspect by modern social scientists. So too was the sense that something important in human terms was lost in the formation of the state. Weber's "disenchantment of the world," the overly rationalized and bureaucratized reality characteristic of the state and modern society, was a concept expressed by many early social theorists. Themes of anomie, alienation, and estrangement pervaded the literature of the nineteenth and early twentieth centuries. These same themes still find faint echoes in mainline social sciences, although the professionalization of these disciplines in the last century has made them very faint indeed. This itself is something that Weber predicted, and lamented, at the same time he helped bring it about.

Of all these early sociological theorists of the modern state, however, Weber has had the most lasting influence in the social sciences, including political science. There is only one rival in this regard, and that is Karl Marx (1818–1883). Indeed, for contemporary theorists of the modern state these thinkers represent the two major theoretical poles of modern state studies. This holds true not only in sociology and political science but in contemporary anthropology as well. The contemporary debate among anthropologists over the sources of state formation essentially revolves around the same issues that divided Marx and Weber. And the same concerns with the perceived processes of alienation and anomie that characterized early sociological analysis find their counterpart in both Marx's and Weber's sociologies.

In order to understand this debate between the Weberian and Marxian theories of the state, it is necessary to shift our perspective from Weber to Marx. This is so not only because Marx pre-dates Weber, but also because Weber's own theory of the state is as much derivative as it is contrary to Marx's views. This is a crucial point because Weber's theory of the state, and much else in his substantive sociology, is often treated as if it were a straightforward rejection of Marxism. In fact, much contemporary theoretical work on the state combines elements of both Marx and Weber. Nonetheless, there are differences, and much of the contemporary debate in political science over the nature and status of the modern state returns, if only implicitly, to these two great founders of modern state studies.

There are two important epistemological and methodological differences that should be noted at the outset. Marx's materialism involves a dialectical undestanding of social relationships. Here, of course, is the obvious influence of Hegel, but stripped of his idealist metaphysics. And while it was Engels rather than Marx who took the dialectic seriously at an ontological and methodological level, Marx's sociological analysis, unlike Weber's, is dialectical through and through.[6] This is important to bear in mind because it means that the state for Marx could never be impersonal, as the liberal ideology of legitimation had to assume, but is always organically connected to the underlying social formations. In this, Marx is one with contemporary anthropology, which has always, and everywhere, defined the state in social terms as a "state form of society." And while Weber certainly does not deny the obvious connection between social formation and political structure, in his analysis the connection is neither dialectical nor as "deterministic" as in Marx's sociology.

The other key difference is even more profound. Marx is an advocate of the unity of theory and practice in which the validity of theory can be confirmed only in revolutionary *praxis*. Developed most explicitly in his *Theses on Feuerbach*, Marx argues that scientific objectivity is premised upon subjectivity, the attempt to change existing reality in line with the predictions of theory. Hence, communism is objectively possible only to the extent that it can actually be created in practice. The attempt to develop theoretical understandings apart from *praxis* is doomed to ideological malformation because the theory will invariably reflect the social (class) relationships of existing society. Classical liberalism's defense of civil society and the supposed impersonal state premised upon individual rights is, for Marx, the key example of this malformation.[7]

Here the difference with Weber, and indeed with traditional social science, is dramatic. Weber utterly rejects *praxis* in the name of "value neutrality." He does not dispute that human activity is embedded in values and that human action cannot be understood apart from its subjective meanings. Indeed Weber parts from the extreme positivism of some earlier (and some contemporary) social sciences precisely in this regard. Empirically observable behavior must be understood in light of its inner meaning (*verstehen*) for Weber despite the difficulties involved.[8] But nowhere does Weber suggest that it is the task of sociology to import theoretical understandings of observable reality into that reality itself. This would violate the scientific principle of objectivity for Weber no less than for his positivist forbears. Value neutrality does not mean that human values and subjective meanings are not valid sources of sociological investigation; it does mean that the sociologist must remain removed from the object of his investigations.

Given that *praxis* is anathema to academic social science, it is hardly surprising that Weber rather than Marx has been the primary influence in the social sciences, including political science. The problem, apart from the fact that Marx is important in his own right, is that Weber cannot really be understood in isolation from Marx. As noted, his sociology is both derivative of and contrary to Marxist views, and this applies with special relevance to his theory of the modern state. Indeed, the Marxist theory of the state has been the most important source of state theorizing in the postwar era, and contemporary debates about the nature of the modern state follow along lines first articulated by Marx and, in response, by Weber.

The difficulty is that Marx's theory of the state is complicated by the fact that there are two variations of it, and the entire debate among contemporary Marxists and neo-Marxists revolves precisely around this issue. What we may term the primary theory has the great advantage of simplicity and clarity.[9] Its most direct, if schematic, presentation is in Marx's *Preface to a Contribution to the Critique of Political Economy*, the basic premise of which is that "the sum total of (the) relations of production constitutes the economic structure of society, the real foundation, on which rises a legal and political superstructure and to which correspond definite forms of social consciousness."[10] The modern state and its ideology of legitimation are thus the superstructural reflections of the capitalist relations of production, that is, of the class system. As such, and in one of Marx's starkest formulations of the primary theory of the state, he asserts that . . ."the executive of the modern *State* is but a committee for managing the common affairs of the whole bourgeoisie."[11] Liberalism is the corresponding ideology of legitimation.

There are several features of the primary theory that require elaboration. First, while it clearly constitutes a class theory of the state, it is hardly the first of its kind. Marx did not discover the class basis of the state; indeed, it was taken for granted from classical thinkers on until the modern theory of contract and the emergence of the liberal ideology. What Marx did was to specify the precise nature of those class relations, not merely as distinctions of wealth and poverty, but as productive relations that constitute the entire structure of economic relations within civil society.

A second important feature of the primary theory is that the relationship between substructure and superstructure is distinctly deterministic. The state is purely epiphenomenal of the class system. And while Marx's materialism is distinguished by its lack of a strict determinism, emphasizing human agency (*praxis*) in historical development, the deterministic side of his materialism is clearly emphasized in the primary theory. This, however, is to be understood only as a general characterization of the state's relationship to the class system, not as a predictor of state policies or any specific political outcomes. Indeed, Marx is quite adamant in noting that while the economic substructure is amenable to predictive scientific analysis, the same cannot be said of the political and ideological superstructure which, beyond determining the general form of state, is exceedingly variable.[12] It is apparent in Marxist analysis, for example, that the modern liberal-democratic state corresponds to (is "determined" by) the capitalist relations of production, but the particular form the ideology of legitimation will take is not entirely predictable. Marx himself saw only the outlines of the shift from classical to modern liberalism as the legitimizing ideology of the modern state, something he had never anticipated.

Finally, it is important to note that the schematic presentation of the primary theory of the state is elaborated in much greater detail, and sophistication, in a variety of other works by Marx and by Engels as well. Indeed, Engel's *The Origin of the Family, Private Property and the State* is clearly the most developed Marxist anthropology of the state. Although the work has been criticized for relying upon the now outdated work of the anthropologist Henry Morgan, it follows the general outline of subsequent anthropologies, tracing the emergence of the modern state from more primitive kinship based communities through the various state forms that pre-date it. Engel's conclusion, however, is consistent with the primary theory that the state's essential function is to preserve the existing class structure.

What may be termed Marx's secondary theory of the state grants to the state a certain autonomy not conceded in the more class deterministic primary theory. The substructure in this view does not inevitably determine the superstructure. There are certain conditions in which the permanent institutions of the state, the bureaucracy and executive organs, are able to assert authority reflecting interests other than those of the dominant class: its own, that of a subordinate class, or in Hegel's ideal, the public interest. These conditions take two forms in Marx. The first is constituted by what is commonly referred to as "oriental despotism," the second by what may be termed the "Bonapartist state."

Oriental despotism is the state form corresponding to the "asiatic mode of production," the earliest type of economic formation in the Marxian typology.[13] Types of state formations are linked to corresponding modes of production, and in Marx's analysis the modern state emerged out of the disintegration of feudalism and the emergence of the bourgeois mode of production. In other words, it was the development of the capitalist class that "produced" the modern state. But this process occurred in this specific way only in the West and was the result of the growth of a monied economy, commodity production, and bourgeois forms of private property. In oriental society (which is never really adequately defined in Marxist historiography) private bourgeois property never developed nor therefore did a capitalist class. A despotic bureaucratic state "owned" the land and organized large-scale economic projects such as irrigation systems (Wittfogel's hydraulic thesis draws upon this analysis) and thus acted as an autonomous political force apart from any property owning social class.[14]

The contemporary version of Marx's secondary or autonomous theory of the state does not, however, draw upon the concept of oriental despotism. Its importance lies elsewhere, in demonstrating the difficulty in attempting to frame any unicausal theory of state formation. Oriental society is class (or caste) divided, but class is not the "cause" of state as in the primary theory. In effect, the issue here is in broad terms the same issue that divides not only Marx and Weber but contemporary anthropologists as well, whether social class is the cause or the result of state formation. Both are persuasive explanations and most likely both state and class have mutually reinforced one another in their development. What nonetheless remains key to the Marxist theory of the state, no less than to contemporary anthropological theories, is that the state is always and everywhere based upon some form of class stratification whatever the specific source of the state's formation.

It is the Bonapartist theory of the state, at any rate, that has had the greatest influence on contemporary debates about the relative autonomy of the modern state. Under certain conditions both Marx and Engels concede that the state may act as an autonomous power rather than exclusively as an executive agency of the bourgeoisie. The term "Bonapartist" is derived from Marx's historical study of the dictatorial regime of Louis Bonaparte (Napoleon III, 1851–1870) during the Second French Empire. In *The Eighteenth Brumaire of Louis Bonaparte*, Marx argues that unique conditions had emerged that prevented either the bourgeoisie or any other class from asserting its dominance. The resulting stalemate in the class struggle thus allowed the state, that is, Louis Bonaparte, to act with relative autonomy.[15]

In *The Origin of the Family, Private Property and the State*, Engels extends this analysis to other historical periods. In Engel's view, the absolute monarchies of the seventeenth and eighteenth centuries were relatively autonomous due to the inability of either the nobility or emerging bourgeoisie to establish dominance. The same holds true he argues for the German Empire under Bismarck. Here neither the capitalists nor workers could establish preeminence. In each of these cases the resulting class stalemate allowed for relative state autonomy.[16] This, however, is an exception and does not obviate Marx's primary theory of the state according to Engels in his summation of both the primary and secondary theories.

> Because the state arose from the need to hold class antagonisms in check, but because it arose, at the same time, in the midst of the conflict of these classes, it is, as a rule, the state of the most powerful, economically dominant class, which, through the medium of the state, becomes also the politically dominant

class, and thus acquires new means of holding down and exploiting the oppressed class . . . . By way of exception, however, periods occur in which the warring classes balance each other so nearly that the state power, as ostensible mediator, acquires, for the moment, a certain degree of independence of both.[17]

Most contemporary neo-Marxists, who have been greatly influenced by the secondary or "relative autonomy" theory of the state, nonetheless follow Engel's lead in affirming the long-term validity of the primary theory. Having said this, however, there is little question that superstructural factors have come to play an increasing role in Marxist theories of the state. While this is particularly the case with contemporary neo-Marxism, it has historical precedents in other varieties of postclassical Marxism as wells.

Most notable in this regard is Antonio Gramsci (1891–1937) who in his *Prison Notebooks* argues that the modern state is not based on mere coercion by the dominant class, but on an underlying consent on the part of all citizens regardless of class position. Gramsci terms this hegemony, a set of beliefs and values created and sustained by elements of the intellectual stratum that act to legitimize the existing state structure and, correspondingly, the existing class system. This means that the essentially epiphenomenal character of the superstructure in the primary theory of the state has become, in effect, almost substructural or, as Gramsci would conceive it, the substructure has taken on characteristics of the superstructure.[18] In Gramsci's analysis, there are "two major superstructural 'levels': the one that can be called 'civil society,' that is the ensemble of organisms called 'private,' and that of 'political society' or 'the State.' "[19] Civil society organizes the ideological justification of class domination; the state imposes direct domination where ideology (consent) fails. In terms of classical Marxism, the relations of production are now understood as a unity of both class structure and ideological formation, and the coercive role of the state is thereby legitimized.

The problem is that even with the continued affirmation of the ultimate class basis of the state, the focus on superstructure whether defined as hegemony or relative autonomy or some other equivalent category, raises serious questions about the sociological viability of Marxism. Carried to its logical conclusion, the state and its entire panoply of legal and ideological appendages would constitute as much an independent variable as had the relations of production in the primary theory of the state. It is not surprising, therefore, that Max Weber's sociology of the state has in some cases been combined with certain variations of Marx's secondary or relative autonomy theory. Weber never doubted the autonomy of the state, and the fact that he has influenced even neo-Marxist views says, perhaps, as much about the nature of the modern state as it does about the power of Weber's analysis. The relative autonomy of the state has become an important issue precisely because the modern state has proven to be more central to modern politics than Marx had perhaps initially assumed.

So too, as Gramsci insisted, has its ideology of legitimation. And, indeed, not only does much contemporary Marxist debate on the state focus on ideological issues, inherently so given the relative autonomy theory of the state and superstructure, but Marx himself argued that the role of ideology is central if only in the negative sense that it prevents a scientific under-standing of the state as it truly is. For this reason, Marx asserts in *The German Ideology* that "all struggles within the State, the struggle between democracy, aristocracy and monarchy, the struggle for the franchise, etc., etc., are merely the illusory forms in which the real struggles of the different classes are fought out among one another."[20] And this illusory struggle applies not only to the key legitimizing ideologies of the state, but to more mundane disputes over public policy as well. For Marx, the source of social ills lies in class domination and exploitation, but he argues that "*all* states seek the cause (of social problems) in *fortuitous* or *intentional defects in the administration* and hence the cure is sought in administrative measures."[21]

As we shall see, this analysis is particularly relevant to current neo-Marxist theories, for they all presume that the problems of class exploita-tion cannot in the long run be resolved by bureaucratic means and that, as a consequence, the ideology of state legitimation will be exposed for what it is, a legitimation of the existing relations of class domination. To pursue these issues further, however, requires that we return to the sociology of Max Weber. As we have noted, Weber cannot be fully understood apart from Marx, for he draws upon Marx as much as he rejects, or better, mod-ifies him. This is particularly so in the case of the sociology of the modern state, and here the epistemological and methodological differences between the two are not really relevant. In terms of the sociological conception of the state, both add enormously to our understanding, and both raise issues that are still the essential source of differing theories of the modern state.

Weber's sociology of the state is similar to Marx's in a number of important ways. Both understand the modern state to be a reflection of the industrial revolution that destroyed feudal and traditional forms of political organization. Both clearly understand the state as a form of domination, strip it of any spiritual or idealist purposes, and in Weber's words reduce it to purely bureaucratic and political means. Moreover, both thinkers conceive the state as a form of social differentiation spawned by the increas-ing division of labor in industrial-capitalist society, and both see in this a process of alienation, that is, of the separation of specifically human quali-ties into structures of domination. This relationship between differentiation and alienation was, of course, characteristic of other early sociological thinkers such as Durkheim and Tonnies, but it has a special significance in Marx and Weber's theories.

The differences in their theoretical views, again setting aside epistemo-logical and methodological issues, are not then so much over the basic facts of modern state formation, but rather over how to interpret those facts. Even then, there is as much agreement as disagreement. This is best understood if we begin where Weber himself does, with a sociology of social action rooted in the concept of domination. In his greatest, though uncompleted, sociological treatise *Wirtschaft und Gesellschaft (Economy and Society)*, Weber argues that "domination is one of the most important elements of communal action."[22] But as a specific form of social power, domination must be legitimized to be politically effective. This is the basis of Weber's definition of the modern state as the *"monopoly of the legitimate use of physical force* within a given territory." The state for Weber is unique in its territorial monopolization of power, but that particular structure of domination must be legitimized no less than other forms of domination.

Perhaps the most well-known aspect of Weber's sociology, certainly among political scientists, is his typology of forms of legitimate domination or authority (the term authority is typically used if the domination is legitimate as opposed to purely coercive). These are detailed in a number of works, but the most comprehensive analysis is to be found in *Economy and Society* where three basic forms or "ideal types" are specified: charismatic, traditional, and rational-legal. The concept of ideal type is a key aspect of Weber's methodology, the object of which is to aid in the investigation of the empirical world by directing attention to the key factors obscured by the complexity of any social situation. It is not meant to be a literal representation of reality, but a guide to empirical analysis. Hence, as an ideal type, charismatic domination is legitimized by the purely personal qualities of the leader as prophet, hero, or some other such form of charisma. Traditional domination is legitimized by custom as in the case of hereditary monarchy. Rational-legal domination is unique in its abstract character in that legitimacy is conferred by legal norms rather than by personal qualities or traditional values. It is, in short, a form of authority characteristic of the modern impersonal state.

These are ideal types however. As Weber emphasizes; "The forms of domination occurring in historical reality constitute combinations, mixtures, adaptations, or modifications of these 'pure types.' "[23] In regard to the modern state as it actually is, then, we should expect to find admixtures of the various forms of authority (recall that this had been Hegel's insight as well and the basis of his constitutional theory). Any contemporary executive is well aware of the power of charisma, should he or she be fortunate enough to possess it, and of the authority conferred when traditional values are appealed to. Nonetheless, we should expect to find the preponderant legitimation of the state to be in rational-legal terms. There is in this no implication of any evolutionary process by which earlier forms of society inevitably give rise to the rational-legal state. Here Weber parts company with Marx, and Hegel before him, whose thinking clearly is premised upon an evolutionary view of history. Weber understands that the structure of the modern state carries with it certain inevitable tendencies, such as increasing centralization and bureaucratization, but he does not accept the idea that these are the outcome of some larger historical process.

Given that the modern state is characterized primarily by rational-legal forms of domination, Weber's analysis of the state focuses on this type of legitimation, that is, on the legitimation conferred by the impersonality and rationality of positive law. For Weber, the term rational does not mean "right," or "morally appropriate," but logically consistent. State law is constituted as a logically coherent system of legal rules such that the ends sought—public order—are inherent in the regularity of the legal means employed. If the law is seen as impersonal and coherent it will be legitimized and thus willingly obeyed, at least by most. Nonetheless, the authority of law in the modern state is always and everywhere backed up by the means unique to the state. Weber is unequivocal in this regard: "Today legal coercion by violence is the monopoly of the state."[24]

Weber's concept of the modern state as a rational-legal system of authority is most clearly reflected in his theory of bureaucracy, surely his major contribution to modern social science. For Weber, the modern state is characterized above all by its increasingly bureaucratized structure, and this is precisely the organizational form that rational-legal authority takes in the modern state. Bureaucracy is rational, in Weber's meaning of that term, and bounded by explicitly articulated legal rules. The basic nature of those rules and organizational structures are delineated by Weber in great detail—permanence, hierarchy, predictability, and so on—and remain to this day the starting point for any scholarly analysis of bureaucracy.[25]

This is not to suggest that bureaucracy does not pre-date the state, or that it cannot be premised upon a different form of authority. Weber discusses a number of such cases: the new empire of ancient Egypt, the later Roman Principate, the Roman Catholic Church of the late medieval period, and the China of his own day. These were all cases of polities whose bureaucratic organization was premised upon patrimonial or prebendal elements rather than a fully developed rational-legal structure. As such, they were incapable of maintaining themselves as pure bureaucratic types and were constantly in danger of being transformed into some other form of political organization such as patriarchal or feudal polities.[26]

For Weber, however, what makes the modern state unique is that it has evolved into a fully developed and permanent form of bureaucratic organization of the rational-legal type. And there is no going back according to Weber; the continued bureaucratic organization of public- and private-life is now inevitable. He is equally certain of the reasons for the rise of modern state bureaucracy: a monied economy, which he sees as "the normal precondition for the unchanged and continued existence, if not for the establishment of pure bureaucratic administrations."[27] The reasons for this are obvious enough; a monied economy ensures a regularized source of taxation and, hence, permanently salaried bureaucratic employees. But a monied economy is the indispensable basis of modern capitalism as well, and for Weber this ultimately is the crucial fact. The bureaucratization of the modern state, as of the large-scale business enterprise itself, is the result of modern industrial capitalism.

Indeed, it is capitalism that spawns the entire social, cultural, and political milieu necessary for the rise of modern bureaucracy according to Weber.

Increasing wealth and the emergence of consumer society characteristic of advanced capitalist society require the organization and systemization that only bureaucratic structures can provide. In addition, modern mass communications engendered by capitalist enterprise require regulation by public authority, and this realistically requires bureaucratic administration. And the state specifically must not only be organized bureaucratically in a capitalist society, its entire mode of policy formation requires the modern mass democratic party which itself, Weber emphasizes, has increasingly become bureaucratized. Just as the remnants of the feudal economy have been obliterated by the large-scale capitalist enterprise organized on bureaucratic lines, so too the modern mass based party has eliminated the last vestiges of the feudal polity. It has replaced rule in parliament by local notables with party leaders who head huge bureaucratic parties organized for electoral purposes.[28]

The nature of the modern mass based party proved to be particularly important to Weber because it manifested a crucial feature of modern—that is, state—politics: its increasing democratization. This too was a consequence of industrial capitalism according to Weber, for capitalism and democracy have gone hand in hand in the development of the modern state. And liberalism, both classical and modern, has always legitimized this connection. Indeed liberal-democratic theory is thoroughly entwined with liberal-capitalist economic theory. And Weber, like Marx before him, clearly grasped the historical paradox inherent in the theory and practice of democracy. On the one hand, the concept of the "equal rights" of the citizen leads to incessant attempts to prevent the centralization of state power. On the other, this selfsame concept is the requisite basis for the development of a centralized state bureaucracy, for the idea of equality presupposes that offices of state are open to all. In this way, Weber argues, "democracy inevitably comes into conflict with the bureaucratic tendencies which, by its fight against notable rule, democracy has produced."[29]

There is much in this analysis, as with Marx's earlier critique of bureaucratic rule, that anticipates the later "crisis of legitimacy" literature on the state that is rooted in Marxist forms of analysis, and indeed there is much in Weber's reasoning that is entirely compatible with Marx's focus on capitalism as the shaping force of modern state and society. Weber in fact extends Marx's analysis of capitalism as an economic system to the broader social and political domain.[30] He sees in the organization of the capitalist enterprise, for example, the model of state forms of bureaucratization as well. But Weber extends Marx's analysis of capitalism at an even more profound level, applying Marx's concept of economic alienation equally to the political domain. This includes, most importantly for Weber, bureaucracy, in which the bureaucrat is alienated (separated) from the means of administration, a precise parallel to Marx's analysis of the modern proletariat who is alienated from the means of production. Neither the worker nor the bureaucrat owns the tools, buildings, or other material means required to perform their particular functions.[31]

But the more profound alienation for Weber is to be seen in the state itself, that is, the state as a centralized structure of bureaucratic control. It is only in this type of political system that the objective legal order is conceptually distinguished from the subjective rights of the individual which, according to Weber, constitutes a complete separation of public and private. But, Weber argues, "this conceptual separation presupposes the conceptual separation of the 'state,' as an abstract bearer of sovereign prerogatives and the creator of 'legal norms', from all personal 'authorizations' of individuals."[32] And, he notes, "These conceptual forms are necessarily remote from the nature of pre-bureaucratic, and especially from patrimonial and feudal, structures of authority."[33]

Weber, of course, is describing the conceptual basis of the modern state: an abstract entity premised upon an impersonal concept of sovereignty that is separate from both ruler and ruled. Here the state is clearly distinguished (separated / alienated) conceptually from society, hence public from private, and authority is rendered entirely impersonal as a rational-legal structure of domination. And it is only with the development of modern bureaucracy that this conceptualization is fully realized. As Weber emphasizes, "It was left to the complete depersonalization of administrative management by bureaucracy and the rational systematization of law to realize the separation of public and private fully and in principle."[34]

Weber's analysis of the underlying class system of capitalism is, as with his sociology of the state generally, more complex than Marx's, but again the differences are more a matter of emphasis and detail than of fundamentals. For Weber, social stratification occurs not only along class lines, but along status and political (party) lines as well. Whereas class stratification is rooted in the economic order and is dependent upon the acquisition of property, status stratification is an aspect of the social order and is premised upon the display of social honor such as ethnic or occupational identification. Political stratification belongs to what Weber terms the legal order and is manifested by the explicit possession of political power. All three, however, " 'classes,' 'status groups,' and 'parties' are phenomena of the distribution of power within a community,"[35] according to Weber.

Nonetheless, insofar as the modern state is concerned, social class remains the crucial form of stratification for Weber no less than for Marx. Hence, while a status group may be predominant in shaping politics at any given time, in a capitalist system status is largely determined by class position. As Weber notes " 'classes' are stratified according to their relations to the production and acquisition of goods; whereas 'status groups' are stratified according to the principle of their consumption of goods as represented by special 'styles of life.' "[36] In a capitalist society, the requisite consumption of goods is largely determined by class position. In the same way, parties may be based on class or status, in most cases they reflect both forms of stratification according to Weber, but the predominance of class in the modern state remains the key fact. Moreover, Weber argues, "Every technological repercussion and economic transformation threatens stratification by status and pushes the class situation into the foreground."[37]

This same difference of emphasis rather than of substance characterizes Weber's treatment of the relationship between social class and forms of social consciousness. Weber no less than Marx sees a clear connection between the two, but for Weber they share what he terms an "elective affinity" rather than the one strictly "determining" the other. Thus, in perhaps his most famous sociological study, *The Protestant Ethic and the Spirit of Capitalism*, he argues that while Protestantism as a form of religious consciousness arose in conjunction with capitalism, it was not merely "determined" by that economic system but had a profoundly shaping influence on it as well.[38] In the same way, it can be said that liberalism shaped the development of capitalism no less than the capitalist relations of production gave rise to the liberal ideology. But while much has been made of Weber's concept of elective affinity relative to Marx's views, in fact Marx is not nearly so deterministic as some have assumed. Class relations of production and ideology, substructure and superstructure, are in fact dialectically related for Marx, and while he would never concede that consciousness alone can determine material conditions, neither would Weber.

It is clear, then, that while there are clear differences between Marx and Weber, they are more matters of detail and emphasis than of substance. Weber's sociology of the state is certainly more developed and complex than Marx's, whether in its primary or secondary form. Marx is not primarily interested in the conceptual basis of the state, except as an ideological formation, or in typologies of legitimate domination, or in the nature of bureaucracy as a rational-legal form of authority. But these elements of Weber's sociology are not contrary to Marx's analysis, indeed are in many ways an extension of it, and are clearly in conformity with Marx's emphasis on the underlying reality of the capitalist relations of production. As we have seen, the entire conceptual and empirical apparatus of the modern state is understood by Weber to be intertwined with the development of modern capitalism. As such, Marx and Weber should be understood together as constituting the two most important social theorists of the modern state to this day. The entire field of modern state studies in the social sciences including contemporary anthropology draws primarily upon one, or both, of these two thinkers.

In the contemporary period, neo-Marxism, drawing largely upon Marx's secondary theory of the state, has been the most predominant influence in the sociology of the modern state. There is in this a certain paradox since the secondary theory granted an autonomy to the state only under exceptional and time limited circumstances. Clearly, if the state has become an important subject for Marxists it is because the state has in fact proven more important than anticipated. The question is why. The answer in general terms has been developed in previous chapters. The theory of the abstract impersonal state, which separated state from civil society, that is, from the class system, produced a situation in which the inequality of the economic system came increasingly into conflict with the demands from the newly, and growing, enfranchised working classes for political resolution to their emiseration. These demands, expressed in the ideologies of modern liberalism and reformist social democracy, were ultimately carried into political practice by the new mass based bureaucratic parties that Weber had analyzed as fundamental to this democratizing process.[39]

This, in its essentials, is the process by which the modern Western state took on its contemporary form as a "welfare state." The resulting increase in the state's functions, as Weber had predicted, contributed even more to those centralizing and bureaucratizing tendencies characteristic of the modern state, and he took issue with those—revolutionary socialists in particular—who believed that democratizing civil society itself would diminish the power of the state. For Marxists, however, the issue posed by the welfare state was even more significant than its increasingly bureaucratic structure. On the face of it, the welfare state seemingly challenged the Marxist assumption, or at least the more radical Marxist assumption, that the state is no more than the "political arm of the ruling class" and its liberal-democratic ideology of legitimation merely a cover for the reality of class rule. Did the welfare state not demonstrate that democratic government could put the sovereign power of the state in the hands of the working classes, and that the state could represent other class interests besides those of the capitalist?

It was in response to this issue that Marxists, and neo-Marxists in particular, began to develop a renewed interest in the state, and that Marx's secondary theory of the state gained increasing prominence.[40] The issue became "to what extent can the state in capitalist society become relatively autonomous from direct class control" such that, at least in the short run, it can represent other class interests besides those of the capitalist.[41] The term "relative" is key here, because the assumption remained that capitalism, either as specific relations of production or the economic system as a whole, must strive to maintain itself. And while debates between various schools of Marxism are, to say the least, tediously complex, the general tendencies are discernable enough.

At one end of the spectrum are the "instrumentalists" who come closest to maintaining Marx's primary theory of the state, although not in a crudely direct way, arguing that the capitalist class in fact continues to use the state as its instrument of class rule.[42] Ralph Miliband's *The State in Capitalist Society* is a classic work along these lines in which members of the capitalist class or their managerial and professional proxies are shown to control the key executive institutions of the state as well as crucial policy-forming institutions such as political parties, the media, and so on.[43] At the same time, Miliband argues that to be effective the state must be able to establish some autonomy from direct class pressure.[44]

At the other end of the spectrum are the "structuralists" such as Nicos Poulantzas who argue that the state is a structural component of the capitalist system whose function is to maintain the system as a whole. This is not done by directly occupying key positions of state power, but by the overall regulation of civil society and ideological manipulation. Although such an arrangement remains in the clear interest of the capitalist class, it does not constitute a direct representation of that interest within the structure of the state. Indeed, it becomes necessary for the state to establish a "relative autonomy" from the various class factions that are striving to capture state power. In this way, superstructural factors become, if not ultimately dominant, at least crucially important, and Poulantzas returns to Gramsci's notion of "hegemony" to explain this increasingly complex relationship between state and civil society.[45]

The initial debate between instrumentalists and structuralists soon led to further developments in the theory of relative autonomy. The tendency was to impute increasing autonomy to the state while, at the same time, insisting upon the ultimate preservation of the interests of the capitalist class if only in the short term. Clauss Offe, for example, argues that the state is an independent entity that acts as a mediator in the class struggle; that through corporatist forms of political organization it attempts to secure both capitalist accumulation and social welfare. That ultimately this is an impossibility for Offe does not obviate the fact that neither the capitalist nor worker is able to establish sufficient class cohesion to control the state.[46]

This analysis, of course, is reminiscent of the original "Bonapartist" or secondary Marxist theory of the state. Taken to its logical conclusion, we arrive at the Weberian theory of the autonomous bureaucratic state.[47] And, indeed, this is precisely where the critics of neo-Marxism arrived, most notably Theda Skocpol who, in *States and Social Revolutions*, argues contrary to the neo-Marxists, and quite in line with Weber's views, that "the state . . . is no mere arena in which socioeconomic struggles are fought out. It is, rather, a set of administrative, policing, and military organizations headed, and more or less well coordinated by, an executive authority."[48] That is, it is an autonomous bureaucratic structure that stands on its own quite apart from the class system.[49] This is not to deny that the state is premised upon class stratification, an obvious fact for Skocpol no less than for Weber, but simply that the state cannot be reduced to the class system, either directly as in the Marxist primary theory of the state, or indirectly as in the secondary or relative autonomy theory.[50] Skocpol, appropriately, terms her views "organizational realism," a term that could easily be applied to Weber's theory of the state.

What for our purposes is ultimately important in this debate, however, is the issue of state legitimacy. While Skocpol dismisses this as an important issue largely of concern to non-Marxists, it is in fact important to Marxists as well, and neo-Marxists in particular who argue that the relative autonomy of the state is the necessary condition for its continuing legitimacy. And certainly it was important to Weber whose typology of domination, including state forms of domination, was premised precisely on the concept of legitimation. It is undoubtedly true, as Skocpol maintains, that in general the state remains legitimate so long as it performs its tasks adequately, and even for a time if it does not, and that it is for the most part only the elites and state administrators that are even concerned with the issue.[51] But our focus has been on the broad historical basis of state legitimacy, its theoretical origins and inherent contradictions, not simply on its ideological viability in immediate terms. In this context, legitimacy remains a crucial issue, for no form of polity can exist long term without an ideology of legitimation that validates its existence.

Marxist based "critical theory" has been particularly concerned with this issue of legitimacy, most notably in the work of Jurgen Habermas, a member of the Frankfurt Institute in Germany of which Offe is also associated. Habermas explicitly focuses on the issue of a potential legitimation crisis in advanced capitalism. The argument Habermas advances is exceedingly complex, probably too complex, but the essence of it is comprehensible enough, and follows in the general lines of the neo-Marxists. The modern welfare state is trapped in an insurmountable contradiction: sustaining capitalist accumulation while, at the same time, responding to the economic demands of the broader citizenry. This it attempts to resolve by shifting the contradictions of the capitalist relations of production from the private sphere of civil society to the state. But this has the effect of politicizing the class system and, potentially, of delegitimizing the state by exposing its universalistic claims of equal rights as little more than a cover for the particular interests of the capitalist.[52]

As a consequence, the state must continuously attempt to depoliticize the public realm. This it cannot do directly; that is, it cannot abolish mass democracy since the contemporary welfare state is legitimized precisely in liberal-democratic terms. Rather, Habermas argues, the political structure of the modern state has the effect of neutralizing mass participation in a way that creates the impression of citizen involvement in decision making but not the reality. It "provides for application of institutions and procedures that are democratic in form, while the citizenry, in the midst of an objectively . . . political society, enjoy the status of passive citizens with only the right to withhold acclamation."[53] The result, Habermas argues, is on the one hand an increasing privatization of life in which individuals begin to shift their focus from public life to economic well being—the consumer society—and on the other an increasing domination of technical elites within the state bureaucracy.

Whether or not the modern state can maintain its legitimacy in this way is problematical, but clearly for critical theorists there is no longer any certainty in this regard. It is not without reason that critical theory is often seen as a form of "pessimistic Marxism." But it is pessimistic only because the structure of the modern state, and its increasing autonomy from democratic controls, has called into question the adequacy of the Marxist theory of the state as such. The state and its legal and ideological superstructure have proven to be more important, and pervasive, than classical Marxist theory presumed, whether in its primary or secondary form. It is for this reason that critical theory, like neo-Marxist theory in general, has focused on the state and, in particular, its ideology of legitimation as important factors in the maintenance of the capitalist system. It is also for this reason that Weber has been particularly influential among critical theorists. Weber not only provides a detailed account of the nature of the modern state as a bureaucratic system of control, but of the specific character of its ideology of rational-legal legitimation.

The problem is that Weber's purely legal-positivism does not establish a sufficient basis of state legitimation according to Habermas. Law, he insists, must be rooted in some ethical principle beyond itself, and this is precisely what Weber, as a modern social scientist, rejects.[54] Habermas's objection, of course, is hardly new; it is in essence the same objection made of Hobbes's foundational theory of the state based upon a purely prudential theory of obligation and an ethically neutral concept of state (positive) law. It is this same objection that lay at the heart of Hegel's attempt to found the state once again upon an ethically "real" basis, upon a concept of a final end. But Habermas's analysis of the modern state is rooted in the materialism of Marx and Weber, and despite his criticisms of these traditions of thought, and of the uncritical empiricism of modern social science, he cannot return to the older tradition of positing some final end beyond the material world.

Habermas's solution to this dilemma is the "theory of communicative competence" that posits the possibility of deriving consensually an obligatory ethical system through open, equal, and mutually unfettered communication, communication free of all forms of domination or ideological distortion. This, "the ideal speech situation" in Habermas's terms, could, he believes, provide an ethical alternative to those existing relations of production and political forms of domination now obscured by ideological justifications of existing reality. Whether or not Habermas is correct in this estimation is obviously open to a variety of objections, not the least of which is that the "consensus theory of truth" itself requires justification. Habermas's response, in its simplest terms, is that the inherent nature of discourse presumes the possibility of establishing ethical truths, and that the pragmatic structure of discursive formation makes free and equal consensus possible, and politically imperative.[55]

What is important for our purposes is the fact that, even within a Marxist materialist framework, Habermas feels compelled to raise again the issue of legitimation and, hence, of the ethical basis of the state. For Habermas, of course, as for neo-Marxists generally, it is the interventionist welfare state characteristic of advanced capitalism that, in attempting to integrate the economy with the political system, has pushed the issue to the forefront. Issues of class have now become political issues whereas, in the classical liberal separation of state and civil society, class relations were formally depoliticized. Consequently, Habermas argues, the modern interventionist state "must, therefore—like the precapitalist state—be legitimated, although it can no longer rely on residues of tradition that have been undermined and worn out during the development of capitalism."[56]

If, as Habermas asserts, the modern state can no longer rely on traditional authority, and if Weber's analysis is correct that rational-legal domination (legal-positivism and bureaucratic control) is the key characteristic of the modern state, then how in the long term can it be legitimated? Habermas's solution is at best debatable, and apart from a radical regression into some temporary form of charismatic authority, no solution is easily apparent. Certainly liberal-nationalism no longer suffices as a legitimizing ideology; it is an ideal that failed long ago. And while it is obvious enough to critical theorists and neo-Marxists that the legitimizing ideology of modern liberalism must somehow be transcended, they do not view this as possible under existing conditions. Either the capitalist relations of production are transformed or we face a bleak future of increasingly bureaucratic and ideological controls.

Perhaps such pessimism is unwarranted, although Weber himself was hardly less pessimistic, but the issue of legitimation is a real political issue, now thrust into the forefront by the democratic welfare state, and cannot simply be dismissed in the name of a value neutral social science. Indeed, the current revival of interest in the state in the social sciences, and hence the reinvigoration of both Marx's and Weber's sociologies, is itself an aspect of the legitimation issue, that is, of the structural and ideological contradictions of the modern state in the contemporary period.

Chapter Eight

The State in Retrospect

One of the more revealing statements in the history of political consciousness, made by the emerging territorial monarchs toward the end of the thirteenth century, is "the king is emperor in his own kingdom." This was a claim that attempted to legitimate the new form of rulership by appeal to an incipient concept of sovereignty inherent in the existing model of supreme authority within Christendom, a concept that reached back to the ancient Roman *imperium* itself. As a political stratagem, it worked well enough. As an accurate reflection of political reality, it was woefully inadequate. Although the king was now clearly something more than a feudal noble first among equals, he was hardly an emperor. And even if he could have claimed authority equivalent to the emperor's, it was of a nature not only entirely different, but also destructive ultimately of the pretensions of the emperor to universal rule within the ancient Christian Republic. It was, in fact, the first stirrings of a concept of state sovereignty.

This misperception of political reality is hardly untypical in the history of political thought, particularly during transitional periods such as the High Middle Ages. The existing form of polity becomes the unwitting, but erroneous, model for the legitimation of a new and emerging political structure. We see this again and again: attempts to found a new ideology of legitimation upon the basis of the old, and increasingly irrelevant, political order. Aristotle attempted to affirm the ideal of a by then moribund classical *polis* at the very time his most famous student was destroying it, as Cicero later sought to reform the emerging Roman Empire with increasingly irrelevant republican ideals. The entire history of medieval political thought is characterized by claims to legitimacy derived from classical Roman and Greek state theory on the part of multiple authorities ruling over a radically nonstate form of society. And, as we have seen, even when the modern state had emerged in clear structural form, political consciousness still tended to reflect traditional, if often contradictory, models of political organization, or at least not to have thought clearly beyond them.

What makes American political science unique in this theoretical history is its claim to have transcended the historical connection between polity and political consciousness. Its definitions and models of politics in the postwar era have been largely premised upon a rejection of the existing form of polity— the modern state—as a valid basis of political analysis. The implication is that a genuine science of politics has been created, or at least the possibility of it now exists, because political theory has finally been severed from what heretofore had always been an ideological reflection or justification of a historically given polity. In this rejection of the modern state, indeed of the concept of the state as such, American political science has not only laid claim to creating a value neutral science of politics freed from normative issues of legitimation, but to the possibility of a universal science no longer tied to the historically given.

When viewed against the historical and ideological background of the modern state, however, this claim becomes at best questionable. As noted in chapter one, postwar political science generated models of political behavior that reflected the most paradoxical feature of the modern state: radical individualism coupled with an extensive centralization of impersonal sovereign authority. The paradox is premised upon the theory of the impersonal state separate from both ruler and ruled, that is, upon the modern theory of sovereignty in which supreme political authority is derived from the consent of individuals equal in the act of consenting despite their inequality within civil society.

This complex of ideas became the basis of the liberal ideology, the essential legitimizing ideology of the modern state, both in classical and, despite its Hegelian roots, in modern form as well. The frequently made criticism of mainline American political science, that it is implicated in the liberal ideology, is therefore to assert that in fact it reflects the state despite its rejection of it. Indeed, it might well be argued that American political science's rejection of the state is simply a contemporary form of state ideology, for it requires a theoretically impersonal and socially distinct political structure to make conceivable a theory of politics divorced from the existing form of polity and its legitimizing ideology.

This same liberal and antistate bias lies behind those related criticisms of American political science that point to its classless and ahistorical approach to political phenomena. The modern state is a historically given entity and, like every other state formation that preceded it, it is based upon a particular form of class stratification. This is what makes American political science so different from, and its critics would argue anemic relative to, Marxian, Weberian, and, for that matter, even Hegelian modes of political theorizing, for these recognized the historicity of the modern state, its sociological grounding in the class system, and the necessity therefore of understanding political behavior within this historical and sociological context.

But what about the contrary tendency within the discipline to reengage the issue of the state? To be sure, this is an important development, but the more prominent state-centric theories such as neo-Marxism and even Weberian based perspectives such as organizational realism are not fully developed theories of the state. While neo-Marxism has drawn upon what we have termed the secondary Marxist theory of the "relatively autonomous" state, this does not in itself constitute a comprehensive state theory.[1] And while organizational realists and neo-institutionalists have "brought the state back in," they tend to understand it only as a set of administrative institutions, as the permanent bureaucratic structure of government, and to leave out of account the conceptual basis of the state and its ideology of legitimation. While for its adherents at least, this constitutes an advance over the nonstatist approach in the discipline, and the "social (class) reductionism" of neo-Marxism, it is to conceive of the modern state in less than its totality.[2]

As a totality, the modern state, like every state formation that preceded it, is a complex of political, social, and ideological structures. What makes the modern state unique is its supposed impersonality. It is this that constitutes the core of its legitimacy, the merging of an abstract concept of the state with a doctrine of popular sovereignty that transcends the purely personal characteristics of the more ancient notion of ruler sovereignty. As such, the modern state is as much conceptual as empirical, a point not merely stressed by thinkers such as Hegel, but by empiricists such as Max Weber as well. Thus, to understand the modern state means to understand it not merely empirically as a set of governing institutions, but as a conceptual and ideological structure that orders those institutions in some particular (constitutional) pattern and upon some sociological (class) basis. Such an understanding, however, cannot be attained in isolation from the historical transformations—political and sociological—that produced these particular features. This, of course, was Hegel's point, and method, and while no contemporary social scientist would—or could—agree with his conclusion that "the state is the actuality of the ethical Idea," it most certainly is the actualization of a historically given structure of social and political institutions, concepts, and ideological legitimations.

A state-centric approach within the discipline of political science does raise some profound epistemological and methodological issues, however. It would mean a much greater reliance on historical data, and a willingness to deal with the fact of historical contingency that is so problematical in any attempt to formulate general and universal theories of political behavior. It would mean an empiricism that is rooted in a broader conceptual framework, not abstracted from the historically given, but explicitly rather than implicitly (ideologically) reflective of it, and a willingness to deal with related legitimation issues, not as normative issues as such, of course, but in the Weberian sense as ideological constructs that have real empirical consequences.

It would also mean a deeper recognition of the shaping influence of social class on the entire field of political behavior, for the anthropological evidence makes clear that the state cannot in reality be impersonal as the legitimizing ideology presupposes, but is always and everywhere a "state form of society," that is, a political structure corresponding to some system of class stratification. This does not, it needs be noted, necessarily lead to a Marxist theory of the state, although that is one possible conclusion to be derived from the evidence. This is an important caveat, for there is a tendency to think that a class analysis of the state is somehow inevitably a Marxist one. It must be remembered, however, that until the theory of the modern state the class basis of the polity was taken for granted, and justice was understood to be precisely the appropriate constitutional structuring of class interests within the state. That this view is debatable is clear enough, but it does not inevitably follow that recognizing the class basis of the state requires delegitimizing it or rendering it purely epiphenomenal to the class system. What ought not to be debatable is that the state, from the archaic to the modern, always corresponds to, and is dependent upon, some system of class stratification.

Could such an approach produce a predictive science of politics capable of generating universally valid understandings of political behavior? This ultimately is the issue for the social and political sciences, and the answer is at best an ambiguous "perhaps" to a more likely "probably not." Certainly a purely neo-positivist ideal of a political science would not be possible, which is no doubt at least an implicit reason why there has been in the postwar era sustained resistance to a state-centric approach in the discipline. It is not simply that the state is viewed as an unnecessary construct in the development of a science of politics; it is seen as a potentially destructive one.[3] But political theory has invariably reflected the existing form of polity, a fact confirmed in even the most cursory historical analysis of state forma- tions, and not proven to be in any way different for contemporary political science despite its methodological rejection of the state. The issue is not whether the state will influence political theorizing, but whether it will do so implicitly (hence ideologically) or, as in Weber and the historical school of sociology, explicitly such that the ideological issue, if never entirely surmountable, can at least be confronted directly. That such an approach will require a humbler, less certain, and more tentative approach to under- standing political behavior is no doubt true, but if the history of political thought is any guide, it is also likely to be a richer and more substantive science of politics than one divorced from what had been, until the behavioral revolution, its own subject matter.[4]

A final consideration, heretofore periphery to our concerns, deserves mention. If history is any guide, the renewed interest in the state, while framed as a methodological issue, is likely reflective of more profound social and political changes. The most profound change that could occur would be a transformation of the existing form of polity itself and, as the preceding chapters have hopefully demonstrated, major shifts in political conscious- ness typically began to occur during transitions from one form of polity to another. It is not, therefore, unreasonable to ask if this is not now occurring and that, despite the changes introduced by the welfare state that seem to undergird much of the renewed interest in the state within the discipline, perhaps the disintegration of the "nation-state" itself is a contributing factor on the other side of the debate. Perhaps the methodological objections to the state concept on the part of the "antistatists" are in reality a reflection of its actual demise.

This possibility has been raised most explicitly within the field of international politics. Some have argued quite strongly in its favor, pointing to the growth of transnational entities such as multinational corporations, the growth of regional economic and political units such as the European Community, and the increasing authority of international organizations such as the United Nations that collectively are diminishing the sovereignty of the state.[5] Not all in the field are so certain however,[6] and debates equivalent, if not always identical, to those in political science over the usefulness of the state concept continue to occur.[7] The "realist" school in particular continues to emphasize the importance of the state in the international domain, particularly in contrast to the normative positions of what might loosely be called "liberal" and "neo-Kantian" theorists.[8]

It goes without saying that it is unlikely that this debate will be resolved any time soon; indeed it will not be resolved at all until the state either disappears or proves so peskily persistent that its detractors withdraw their objections to it. It is a reasonably safe prediction at any rate that those involved in the debate will not be around to confirm the outcome one way or the other. This at least would be the conclusion to be drawn from past experience, for the major forms of polity that have existed over historical time have persisted long after historians of a later age discovered the seeds of their disintegration. We, however, live in an age that, unlike any previous, announces major historical transformations while we are supposedly in the midst of them: postindustrial, postmodern, and even posthistorical. Post–nation-state is of a kind, and the problem is not that it may not be a valid characterization in the long term, but that the long term may be very long indeed.

But for our purposes the important point is not whether or not the modern state is in a condition of decline, but whether or not it will continue to influence how we think about politics even if it is being superseded or transcended by extrastate organizations or by some new and emerging form of polity. Here once again the historical record is illuminating: In past transformations the existing form of polity became the model for the emerging form and, of course, it was invariably the wrong model. We have noted this fact throughout this book, but it bears repeating, and in the case of international politics the question can legitimately be raised as to the extent that the state concept will continue to influence those theoretical constructs premised upon its demise.

Surely this has been the case for American political science despite its attempt to jettison the state as a useful concept. So many of its key concepts are absolutely implicated in the state, from its concept of power to that of politics itself. When seen against the historical background from which these concepts evolved, which has constituted the primary focus of this book, this all becomes apparent. And, in the domain of normative theory, this is even more obviously the case, in international political theory as well as political science generally. Current notions of human rights, for example, are derivative of an older natural right tradition that, despite its assertion of universality, was and is a product of the modern state. And demands for international forms of governance—from parliamentary organizations to juridical structures—invariably draw upon models that, while pre-dating the modern state, were fully developed and legitimized within it.

That the pervasiveness of the modern state in our political consciousness poses difficulties in the development of a science of politics is clear enough. To ignore its influence on our political thinking, however, is to perpetuate it in the very theoretical constructs aimed at transcending it. It cannot simply be eliminated by theoretical fiat; it must first be comprehended before attempts are made to transcend it, and a persistent awareness of the limitations inherent in such a project always borne in mind. This in the broadest terms is simply to recognize and accept our own historicity and the inherent limitations it imposes on any theoretical endeavor that deals with the social and political worlds. Certainly this must be the case for any science of politics that wishes to avoid being the unwitting ideological mirror of its age that a future historian will conclude, as the feudal monarch who claimed to be "emperor in his own kingdom," really missed the point.

Notes

Chapter One   State and Ideology

1. See R.M. MacIver, *The Modern State* (Oxford: Oxford University Press, 1926). MacIver and Wilson's concern with the state had a more pragmatic bent, to reform the administrative apparatus. See Raymond Seidelman and Edward J. Harpam, *Disenchanted Realists: Political Science and the American Crisis, 1884–1984*, in series: *SUNY Series in Political Theory: Contemporary Issues*, ed. John G. Gunnell (Albany: State University of New York Press, 1985), 49–50.
2. Postwar political science rejected the concept of the state as unscientific not only because it was considered an empirically void abstraction, but also because it had been historically implicated in normative issues.
3. See Peter T. Manicas, *A History and Philosophy of the Social Sciences* (Oxford: Basil Blackwell, 1987), 216–221, for a concise analysis of this new empiricism, and the break from the predominant influence of German political thought it entailed.
4. See Raymond Seidelman and Edward J. Harpham, *Disenchanted Realists*, 67–74, for an analysis of the extreme empiricism inherent in Bentley's rejection of "soul stuff," particularly in his early work *The Process of Government*. What is rejected is not only the state, but also any institutional concept beyond the immediately observable behavior of individuals.
5. See, e.g., Gabriel Almond, "The Return to the State," *American Political Science Review*, v. 82, no. 3, September 1988.
6. Peter B. Evans, Dietrich Rueschemeyer, and Theda Skocpol, eds., *Bringing the State Back In* (New York: Cambridge University Press, 1985), for a series of chapters on refocusing the discipline of political science on the various facets of the modern state.
7. Harold Laswell, *Politics: Who Gets What, When, How* (New York: P. Smith, 1950).
8. George Armstrong Kelly, "Who Needs a Theory of Citizenship," *Daedalus*, v. 108, no. 4, Fall 1979, 22.
9. Robert A. Dahl was the most prominent of the pluralist theorists. See, e.g., his *A Preface to Democratic Theory* (Chicago: University of Chicago Press, 1956), and *Who Governs? Democracy and Power in an American City* (New Haven: Yale University Press, 1961). See also Seidelman and Harpham, *Disenchanted Realists*, 159, for an analysis of Dahl's pluralist-behavioralist tradition.
10. See John S. Nelson, "Education for Politics: Rethinking Research on Political Socialization," *What Should Political Theory Be Now: Essays from the Shambaugh Conference on Political Theory*, ed. John S. Nelson, in series: *SUNY Series in Political Theory: Contemporary Issues*, ed. John G. Gunnell (Albany: State University of New York Press, 1983), 419–428, for a brief but illuminating analysis of the combined theoretical perspectives of structural functionalism and

systems theory, and particularly of the influence of Talcott Parsons and David Easton in the development of the two approaches.

11. See David Easton, *The Political System* (New York: Alfred Knopf, 1953), for an example of the system analytic approach. Easton was the premier systems theorist in the period.

12. See Jeffrey Friedman, "Economic Approaches to Politics," *Critical Review: An Interdisciplinary Journal of Politics and Society*, v. 9, no. 1–2, 1995. Friedman argues that while the focus of public choice is narrower than rational choice, the latter applying its analysis beyond the political, the basic assumptions are identical in both: that human behavior can be reduced to purely economic forms of calculations.

13. The microphysics of power is a theme in most of Foucault's works. Perhaps the most accessible of his writings in this regard is Michel Foucault, *Discipline and Punish: The Birth of the Prison*, trans. Alan Sheridan (New York: Vintage Books, 1995). Foucault does not deny, however, that the state remains a crucial component of the overall structure of power in society. See Barry Smart, *Michel Foucault*, in series: *Key Sociologists*, ed. Peter Hamilton (London: Routledge, 1988), 131–132.

14. See Mark Irving Lichbach and Alan S. Zuckerman, *Comparative Politics: Rationality, Culture, and Structure* (Cambridge: Cambridge University Press, 1997), 5–8, for a brief summary of the basic approaches in contemporary comparative theory. These, according to the authors, are rational choice and cultural and structural forms of analysis. The latter includes those in the Marxian and Weberian traditions who are attempting to revive interest in the state.

15. Arthur Goldhammer, "Introduction," in *The Sociology of the State*, ed. Bertrand Badie and Pierre Birnbaum, trans. Arthur Goldhammer (Chicago: University of Chicago Press, 1983), ix–xx.

16. Ibid., ix.

Chapter Two   State Formations

1. Joseph R. Strayer, *On the Medieval Origins of the Modern State* (Princeton: Princeton University Press, 1970). Strayer also points to the difficulty in framing a satisfactory definition of the state, and lists in its stead a number of its key elements that overlap those we have detailed.

2. Max Weber, "Politics as a Vocation," in *From Max Weber: Essays in Sociology*, ed. trans. H.H. Gerth and C. Wright Mills (New York: Oxford University Press, 1946), 78.

3. The absence of private property and class stratification in pre-state societies led Marx and Engels, among others, to argue that in the beginning a certain "primitive communism" prevailed. See Frederick Engels, "The Origins of the Family, Private Property, and the State," in *Selected Works in One Volume*, Col. Karl Marx and Frederick Engels (New York: International Publisher, 1968).

4. The first to recognize that governance in pre-state societies is rooted in kin relations was Sir Henry Maine, the nineteenth century father of comparative jurisprudence who, in his *Ancient Law*, posited kinship rather than territoriality as the basis of the primitive polity. Another lawyer, Louis Henry Morgan, followed Maine's lead in his *Ancient Society*, a work that greatly influenced later anthropologists and political scientists as well as the thinking of Friedrich

Engels and Karl Marx. See Ted C. Lewellen, *Political Anthropology: An Introduction*, 2nd ed. (Westport: Bergin and Garvey, 1992), 8–10, for an analysis of the thought, and influence, of Maine and Morgan. And while not all have accepted the Maine–Morgan thesis uncritically, for early on there were those, such as Robert Lowie, who argued that other relationships beyond kinship played a role in social and political cohesion of pre-state societies, no one has disputed that kinship is the primary basis of the primitive polity. See Robert Lowie, *The Origin of the State* (New York: Russell and Russell, 1962).

5. See Pierre Clastres, *Society Against the State*, trans. Robert Hurley (New York: Mole Editions, 1974), 148–158. Clastres goes so far as to argue that primitive "law" is designed precisely to prevent the emergence of a centralized coercive power and, as such, is literally "written" upon the body in ceremonial initiation rites.

6. The term "segmentary" is derived from a particular form of kinship structure called "segmentary lineage" typical of some tribes, particularly in Africa. The tribe is composed of lineage segments that are autonomous, but that are capable of coming together for specified social or political purposes, most importantly for the regulation of conflict. Disputes among lower kinship segments are raised to higher segments for resolution, a process known as "segmentary opposition." See, e.g., Max Gluckman, *Politics, Law, and Ritual in Tribal Society* (Chicago: Aldine Pub. Co., 1965), 163–166, and Lawrence Krader, *Formation of the State* (Englewood Cliffs, NJ: Prentice Hall, 1968), 35. We employ the term in its broadest sense, however, to refer to stateless societies that are organized politically in autonomous units. This would include Western society during the feudal period. It is possible, however, that in the early formation of the state it will not entirely overcome segmentation and the term "segmentary state" may be appropriate. For an analysis of the concept of segmentary state see F.H. Hinsley, *Sovereignty* (New York: Basic Books Inc., 1966), 18.

7. Hinsley, *Sovereignty*. Hinsley employs the concept of segmentary society and the "segmentary state" to analyze the structure of medieval society and the impediment to a theory of state sovereignty that structure entailed.

8. See Morton H. Fried, *The Evolution of Political Society: An Essay in Political Anthropology* (New York: Random House, 1967), Chap. 4, for a general characterization and analysis of these and other elements of more centralized pre-state formations, what Fried terms rank societies.

9. See I. Schapera, *Government and Politics in Tribal Societies* (London: C.A. Watts and Co., 1956), 211–212, for an example of titular and strong chieftainships in South Africa. Shapera derives the distinction from Lowie.

10. See Jonathan Haas, *The Evolution of the Prehistoric State* (New York: Columbia University Press, 1982), 212–213. Haas notes that not all chiefdoms become states, and that under some circumstances the state may evolve out of more "primitive" social organizations.

11. Lewellen, *Political Anthropology*, 47–51.

12. See Lowie, *The Origin of the State*, for a classic example of an early integration theory.

13. See Haas, *The Evolution of the Prehistoric State*. These are Haas's categories; we employ them as well as his general framework of analysis of theories of state formation.

14. See ibid., 123. While attempting to combine elements of both integration and conflict theories, Haas admits that the conflict theory is empirically the more persuasive of the two.

15. Ibid., 216–217.

16. See Elman R. Service, *Origins of the State and Civilization: The Process of Cultural Evolution* (New York: W.W. Norton, 1975), 282–308. See also Clastres, *Society Against the State*. Clastres argues that "The economic derives from the political; the emergence of the State determines the advent of classes" (168).

17. What might be termed modern empire states could be included here as well given the imperial expansion of some early-formed nation-states, but these were not true empire states in their structure or ideologies of legitimation. In the long run they did not last in any case, and precisely because the modern concept of state (and popular) sovereignty delegitimized imperial rule by foreign powers.

18. Hendrik Spruyt, *The Sovereign State and Its Competitors: An Analysis of Systems Change* (Princeton: Princeton University Press, 1994), 129.

19. Karl Wittfogel, *Oriental Despotism: A Comparative Study of Total Power* (New Haven: Yale University Press, 1957).

20. See Chester G. Starr, *A History of the Ancient World*, 4th ed. (Oxford: Oxford University Press, 1991), 1. According to Starr, "This was the first empire in history, in the sense that it had the first imperial administration" (131).

21. There are a number of typologies of state formations, but the typology used here corresponds to the actual historical development of states in the archaic Near East, the classical Mediterranean area, and Western Europe in the late medieval and Renaissance periods. There are forms of empires that have existed, but that do not fit the definition of state in the strictest sense, such as patrimonial empires (e.g., the Carolingian Empire) and nomadic conquest empires (e.g., the Mongol Empire). See S.N. Eisenstadt, *The Political Systems of Empires* (New York: The Free Press of Glencoe, 1963), 10–11.

22. See Patricia Springborg, "Politics, Primordialism, and Orientalism: Marx, Aristotle, and the Myth of the Gemeinschaft," *American Political Science Review*, v. 80, no. 1, March 1986, 187–188. Springborg argues that the Near Eastern states were much more open and political than traditional Western scholarship had assumed. Recent archaeological investigations now suggest that the political structure of the very earliest Sumerian states was most likely based upon an assembly of all citizens and, despite class distinctions, a relatively egalitarian social structure. This political structure, however, and that of subsequent Mesopotamian city and empire states, gave way by about 2800 BCE to theocratic monarchies and rigidly class divided societies. The reason for this transformation is not entirely known, but it appears that exogenous factors were predominant, most importantly the ceaseless warfare between the various cities. This at least seems to be the case for the larger states of Sumer. See Starr, *A History of the Ancient World*, 41–42.

23. C. Leonard Woolley, *The Sumerians* (New York: W.W. Norton, 1965), 18.

24. This, at least, was true for Egypt. While it underwent a number of transformations, including conquest and disunity through the old, middle, and new kingdoms (2700 BCE–1090 BCE), the basics of this theocratic ideology remained. See Henri Frankfort, *Kingship and the Gods: A Study of Ancient Near Eastern Religion as the Integration of Society and Nature* (Chicago: The University of Chicago Press, 1978), 52.

25. Ibid., 3.

26. Ibid., 9, 157.

27. Hammurabi, *The Hammurabi Code and the Sinaitic Legislation; With a Complete Translation of the Great Babylonian Inscription discovered at Susa*, trans. Chilperic Edwards (Port Washington, NY: Kennikat Press, 1971), 23.

28. Ibid., 62. For example, if a man strikes a superior he will be publicly whipped, but only pay a nominal sum if he assaults an equal.
29. Starr, *A History of the Ancient World*, 149–152.
30. Not until the dominance of Persia in the Near East did the remnants of the people of Judah (the Jews) reestablish a semiautonomous state in Palestine that was subsequently absorbed by the Roman Empire.
31. Frankfort, *Kingship and the Gods*, 343.
32. Ibid., 341–342.
33. Ibid., 342.
34. Quentin Skinner, *The Foundations of Modern Political Thought: The Age of Reformation*, v. II (Cambridge: Cambridge University Press, 1978), 349–358. In Skinner's analysis, the preconditions for the emergence of the modern impersonal state also include the development of political theory as a "distinct branch of moral philosophy."

Chapter Three   The Ideal State

1. See Ralph Sealey, *A History of the Greek City-States: 700–338 B.C.* (Berkeley, CA: University of California Press, 1976), 99, for a discussion of some other great lawgivers of the classical period, including the infamous Dracon of Athens.
2. Ibid., 154. This was particularly the case following Cleisthenes' return in 508–507 BCE, although Sealey suggests that the tribes likely continued to play a prominent political role until the late fifth century. These tribes, however, were based on geography rather than kinship.
3. Victor Ehrenberg, *The Greek State*, 2nd ed. (London: Methuen and Co., 1969), 47.
4. This "desacralization" of religious ideology was in part connected to the decline of Greek kingship that, like kingship in the archaic Near Eastern states, was initially the source of divine knowledge. See Jean-Pierre Vernant, *The Origins of Greek Thought*, Chap. VII. (Ithaca: Cornell University Press, 1982).
5. *Politeia* is the term for constitution and, as Aristotle notes, "The term 'constitution' (*politeia*) signifies the same thing as 'civic body' (*politeuma*)." See Aristotle, *The Politics of Aristotle*, ed. trans. Ernest Barker (Oxford: Oxford University Press, 1962), Book III, Chap. VII, 114. In Aristotle's analysis, the civic body is constituted by the whole body of citizens that are, in turn, defined as those who have a share in political power. The breadth of these terms corresponds to the Greek theory of the state (regime) that conflates constitution, citizen (*polites*), and civic body (ruling group) into one overall concept. As Ehrenberg notes, *politeia* in fact refers to "the whole structure of the state." See Victor Ehrenberg, *The Greek State*, 38.
6. See John Thorley, *Athenian Democracy* (London: Routledge, 1966), Chaps 2–4; also, Lawrence A. Scaff, *Participation in the Western Political Tradition: A Study of Theory and Practice*, Political Theory Studies, no. 2, The Institute of Government Research (Tucson: The University of Arizona Press, 1975), 19–35, and Sealey, *A History of the Greek City-States*, Chaps 5–6, for more detailed analysis of the rise of democratic Athens and Cleisthenes' reforms in particular.
7. See Arlene Saxonhouse, *Athenian Democracy: Modern Mythmakers and Ancient Theorists* (Notre Dame: University of Notre Dame Press, 1996). From

a somewhat different perspective, Saxonhouse argues that this tendency to romanticize the democracy of Athens, and to employ it to justify or criticize existing democratic practices, fails to take account of the real complexity of those institutions and the subtlety of those ancient theorists who attempted to comprehend them.

8. The most important of these federal systems were the Achaean League and the Aetolian League, but even had they prevailed in the long term, they would have destroyed the self-sufficiency of the *polis* and, hence, its unique character as a state form. As Ehrenberg notes in *The Greek State* "fundamentally the federal development meant the end of the idea of the *Polis*" (131).

9. This, at least, was the position of the more radical Sophists, and is perhaps best expressed by the Sophist Thrasymachus in Plato's *Republic*. The Sophists were by no means all of one mind, however, and some were more moderate in their views than others.

10. Democracies did not exclude the leadership of aristocrats, so long as they did the bidding of the people, and there were plenty of these around. Solon and Cleisthenes were from aristocratic families, as was Pericles, the greatest democratic leader in Athens from 460 – 429 BCE.

11. Plato's theory of constitutions is modeled on the actual evolution of Greek constitutionalism, which Plato describes as a decline in the ethical basis of the *polis*. What is unique in Plato's analysis, however, is that he reverses the historical pattern in terms of democracy and tyranny, arguing contrary to the historical facts that democracy ultimately leads to tyranny, the most unjust constitution for Plato. See Plato, "Republic" in *The Dialogues of Plato*," v. II, Books VII–IX, 4th ed., trans B. Jowett (Oxford: The Clarendon Press, 1953).

12. See Brian R. Nelson, *Western Political Thought: From Socrates to the Age of Ideology*, 2nd ed. (Englewood Cliffs: Prentice Hall, 1996), 130–132.

13. The lack of any distinction between the state and the family in Plato's theory of the ideal state is a source of major criticism on the part of Aristotle. While Aristotle also integrates the social order (class system) into the constitutional structure of the state, he nonetheless maintains a clear distinction between the family (household) and the *polis*. This idea that the public sphere is not merely an extension of the family will prove to be a crucially important idea in late medieval thought and, indeed, in Western political thought generally, for it will liberate political thinking from patriarchal concepts of rulership and purely private (feudal) concepts of power. Without this, the concept of the modern state could not have evolved as it did. See Aristotle, *Politics*, Book I; Chap. XII; Book II, Chaps I–V.

14. See Aristotle, *The Athenian Constitution*, trans. P.J. Rhodes (New York: Penguin Books, 1984) for an analysis of the development of Athenian democracy that corresponds to its description earlier in this chapter, from Salon on. It is generally conceded that this work was by a student of Aristotle rather than Aristotle himself, as the *Politics* was a compilation of Aristotle's lectures by his students, but both works seem clearly to represent Aristotle's views.

15. See Aristotle, *The Ethics of Aristotle*, trans. J.A.K. Thomson (Harmondsworth: Penguin Books: 1955), 27.

16. Aristotle, *Politics*, Book I, Chaps I–II.

17. The *Laws* replace the philosophic rulership of the *Republic* with legal rules. Yet, even here, Plato remains in thrall to his ideal by introducing a "Nocturnal Council" to oversee the state. See Plato, "Laws" in *The Dialogues of Plato*, v. IV, Book XII, 542.

18. Aristotle, *Politics*, Book III, Chap. 1, 93.
19. Ibid., Book III, Chap. VII. Aristotle's classification of constitutions closely parallels that of Plato's in the *Republic* and even more so in Plato's *Statesman*. This indicates that, despite their differences, both thinkers were working within the same framework of assumptions that defined the ideal of the *polis* and therefore the classical theory of the state.
20. Ibid., Book III, Chap VII. The classification of constitutions by class is not systematically extended beyond oligarchies and democracies however. See Sir Ernest Barker, *The Political Thought of Plato and Aristotle* (New York: Dover Publications: 1959), 312.
21. Aristotle *Politics*, Book IV, Chaps VII–IX.
22. Assuming the "perfectly" virtuous (just) man could be found, monarchy would logically be the ideal state since the ideal is precisely the rule of virtue (ibid., Book III, Chap. XVII). But Aristotle sees this perfection possible in a properly constructed aristocracy as well and, in fact, this is most likely his real ideal. Among other things, it allows for political participation that, for Aristotle, is the key means by which virtue is attained. See Curtis N. Johnson, *Aristotle's Theory of the State* (New York: St. Martin's Press, 1990), 155–156. Johnson stresses that Aristotle is not entirely clear or consistent on precisely what his concept of the ideally best state is, shifting between an almost Platonic conception of the philosopher king and a more participatory model in which the citizen "rules and is ruled in turn." Whatever the precise constitutional structure of his ideal state, however, it is one in which the good citizen and the good man must be identical, unlike all other less than ideal constitutions.
23. Aristotle, *Politics*, Book IV, Chap. XI.
24. See Quentin Skinner, *The Foundations of Modern Political Thought: The Age of Reformation*, v. II (Cambridge: Cambridge University Press, 1978). Skinner argues that a key precondition for the emergence of the modern concept of the state is that "the sphere of politics should be envisaged as a distinct branch of moral philosophy, a branch concerned with the art of government" (349), and that the recovery in the West of Aristotle's Politics was the crucial factor in this regard.
25. Territoriality is an important issue for Aristotle in terms of establishing the appropriate size of the political community. Clearly, a *polis* too large ceases to be a *polis* in Aristotle's terms. But the territory does not define the state; as Aristotle puts it in his *Politics*: "The identity of a *polis* is not constituted by its walls," Book III; Chap. 3, 98. Its identity is that of a community of citizens. See Ehrenberg, *The Greek State*, 26.
26. See Aristotle, *Politics*. Aristotle discusses the general concept of sovereignty from several different perspectives, as rooted in law when it is rightly constituted Book III, Chap. XI, 127, or in the ruling civic body (*politeuma*) Book III, Chap. VI, 110. Since in Aristotle's constitutional theory the civic body is the ruling class, and since it is the source of law making authority, it follows in the final analysis that sovereignty resides in the ruling class or, where class interests overlap, in the majority of those interests (261).
27. See F.H. Hinsley, *Sovereignty* (New York: Basic Books, 1966), 37, for a contrary view of the Roman Republic's contribution to the concept of sovereignty. Hinsley argues that the republic did not go any further in this regard than the Greek city-states. There is something to be said for this position, but we argue that the concept was there in outline form in the political works of Cicero.

28. See Mason Hammond, *City-State and World State in Greek and Roman Political Theory Until Augustus* (Cambridge: Harvard University Press, 1951), 56–57. According to Hammond, even in the earliest stages of Rome's political development during the period of kingship, the sovereignty of the people was explicit.

29. It is worth noting here the profound influence of the Greeks, both of the Hellenic and Hellenistic periods, on Cicero's political thinking. Cicero considered himself a follower of the Platonic Academy, although it was at that time the center of the Skeptical philosophy that Cicero rejected, and not only entitled his *Republic* in honor of Plato's great work, but also imitated its dialogue format. Other Greek thinkers of the Hellenistic period also had a profound influence on Cicero, particularly on his legal theory. And this influence was not unique to Cicero. The Romans were not original political thinkers; in their view the state was a practical institution to be understood in pragmatic legal terms. Were it not for the Greeks, Roman political theory would have been exceedingly impoverished, and its subsequent influence on Western theories of the state greatly reduced. See Nelson, *Western Political Thought*, Chap. 4.

30. See Polybius, *The Rise of the Roman Empire*, ed. Frank W. Wallbank, trans. Ian Scott-Kilvert (New York: Penguin Books, 1979), Book VI, 302–318.

31. The monarchical element in Cicero's ideal composite state is ambiguous. In the *Republic*, he advocates a new type of magistrate called the rector as the monarchical element; in the *Laws* he suggests the consuls. See George Holland Sabine and Stanley Barney Smith, "Introduction," in *Marcus Tullius Cicero: On The Commonwealth*, trans. George Holland Sabine and Stanley Barney Smith (Indianapolis: The Bobbs-Merrill Company), reprinted from the original edition (Columbus: The Ohio State University Press, 1929), 92–98, for a discussion of Cicero's varying views on the monarchical principle.

32. Ibid., 129.

33. For this reason, Cicero defends both the people's assemblies and, more controversially, the increased power of the people's tribunes that he views as crucial to the liberty of the people, another key element in his republican constitution. Cicero's defense of the tribuneship is most clearly developed in the *Laws*. See Marcus Tullius Cicero, "The Laws" in *The Loeb Classical Library, Volume XVI: De Re Publica-De Legibus*, ed. G.P. Gould, trans. Clinton Walker Keyes (Cambridge: Harvard University Press, 1928), 487.

34. Cicero, *Laws*, 461.

35. Ibid., 323.

36. See Hinsley, *Sovereignty*, 41. Hinsley argues that the Romans of the late first century CE possessed the basic elements of a theory of sovereignty, most notably that the emperor was now understood to be above the law.

37. Cicero, *On The Commonwealth*, 129.

38. Hammond, *City-State and World State*, 61.

39. See Charles Howard McIlwain, *The Growth of Political Thought in the West: From the Greeks to the End of the Middle Ages* (New York: The Macmillan Company, 1932), 117. McIlwain notes that Cicero's concept of consent does not necessarily imply a formal contract. This is almost certainly the case. An act of consent, or in Cicero's words an agreement, carries with it the implication that the state is conventional rather than, as in Plato and Aristotle, natural, something that was clearly understood by Cicero and indeed by Greek thinkers from the Sophists to the Epicureans. These thinkers even proposed an explicit theory

of contract, and in the *Republic* Cicero raises the issue of the contractual basis of the state that, however, he is quick to reject. For Cicero, the "agreement" or consent to the formation of the state is understood to mean an implicit understanding of its ethical basis and moral propriety, something essential for the existence of any political order, not a contractual act, express or tacit.

40. The *Legeis Curiatae*, however, set strict limitations on the exercise of power. So did the *Lex Regia* in constitutional theory, but in political fact the emperor's claim to full *potestas* and *imperium* had become a claim to absolute and irrevocable sovereign authority. See McIlwain, *The Growth of Political Thought in the West*, 136–137.

41. The *ius gentium* and the *ius naturale* were initially considered almost identical. Later, the two were understood to be distinct forms of law.

42. The *Corpus Iuris Civilis* was composed of four parts: The *Digest*, a compilation of selected writings of Roman jurists during the classical period of Roman law from the late first century BCE to the mid-third century CE; the *Code*, a collection of imperial legislation from the early second century CE to Justinian; the *Institutes*, a textbook on Roman law for first year law students, drawn in large measure from the *Institutes* of Gaius, and surely the most influential university textbook ever written; and the *Novels*, a collection of Justinian's own legislation. See *The Institutes of Gaius*, trans. W.M. Gordon and O.R. Robinson with the Latin text of Seckel and Kuebler (Ithaca: Cornell University Press, 1988), 7–8.

43. Roman law, first studied at the University of Bologna, had its initial reception in Southern Europe where Roman law and customary law were essentially compatible. Its reception in Northern Europe took longer. In England, Roman law was known and taught, but Common law prevailed and became the basis of the legal system. See Barry Nicholas, *An Introduction to Roman Law*, in series: *Clarendon Law Series*, ed. H.L.A Hart (Oxford: Clarendon Press, 1962), 48–50.

44. See Giovanni Reale, *The Systems of the Hellenistic Age*, 3rd ed., ed. trans. John R. Catan, (Albany: State University of New York Press, 1985), 12–13, for an analysis of the Hellenistic ideal of autonomy (*autarcheia*) and inner peace (*ataraxy*).

45. Plotinus spiritualizes Plato, so to speak, wishing only to live in Plato's "intelligible world" and to unite with the "One." See Plotinus, "Enneads," VI, ix , in *The Philosophy of Plotinus: Representative Books from the Enneads*, ed. trans. Joseph Katz, in series: Appleton-century Philosophy Source Books, ed. Sterling Lamprecht (New York: Appleton Century Crofts, 1950), Chap. 6.

Chapter Four   The Christian Republic

1. Joseph Strayer, *The Medieval Origins of the Modern State* (Princeton: Princeton University Press, 1970), 5. Strayer argues that the basic structure of the modern state had emerged as early as the thirteenth century.

2. Walter Ullmann, *Medieval Political Thought* (Harmondsworth: Penguin Books, 1975), 18.

3. Mathew 16:19. See Ullman, *Medieval Political Thought*, 24–25. If the Petrine commission precluded secular rulers from priesthood, it conferred at the same time monarchial authority upon the pope. Pope Leo I (440–461) made the Petrine commission a matter of doctrine and, as Ullmann notes, this conferring of monarchical powers upon the papacy was accepted by both pro- and

antipapal forces throughout the Middle Ages. The dispute was over the "scope and extent" of the pope's powers, not over his monarchical authority as such.

4. After 395, the division between the eastern and western halves of the empire became permanent.

5. J.M. Wallace-Hadrill, *Early Germanic Kingship in England and on the Continent* (Oxford: Oxford University Press, 1971), 14–15.

6. That the king partook of the sacred was not a novel idea to the barbarian kings; they may have been in the early stages merely war leaders chosen by an assembly of warriors and kinsmen (the Germanic *Thing*), but they typically traced their lineage back to the gods. See ibid., 7–14. Hence, the idea of kingship that the church wished to promote fell on already fertile ground, and carried with it a potentially serious challenge to the church's eventual claim to an exclusively priestly power centered in its chief priest, the bishop of Rome.

7. While Charlemagne did retain the idea of emperorship in establishing rules of succession that imposed upon his heirs a collective responsibility to defend the faith, he did not transfer the emperorship as such to any of his sons. See Francois Louis Ganshof, *Frankish Institutions Under Charlemagne*, trans. Bryce and Mary Lyon (New York: W.W. Norton and Company, 1970), 16–17.

8. Matthew 22:21

9. See "the myth of Er" in Plato's *Republic* and Cicero's allusion to it in his *Republic*, as well as "the dream of Scipio" in that same work, for their belief in an afterlife of reward for those who serve the state justly.

10. Romans 13:1–7. See Lawrence A. Scaff, *Participation in the Western Political Tradition: A Study of Theory and Practice*, The Institute of Government Research, Political Theory Studies, no. 2 (Tucson: The University of Arizona Press, 1975), 37. As Scaff notes, this Pauline doctrine constitutes the origin of the theocratic conception of authority.

11. St. Augustine, *Concerning the City of God against the Pagans*, trans. Henry Bettenson (London: Penguin Books: 1984), 216.

12. Ibid., 205.

13. Sidney Painter, *The Rise of the Feudal Monarchies*, in series: The *Development of Western Civilization: Narrative Essays in the History of Our Tradition from its Origins in Ancient Israel and Greece to the Present*, ed. Edward W. Fox (Ithaca: Cornell University Press, 1951), 8–9. See this work also for a general analysis of the rise of feudalism and feudal monarchy in the major Germanic kingdoms of Western Europe and the empire.

14. Indeed, the medieval period was premised upon a fundamental contradiction between the prevailing theocratic theory of political authority and the actual facts of political decentralization inherent in the feudal system. See Scaff, *Participation in the Western Political Tradition*, 36.

15. Marshall W. Baldwin, *The Medieval Church*, in series: The *Development of Western Civilization: Narrative Essays in the History of Our Tradition from Its Origins in Ancient Israel and Greece to the Present*, ed. Edward W. Fox (Ithaca: Cornell University Press, 1953), 4–5.

16. F.H. Hinsley, *Sovereignty* (New York: Basic Books, 1966), 58.

17. See John B. Morrall, *Political Thought in Medieval Times* (London: Hutchinson University Library, 1958), 39–40.

18. Gelasius's argument for the superiority of sacred over temporal authority was in part rooted in Roman law, an early indication of how important the Roman legal tradition would become in the dispute between the church and secular

authority. In Gelasius, the spiritual authority of the pope was in Roman legal terminology of the nature of ultimate sovereign authority (*auctoritas*), not the merely delegated authority granted to secular rulers (*potestas*). See ibid., 22.

19. The ambiguity of the two swords doctrine was there from the beginning in Gelasius's dualism. See ibid., 23.

20. The papacy further bolstered this reasoning by the fraudulent claim that the Roman Emperor Constantine, recognizing the superior status of the church, had turned over to Pope Sylvester I (314–335) the Western Empire, thereby conceding to him supreme temporal as well as spiritual authority. This claim was based on the most influential, though not only, forged document of the Middle Ages: the "Donation of Constantine." Created in the mid-eighth century, it was not employed by the papacy in a serious way in its struggle with the empire until the eleventh and twelfth centuries, but its early formulation indicates how, from early on, the papacy feared the potential threat posed by a rival claimant to supreme authority. See Walter Ullmann, *Law and Politics in the Middle Ages: An Introduction to the Sources of Medieval Political Ideas* (Ithaca: Cornell University Press, 1975), 129–131, for an analysis of the Donation of Constantine and other medieval forgeries.

21. See translator's "Introduction," *The Institutes of Gaius*, trans. W.M. Gordon and O.R. Robinson with the Latin text of Seckel and Kuebler (Ithaca: Cornell University Press, 1988), in series: *Texts in Roman Law*, ed. Peter Birks, 7–8, and also translator's "Introduction," in *Justinian's Institutes*, trans. Peter Birks and Grant McLeod (Ithaca, Cornell University Press, 1987), 7–13, for an analysis of the component parts of the *Corpus Iuris Civilis*.

22. While elements of the *Corpus Iuris Civilis* had been available in parts of Europe in the early Middle Ages, its full recovery, which was essential for its development and elaboration in the later Middle Ages, did not occur until the late eleventh through middle twelfth centuries. See Joseph Canning, *A History of Medieval Political Thought: 300–1450* (London: Routledge, 1996), 115.

23. See Hinsley, *Sovereignty*, 42–44.

24. Ibid., 42.

25. According to Ullmann, the papal doctrine of the "fullness of power" was enunciated initially by Pope Leo I as a logical extension of his existing Petrine authority. Unlike his Petrine powers, however, which related essentially to sacramental matters, the *plentitudo potestatis* had to do with government and law. It meant that the pope was *principatus* within the church, a term derived from Roman law that clearly establishes the supremacy of the pope within the ecclesiastical hierarchy. See Walter Ullmann, *Medieval Political Thought*, 27. Later, this incipient doctrine of papal sovereignty would be extended to a claim of sovereign authority over temporal rulers as well. For an analysis of this later development in the thirteenth and fourteenth centuries, See Canning, *A History of Medieval Political Thought*, 32, and Morrall, *Political Thought in Medieval Times*, Chap. VI.

26. See Canning, *A History of Medieval Political Thought*, 10.

27. Ibid. The legal basis of this principle had to do with the private relationship between guardians and wards specified in a constitution of Justinian, not with political matters, but medieval jurists employed it "in a political sense as part of the development of theories of consent" (10).

28. See Hinsley, *Sovereignty*, 42–43. Hinsley shows that from the middle of the second century the doctrine of popular sovereignty (the *imperium* of the Roman

people) became inexorably transmuted into a doctrine of the absolute sovereignty of the emperor, despite the objections of those who hearkened back to the earlier concept that sovereignty was constituted by the will of the people.

29. See Brian Tierney, *Religion, Law, and the Growth of Constitutional Thought: 1150–1650* (Cambridge: Cambridge University Press, 1982), 14–19, for an analysis of medieval canonist theories on the sovereign authority of the pope, and the impact of Gratians's *Decretum* in this development.

30. Morrall, *Political Thought in Medieval Times*, 49–50.

31. A great deal has been written on medieval corporation theory, and for good reason. It had a crucial impact on the subsequent Conciliar movement and, subsequently, on early modern constitutional theory. For some sense of its importance in this regard, see Tierney, *Religion, Law, and the Growth of Constitutional Thought*, 19–28.

32. See translators "Introduction," John of Salisbury, *Policraticus*, ed. Lindsay Rogers, trans. John Dickinson (New York: Russell and Russell, 1955), xliii.

33. According to Tierney, the radical formulation, which was derived directly from Roman corporation law, constituted a pure republican model of church governance. The more conservative formulation, which was derived from canonistic corporation law, constituted a mixed monarchy model. See Tierney, *Religion, Law, and the Growth of Constitutional Thought*, 26–27.

34. Ibid., 23–24.

35. Ibid., 23.

36. Ibid., 25.

37. Morrall, *Political Thought in Medieval Times*, 66.

38. Ibid., 46–47.

39. Ullmann argues that all theocratically made law was sacred to the medieval mind, and that a prime reason for the growth of both Roman and canon law studies during the High Middle Ages was to develop methods to reconcile apparently conflicting legal norms, apparently because, of course, sacred law could not in reality be inconsistent. The development in the medieval university of the scholastic or dialectical method, when applied to jurisprudence, was to do precisely this. See Ullmann, *Law and Politics in the Middle Ages*, 87.

40. Ibid., 25–28.

41. See Quentin Skinner, *The Foundations of Modern Political Thought: The Age of Reformation*, v. 2 (Cambridge: Cambridge University Press, 1978). This is precisely Skinner's point in regard to the modern concept of the state, for it requires that "the sphere of politics should be envisaged as a distinct branch of moral philosophy" as it was in classical-Aristotelian thought before it was lost with St. Augustine's otherworldly emphasis in his *The City of God*, 349.

42. Averroes (1126–1198) was an Arab scholar of Aristotle who offended the church on a number of counts, but most importantly in denying the compatibility of reason and faith. It was in great part St. Thomas Aquinas's insistence that Aristotelian rationalism was not contrary to the dictates of faith that made the acceptance of Aristotle by the church ultimately possible.

43. See Fernand Van Steenberghen, *Aristotle in the West*, trans. Leonard Johnston (Louvain: Nauwelaerts Publishing House, 1970), 66–88, for an analysis of the church's concern over the increasing influence of Aristotle and of periodic attempts to ban his works.

44. See Thomas Gilby, The *Political Thought of Thomas Aquinas* (Chicago: University of Chicago Press, 1958), 107–111, for a good analysis of the

consonance of natural and supernatural in Thomas's thinking, and of its value in demonstrating the compatibility of natural and divine law.

45. See Etienne Gilson, *The Philosophy of St. Thomas Aquinas*, rev. ed. G.A. Elrington, trans. Edward Bullough (Freeport: Books for Libraries Press, 1937), 52. While faith and reason are distinct in Thomas, they can never contradict each other.

46. This harmony of faith and reason is particularly important in regard to Thomas's theory of the unity of divine and natural law. See St. Thomas Aquinas, "Summa Theologica," I–II, in *The Political Ideas of St. Thomas Aquinas*, ed. Dino Bigongiari (New York, Hafner Press, 1953), 29–54.

47. *On Kingship* may, in fact, have been written by a student of St. Thomas, although there does not appear to be certainty in this regard. Nonetheless, it is generally conceded that the work was clearly influenced by Thomas. See Anthony Black, *Political Thought in Europe: 1250–1450*, (Cambridge: Cambridge University Press, 1992), 22.

48. St. Thomas Aquinas, "On Kingship," Bigongiari, *The Political Ideas of St. Thomas Aquinas*, 180. In *On Kingship*, Thomas argues that monarchy is the ideal constitutional form, not only because it is the most likely to maintain peace and unity in this world, but because it corresponds to God's monarchical rulership of the universe. And while agreeing with Aristotle that monarchy, when degraded into tyranny, is the worst possible constitution, his solution to this potentiality, while based on Aristotle's analysis, also draws upon sacred sources Hence, in "Summa Theologica," 86–91, Thomas proposes constraining monarchical rule with elements of the classical "mixed constitution," a concept derived from Aristotle and probably Cicero as well, but also from biblical sources that conferred the requisite supernatural sanction to an otherwise worldly constitutional analysis. This analysis, Thomas argues, accords with divine law as shown in the biblical account of the Hebrew "regime" under the leadership of Moses. See ibid., "Summa Theologica," 88.

49. Ibid., 4.

50. See ibid., 14–20. Divine law (biblical law) is also included in Thomas's great hierarchy of law.

51. Ibid., 13.

52. This liberation from Augustinian views transcended politics; it included philosophy, science, indeed the whole realm of human endeavor. See Alexander Passerin D'Entreves, *The Medieval Contribution to Political Thought: Thomas Aquinas, Marsilius of Padua, Richard Hooker* (New York: Humanities Press, 1959), 20–21.

53. See Ullmann, *Law and Politics in the Middle Ages*, 182–183. See also Canning, *A History of Medieval Political Thought*, 124–125, for a discussion of both the canonist and civilian sources of this doctrine, and its importance in supporting the "sovereign authority" of kings within their own territories.

54. See Strayer, *The Medieval Origins of the Modern State*. Strayer argues that the basic structure of a state form of polity had emerged in France by the late thirteenth century. Tierney goes further, arguing that a state form of political consciousness had also emerged by this time, although this view is not widely held. See Tierney, *Religion, Law, and the Growth of Constitutional Thought*, 22. Certainly the modern theory of state sovereignty did not develop until the sixteenth century at the earliest, and not fully until the seventeenth century.

55. The conflict also involved Edward I (1272–1307) of England, another emerging territorial state, although not as dramatically.
56. Pope Boniface VIII, the Bull "Unam Sanctam," in Brian Tierney, *The Crisis of Church and State, 1050–1300* (Toronto: The University of Toronto Press, in association with the Medieval Academy of America, 1988), 189.
57. Tierney, *Religion, Law, and the Growth of Constitutional Thought*, 30.
58. Translator's "Introduction," in John of Paris, *On Royal and Papal Power*, trans. J.A. Watt (Toronto: The Pontifical Institute of Medieval Studies, 1971), 52.
59. See ibid., 118. John provides a number of references in support of the separation of the "two swords," but gives two key reasons for this position. First, and a relatively weak argument in this regard, is that separation requires mutual support between pope and secular ruler (including emperor) and thus encourages the Christian virtues of love and charity. A more powerful, and certainly a more realistic, argument is that a papacy involved in secular affairs is less likely to be concerned with the spiritual.
60. It may be that Dante's hopes for a restored empire rested upon the attempt by Emperor Henry VII (1308–1313) to restore imperial authority in Italy. His major work *Monarchia* was written around this time, but it is not clear whether before or after Henry's attempt failed. See editor's "Introduction," Dante, *Monarchy*, ed. trans. Prue Shaw (Cambridge: Cambridge University Press, 1996), in series: *Cambridge Texts in the History of Political Thought*, ed. Raymond Geuss and Quentin Skinner, x.
61. Ibid., ix.
62. See Tierney, *Religion, Law, and the Growth of Constitutional Thought*, 36–37, for a discussion of the new emphasis, beginning with John of Paris, on the origins of government as the real basis for political legitimacy, and the influence of this mode of thinking on seventeenth and eighteenth-century contract theorists.
63. John of Paris, *On Royal and Papal Power*, 160
64. Ibid., 93.
65. Ibid., Chap. 4. John admits that kingship and priesthood arose contemporaneously if we include pagan forms of priesthood, but these are purely figurative; true priesthood begins with Christ, which means that kingship in the proper sense preceded priesthood.
66. Ibid., 93.
67. See ibid., 196–198. John points out what would be obvious to us, but less so to the medieval mind steeped in allegorical forms of reasoning, that the allegory of the "two swords" can stand for any number of things (e.g., the old and new testaments), and is not therefore a sufficient basis for proving anything; certainly not for what the papacy wanted to prove.
68. Ibid., 115.
69. At least this is so when it comes to the issue of a pope's abdication, for here John believes that the College of Cardinals can legitimately make the requisite decisions. On the more serious issue of deposing a pope, John argues that a general council of the church is perhaps more appropriate, but even here the College of Cardinals is sufficient, for since it made the pope as representative of the Church as a whole, it can depose him in the name of the church as well. See ibid., 242–243.
70. Morrall, *Political Thought in Medieval Times*, 91–92.
71. See Tierney, *Religion, Law, and the Growth of Constitutional Thought*. According to Tierney, the theory of popular consent might seem incompatible

with "the universally held belief that all power came ultimately from God . . . . But here the canon and civil lawyers had already prepared the ground for the position—very commonly asserted in early modern constitutional theory—that power came from God through the people" (41).

72. John of Paris, *On Royal and Papal Power*, 87. See Chap. 3 for a more detailed analysis of the differences John posits between church and secular government.

73. Dante, *Monarchy*, 67–68.

74. Ibid., 87.

75. Even Dante, however, seems incapable of fully transcending these assumptions inherent in the Christian Republic. In the concluding words of the final chapter of *Monarchy*, Dante states, in words that have remained controversial to this day, that in some never quite defined manner the Roman Prince is subject to the Roman Pontiff "since this earthly happiness is in some sense ordered toward immortal happiness" (Dante, *Monarchy*, 94).

76. See editor's "Introduction," Marsilius of Padua, *Defensor Pacis*, ed. trans. Alan Gewirth (Toronto: University of Toronto Press, 1980), xxxvii, for a discussion of the importance of this shift from final to efficient cause in the legitimation of the state. This is not to suggest that Marsilius does not possess a concept of the final end of the state. Clearly he does (see Discourse I, Chap. IV) and essentially follows Aristotle in this regard, but emphasizes at the same time the need for coercive authority for any state to exist (which, subsequently, he shows to be government, the efficient cause of the state). In effect, the efficient cause is primary for Marsilius in the sense that the final cause would exist only as an ideal without it. For the other Aristotelian causes of the state (material and formal), see Discourse I, Chap. VII.

77. Ibid., Discourse I, Chap. XV.

78. Ibid., Chap. XVII, 80–86.

79. While the basic Aristotelian view, and the later medieval view based upon Aristotle's works, was that law is a rule of moral reason, Marsilius manages to appropriate Aristotle to his definition of law as "coercive will." See ibid., Chap. X, 36.

80. While Marsilius defines law in terms of coercion, Morral argues that he nonetheless retains the medieval emphasis on its moral character. See Morral, *Political Thought in Medieval Times*, 111.

81. Marsilius, *Defensor Pacis*, Discourse I. Chap. X, 36. Law retains its legitimacy for Marsilius even if it is morally flawed, but perfect law he insists must conform to principles of justice.

82. Ibid., Discourse II, Chap. XXIX, 405.

83. Ibid., Chap. X, 178.

84. Ibid., Discourse I, Chap. XV, Discourse II, Chap. XXI.

85. See ibid., Discourse I, Chap. XV, for a complete discussion of the efficient cause of the various parts of the state. In this chapter, Marsilius' makes a distinction between the "primary" efficient cause (the human legislator), and the "secondary" efficient cause (government) (62). For his discussion of the legislator as the efficient cause of law, see Chap. XII, 45.

86. See ibid., editor's "Introduction," liv–lv, for an analysis of Marsilius's views on the divine source of political authority expressed through the will of the people.

87. See ibid., Chaps XII, XIII.

88. See ibid., editor's "Introduction," liv–lv.

89. See ibid. Gewirth argues that Marsilius's concept of political power is ultimately unlimited, and that "the modern theory of sovereignty, in its extreme Hobbesian

and Rousseauian form, derives from Marsilius" (lix). At the same time, Gewirth stresses that Marsilius's emphasis upon coercive power as the basis of the state does not obviate his republicanism (xxxiii–xlv) or libertarianism (lx–lxi). In fact, Marsilius has been interpreted as both an authoritarian and a libertarian (lx), depending on which aspect of his political theory one focuses on. See also Morrall, *Political Thought in Medieval Times*, 112–113, for a discussion of the scholarly dispute over these issues. Morrall argues that Gewirth's translation and interpretation of Marsilius, which recognizes that the role of the "weightier part" in the formulation of law includes the vast majority of citizens, demonstrates that his republicanism is genuine. The issue here is whether or not Marsilius had not in fact given real power to a minority, thus undermining the popular republican elements in his political thought. If, however, the "weightier part" is itself democratized, the issue is moot. The potential authoritarianism of the people despite the republican form of the polity, however, what came to be known as the problem of "majority tyranny" in the nineteenth century, is not so easily dismissed. A doctrine of popular sovereignty does not in itself exclude authoritarian forms of rule.

90. See editor's "Introduction," Marsilius, *Defensor Pacis*, xli–xlii, for a discussion of Marsilius's corporatism and its potential absolutist, anti-individualistic, consequences.

91. Not only does Marsilius distinguish government from state, he understands that the offices of government constitute a single source of authority. Hence, in asserting that only one government can exist, he does not fall into the logical error of earlier medieval thinkers in assuming that only monarchy can constitute supreme authority, that is, in confounding government with what would later be understood as sovereign authority. For Marsilius, a government of many, such as *polity*, is still a single unity of one in "respect to office" regardless of the number of persons involved in governing. See ibid., Discourse I, Chap. XVII, 80–81.

92. St. Paul had described the church as the "body of Christ," and its designation as the "mystical body of Christ" had become commonly used by the twelfth century. By the middle of the thirteenth century the phrase had been extended to the "mystical body of the commonwealth," an indication of how influential theoretical developments within the church were to emerging concepts of the state and secular authority. See Brian Tierney, *Religion, Law, and the Growth of Constitutional Thought*, 20.

93. Ernst H. Kantorowicz, *The Kings Two Bodies: A Study In Mediaeval Political Theology* (Princeton: Princeton University Press, 1985).

94. Much has been written on the depersonalization of the crown, and rightly so. Once the crown was conceived impersonally, expressed in such common yet paradoxical sayings as "the king is dead, long live the king," we know that a concept of the impersonal state is close at hand. Perhaps the most paradoxical, yet revealing example of conceiving the crown impersonally yet recognizing the human dimension involved, that is, of the "king's two bodies," is Kantorowicz's description of a coronation ceremony in which the formula is " ' I crown and mitre you over yourself.' " Ibid., 495. See Black, *Political Thought in Europe*, 189–190, for an analysis of the key concepts involved in the impersonal crown, such as the idea of the ruler as a public person, the distinction between person and office, and the notion of impersonal sovereignty. For Black, the concept of the impersonal crown thus indicates that the state concept itself was implicated in medieval political consciousness.

95. See Tierney, *Religion, Law, and the Growth of Constitutional Thought*, 30–34. Tierney argues that the modern concept of sovereignty was implicit in the emerging meaning of jurisdiction as "the power of ruling in general."

Chapter Five   The Making of Leviathan

1. There is a vast literature on the Renaissance Italian city-states and the evolution of republican ideals. For a good general introduction to these topics, see Jacob Burckhardt's classic study, *The Civilization of the Renaissance in Italy*, v. I (New York: Harper & Row Publishers, 1958), as well as Lauro Martines, *Power and Imagination: City-States in Renaissance Italy* (New York: Vintage Books, 1980).

2. See Bernard Guenee, *States and Rulers in Later Medieval Europe*, trans. Juliet Vale (Oxford: Basil Blackwell, 1985), 157–170, for a brief but substantial analysis of the formation of the modern tripartite estate system of nobility, clergy, and bourgeoisie.

3. The bourgeoisie, in brief, supported whatever was in their economic interest and, given the circumstances, there were advantages to be had in both cases. Whether supporting the centralizing monarchs of England and France, or the city-states of Italy and Germany, the emerging middle classes were able to assert their independence from the nobility. The circumstances themselves, however, were largely beyond their control. Long-standing historical conditions determined these. The monarchies of France, and particularly England following the Norman invasion, e.g., were not burdened with the resistance of the papal states to national consolidation, as in Italy, nor with the entirely inappropriate model of the Holy Roman Empire with which the German king was associated. See Robert Ergang, *Emergence of the National State*, ed. Louis L. Snyder (New York: Van Nostrand Reinhold Company, 1971), 26–35.

4. See Hendrik Spruyt, *The Sovereign State and Its Competitors: An Analysis of System Change* (Princeton: Princeton University Press, 1994). Spruyt argues that the city-league, city-state, and sovereign territorial state constituted the three basic forms of polity that emerged out of the late Middle Ages, and that the ultimate triumph of the sovereign state was the result of the superiority of its territorial form of organization.

5. See Machiavelli, "Discourses on the First Ten Books of Titus Livius," *The Prince* and *The Discourses* (New York: The Modern Library, 1950). It is clear that the advantages of a republican system do not obviate the reality of politics for Machiavelli, therefore the necessity of *realpolitik*.

6. Machiavelli, *The Prince*, ed. trans. Robert M. Adams, 2nd ed. (New York: W.W. Norton & Company, 1992), 42.

7. Bernard Guenee, *States and Rulers*, 4–6.

8. Alexander Passerin D'Entreves, *The Notion of the State: An Introduction to Political Theory* (Oxford: Oxford University Press, 1967), Chap. 3. D'Entreves stresses this fact that the new term "state" provided for a new conceptual framework, and that Machiavelli was crucial in the spread of the new term in Italy and eventually throughout Europe.

9. See, e.g., Harvey C. Mansfield, Jr. "On the Impersonality of the Modern State: A Comment on Machiavelli's Use of Stato," *American Political Science Review*, December 1983, v. 77, no. 4, 849–856. Mansfield disputes Quentin Skinner's

thesis that the concept of the modern state evolved from Machiavelli's mainly, though not entirely, traditional view of the state as, in effect, the "status" of the prince (Quentin Skinner, *Foundations of Modern Political Thought: Volume Two, the Age of Reformation* (Cambridge: Cambridge University Press, 1978), 353–354. Mansfield argues that in fact Machiavelli held neither a traditional view of *lo stato*, nor the classical concept of the regime, but understood the state as something to be acquired, hence the "acquisitive personal state." This view, Mansfield insists, was nonetheless a clear transition to the impersonal concept of the state since the advice Machiavelli gives to the prince to acquire where possible is by its nature impersonal, i.e., "neutral between the parties he advises."

10. See Joseph R. Strayer, *On the Medieval Origins of the Modern State* (Princeton: Princeton University Press, 1970), 36. Strayer argues that the basic outlines of the modern state were in place in Western Europe (specifically in France and England) as early as the late thirteenth century.

11. Perry Anderson, *Lineages of the Absolutist State* (London: Verso, 1979), 35–40.

12. See ibid., 15–42, for a Marxist based analysis of the character of the absolutist state in the West as the state of the feudal nobility in transition to the capitalist state of the emerging bourgeoisie.

13. J.W. Allen, *A History of Political Thought in the Sixteenth Century*, rev. ed. (London, 1957), 68. Indeed, in Calvin's thinking, the state is itself a church, and we find in his *Institutes of the Christian Religion* a fully developed theocratic theory of the state.

14. See Owan Chadwick, *The Reformation*, in series: *The Pelican History of the Church*, ed. Owen Chadwick (Middlesex: Penguin Books, 1964), 172–173. Knox's radicalism was, in part, a reflection of the disjunction in Scotland between Protestant subjects and Catholic monarch.

15. See Skinner, *The Foundations of Modern Political Thought*, v. 2, Chap. 7, for a discussion of the doctrine of resistance as it applied to inferior magistrates and to its later development into a revolutionary theory of popular resistance.

16. F. Parkinson, *The Philosophy of International Relations: A Study in the History of Thought, Sage Library of Social Research*, v. 52 (Beverly Hills: Sage Publications, 1977), 33.

17. Ibid., 32–37.

18. Hugo Grotius, *The Rights of War and Peace: Including the Law of Nature and of Nations*, trans. A.C. Campbell, A. M. (Washington: M. Walter Dunnes Publisher, 1901), 22.

19. Parkinson, *The Philosophy of International Relations*, 36.

20. Samuel Pufendorf, *On the Duty of Man and Citizen According to Natural Law*, ed. James Tully, trans. Michael Silverthrone, in series: *Cambridge Texts in the History of Political Thought*, ed. Raymond Geuss and Quentin Skinner (Cambridge: Cambridge University Press, 1991), 36.

21. While Grotius is considered by many to be the founder of the modern school of natural law, Pufendorf expresses it in its most developed form. See James Tully's "Introduction," ibid., xxii, xxiv–xxix, for a discussion of Pufendorf's imposition theory and for disputes surrounding this modern school of natural law.

22. John Plamenatz, *Man and Society: A Critical Examination of Some Important Social and Political Theories from Machiavelli to Marx*, v. I (New York: McGraw-Hill Book Company, 1963), 167.

23. See ibid., 156. Plamentaz correctly points out that, contrary to the modern theory of "divine right," medieval concepts of kingship, whether applied to king,

emperor, or pope, assumed that sovereign authority is by its nature limited. In this, the theory of divine right clearly went beyond medieval views. The point emphasized here, however, is simply that the idea of the divine origin of all authority, temporal or spiritual, had its roots in the medieval world, without which the modern theory of divine right would have never developed. Indeed, as Plamenatz notes (167), the popularity of the doctrine was due in large measure precisely to its compatibility with prevailing religious beliefs.

24. See ibid., 169. The theory of divine right emerged first in France because the wars of religion began earlier there and were more devastating than in England.

25. F.H. Hinsley, *Sovereignty* (New York: Basic Books, 1966), 109. Hinsley argues that the concept of sovereignty is incompatible with the concept of divine right and with theocratic doctrines of rulership in general.

26. Skinner, *The Foundations of Modern Political Thought*, 284.

27. Jean Bodin, *The Six Books of a Commenweale*, ed. Kenneth Douglas McRae, in series: ed. J.P. Mayer et al. *European Political Thought: Traditions and Endurance* (New York: Arno Press, 1979), A9.

28. Jean Bodin, *On Sovereignty: Four Chapters From the Six Books of the Commonwealth*, ed. trans. Julian Franklin (Cambridge: Cambridge University Press, 1992), Book I, Chap. 8, 1.

29. Ibid., 44

30. Ibid., 15. Bodin clearly distinguishes between law, the product of absolute sovereign authority that binds the sovereign not at all, and contract (consent) that creates mutual obligations between subject and sovereign. As such, contract cannot be the source of sovereign authority for Bodin. The later mature theory of contract beginning with Hobbes, however, would understand that the contract that creates sovereign authority is not between subject and government, but between the subjects themselves. In this way, in Hobbes at least, Bodin's objection to the theory of consent or contract is overcome.

31. Ibid., Book II, Chap. 1.

32. See Franklin, *Jean Bodin and the Rise of Absolutist Theory*, in series: *Cambridge Studies in the History and Theory of Politics*, ed. Maurice Cowling et al. (Cambridge: Cambridge University Press, 1973), 26–29, for an analysis of Bodin's confusion regarding sovereignty and the mixed constitution.

33. Jean Bodin, *On Sovereignty*, editor's "Introduction," xiii. Franklin argues that Bodin proposes a concept of ruler sovereignty precisely because his notion of the indivisibility of sovereignty is premised upon the idea that sovereignty resides in the government. See also Franklin, *Jean Bodin and the Rise of Absolutist Theory*. "Bodin wrongly assumes that . . . (sovereign) authority must be vested in what we would today call government. But it is with Bodin's work that discussion of this issue was effectively initiated" (108). At the same time, Quentin Skinner in *The Foundations of Modern Political Thought*, argues that Bodin made major strides in articulating a concept of sovereignty that presumed a concept of the state as such, 284–301.

34. Franklin, *Jean Bodin and the Rise of Absolutist Theory*, 79. Franklin argues that natural law was assumed by Bodin to be purely a moral obligation of conscience, not a political limitation of sovereign authority. In the same way, while the prince may find it wise to respect customary law, he is not bound by it. Indeed, Bodin, *On Sovereignty*, Book I, Chap. 8, unequivocally states that "a prince is not obligated by the common law of peoples any more than by his own edicts, and if the common law of peoples is unjust, the prince can depart from it

in edicts made for his kingdom and forbid his subjects to use it" (45). At the same time, there are other limitations that Bodin asserts apply to the sovereign authority. Private property cannot be taken by public authority without the consent of the owner, and private contracts between the ruler and subject are binding on both. The latter constraint is in fact premised upon a crucially important recognition that sovereign authority is public in nature, and does not relieve the ruler acting as a private person from the accepted limitations imposed on any other private person. The medieval confusion of power as private own-ership (*dominium*) rather than as public authority (*imperium*) is clearly tran-scended in Bodin's analysis. And while private property had always been an accepted right that like other common rights and usages Bodin assumes will continue to be accepted as binding on the part of the sovereign authority, in the final analysis he never grants a right of resistance when the sovereign violates accepted rights, practices, or customary law. See Bodin, *On Sovereignty*, Book I, Chap. 8, 40–42.

35. Skinner, *Foundations of Modern Political Thought*, 301.
36. See George H. Sabine and Thomas L. Thorson, *A History of Political Theory*, 4th ed. (Hindsale: Dryden Press, 1973), 352–357, for a brief but excellent analysis of the *Vindiciae*.
37. Ibid., 389. This was Althusius's view of the contract and, correspondingly, he asserted that the right of resistance can be exercised only by the magistrates, not by individuals.
38. Thomas Hobbes, *Leviathan or the Matter, Forme and Power of a Commonwealth Ecclesiastical and Civil*, ed. Michael Oakeshott (New York: Collier Books, 1962), 37.
39. Ibid., 100.
40. Ibid., 80.
41. Ibid., 100.
42. Ibid., 132.
43. Ibid.
44. That Hobbes provides the first completely unambiguous theory of the modern state is generally conceded. See, e.g., Leo Strauss, *The Political Philosophy of Hobbes: Its Basis and Genesis*, trans. Elsa M. Sinclair (Chicago: The University of Chicago Press, 1952), 1. The debate revolves around the issue of who laid the foundations for what Hobbes eventually completed. Skinner, *Foundations of Modern Political Thought*, 351–358, while viewing Machiavelli as the transi-tional thinker in the evolution of the theory of the modern state, considers Bodin to be the key figure. Others such as Mansfield (Mansfield, "On the Impersonality of the Modern State"), argue that Machiavelli was the decisive theorist in this regard. The debate will likely never be resolved to everyone's satisfaction, but while recognizing the importance of late medieval thinkers in the development of the modern theory of the state, it is generally accepted that the theory developed somewhere between Machiavelli and Hobbes.
45. See Hinsley, *Sovereignty*, Chap. IV, for an analysis of the reasons why the initial doctrine of popular sovereignty was supplanted by the doctrine of state sovereignty.
46. Hobbes, *Leviathan*, 161.
47. Ibid., 104.
48. Ibid., 200.
49. Ibid., 129.

50. Ibid., 80.
51. Max Weber, "Politics as a Vocation," *From Max Weber: Essays in Sociology,* ed. trans., H.H. Gerth and C. Wright Mills (New York: Oxford University Press, 1946), 77–78.
52. See John Locke, "Second Treatise on Civil Government," *Two Treatises of Government,* ed. Peter Laslett (New York: New American Library, 1965), 308–309, for Locke's distinction between paternal and political power.
53. Ibid., 311.
54. Locke, "Essay Concerning Human Understanding," *John Locke: Works* (Germany: Scientia Verlag Aalen, 1963), v. I. Locke argues that natural law is not innate but learned by reasoning from sense experience. In "The Second Treatise," however, he relies upon Hooker, a sixteenth-century political thinker who drew upon St. Thomas Aquinas and the medieval conception of natural law. See John W. Yolton, *Locke and the Compass of Human Understanding* (Cambridge: Cambridge University Press, 1970), for further analysis of Locke's view of natural law.
55. Locke, "Second Treatise," 395.
56. Most notable in this regard is C.B. Macpherson, *The Political Theory of Possessive Individualism: Hobbes to Locke* (Oxford: Oxford University Press, 1962).
57. Locke, "Second Treatise," 395.
58. Ibid.
59. Ibid., 375–376, 413.
60. See Richard Hooker, *Of The Laws of Ecclesiastical Polity: Preface, Book I, Book VIII,* ed. Arthur Stephen McGrade (Cambridge: Cambridge University Press, 1989). Says Hooker, "God doth ratify the works of that Sovereign authority which Kings have received by men" (142). Thus, while Hooker defended the authority of the king in both temporal and ecclesiastical domains against those advocating a right of resistance, he did not deny their assertion that sovereign authority is derived from some form of (corporate) consent of "the whole body politic" (144). In this way Hooker was able to legitimize the authority of the king against the radical reformers, yet recognize its basis in consent and the limitations on political power that this entailed. The genius of the English system for Hooker was that its institutions had evolved in such a way that "though no manner person or cause be unsubject to the *King*'s power, yet so is the power of the *King* over all and in all limited that unto all his proceedings the law itself is a rule" (147). While this doctrine of consent had medieval roots, it marked a break from Hooker's heavily Aristotelian (and Thomistic) perspective (see editor's "Introduction," xxiii).
61. See A.F. Pollard, *The Evolution of Parliament,* 2nd ed. rev. (London: Longmans, Green and Co., 1964) for an analysis of the origins and development of parliamentary institutions, and the particular importance of England in this regard.
62. See John Locke, "Second Treatise," Chaps X-XIII, for the basic elements of Locke's constitutional theory.
63. See *The Levellers in the English Revolution,* ed. G.E. Aylmer, in series: *Documents of Revolution,* ed. Heinz Lubasz (Ithaca: Cornell University Press, 1975), 9. It is not entirely clear how far the Levellers went in their demands for an extension of the franchise, whether to full manhood suffrage or to a more limited suffrage premised upon at least a limited possession of property. See also Richard Overton, "An Arrow Against all Tyrants," in this same work for an

example of the obvious influence of the Levellers on Locke's views on consent, property, popular sovereignty, and constitutionalism.

64. See Macpherson, *The Political Theory of Possessive Individualism*, 272–274. This is in its essentials Macpherson's argument, that the extension of the franchise destroyed that class cohesion necessary for a valid theory of political obligation. Some critical theory and neo-Marxist analysis of the contradictions of the modern liberal-democratic welfare state pursue a similar form of reasoning.

65. See, e.g., Willmore Kendall's analysis in Jean Jacques Rousseau, *The Government of Poland*, trans. Willmoore Kendall (New York: The Bobbs Merrill Co, 1972), ix–xxxix, for the view that Rousseau's political theory did constitute a rejection of the modern state. For contrary views see Robert Nisbet, *The Quest for Community* (New York: Oxford University Press, 1969), 140–152, and Alfred Cobban, *Rousseau and the Modern State* (London: George Allen and Unwin, 1964), 166–165.

66. Jean Jacques Rousseau, *The Social Contract*, rev. Charles Frankel (New York: Hafner Press, 1947), 14–15.

67. Jean Jacques Rousseau, "Second Discourse: On the Origin and Foundations of Inequality Among Men," in *The First and Second Discourses*, ed. Roger D. Masters, trans. Roger D. Masters and Judith R. Masters (New York: St. Martin's Press, 1964), 128.

68. Ibid., 130.

69. See ibid., 151–152, for Rousseau's analysis of the emergence of property as a potential source of the contractual act. For Rousseau's notion that natural disasters cause human beings to contract out of the state of nature, see his "Essay on the Origin of Languages Which treats of Melody and Musical Imitation," *On the Origin of Language*, trans. John H. Moran and Alexander Gode (New York: Frederick Ungar Publishing Co., 1966), 40.

70. Rousseau, *The Social Contract*, 18.

71. Rousseau, "Second Discourse," 102.

72. That inequality is the fundamental political problem in Rousseau's political theory is clear enough. His "Second Discourse" confronts the issue most directly, but the theme of this work defines the essential basis of his political thought in the "First Discourse: On the Sciences and Arts," *The Social Contract*, and other of his most important works as well.

73. See Rousseau, *The Social Contract*, 19–22.

74. Ibid., 47.

75. It is one of the key functions of government for Rousseau to prevent gross inequalities by preventing too great an accumulation of wealth by the citizenry. In this, his economic theory is premised upon maintaining the general will, that is, the ethical basis of the community, not, as in the emerging economic theory of liberalism, expanding the "wealth of nations." See Jean Jaques Rousseau, "Discourse on Political Economy," in *On the Social Contract with Geneva Manuscript and Political Economy*, ed. Roger D. Masters, trans. Judith R. Masters (New York: St. Martin's Press, 1978), 221.

76. Rousseau is insistent that the entire social order is "founded on conventions" and absolutely rejects the doctrines of natural law and natural right as philosophically valid and, therefore, as a basis for the legitimation of the state. See Rousseau, *The Social Contract*, 6.

77. Ibid., 16.

78. Ibid.
79. Ibid., 26.
80. Ibid., 18.
81. Rousseau is particularly adamant that the government is not contractual in origin, but the legal creation of the sovereign authority (general will) of the state. Not only is this recognition of the key modern distinction between state and government, but also of the inherent problem that government poses in the modern state: its potential usurpation of sovereign authority. See ibid., 76–79, 88–91.
82. Ibid., 61. Rousseau, however, recognizes that the ideal of an elective aristocracy is not possible in all circumstances and, following the insights of Montesquieu, that the form of government will vary with the character of the people, the wealth of the populace, and of particular importance to Rousseau, the size of the state. Larger states require more external controls and hence smaller governments (e.g., monarchy) capable of making decisions quickly and decisively; smaller states are more compatible with larger governments of a democratic kind. Rousseau's ideal is a medium size state and an (elected) aristocratic form of government. See Book III, Chaps I–XI in particular, for the development of these and related views.
83. Rousseau, "Discourse on Political Economy," 221.
84. See Harrington, "The Commonwealth of Oceana," in *The Political Writings of James Harrington: Representative Selections*, ed. Charles Blitzer, The Library of Liberal Arts, no. 38, ed. Oskar Piest (New York: The Liberal Arts Press, 1955).
85. Ibid., 40–81. Harrington employs Aristotle's typology of constitutions but with modifications, and implicitly states that, while he follows the ancients, he yet "goes his own way." Most importantly, he proposes to create the just state (republic) by the appropriate balancing of classes (through the requisite distribution of land) that, in his time, was quite different from that which had existed in the classical *polis* or the Renaissance city-states. The latter had revived republican ideals, finding their theoretical comprehension most notably in Machiavelli. The influence of Machiavelli is equally apparent, therefore, and while Harrington's analysis modifies Machiavelli in some important ways, it could be viewed, as Pocock has suggested, as a "Machiavellian meditation on feudalism." See J.G.A. Pocock, *The Machiavellian Moment: Florentine Political Thought and the Atlantic Republican Tradition* (Princeton: Princeton University Press, 1975), 385. See also pages 383–400 for an excellent analysis of these and related issues.
86. See Richard Olson, *The Emergence of the Social Sciences: 1642–1792*, in series: *Twayne's Studies in Intellectual and Cultural History*, Michael Roth, ed. (New York: Twayne Publishers, 1993). Olson argues, with some merit, that Harrington initiated the "sociological tradition" in social and political thought (192). Certainly, it can be argued, he has more in common with contemporary sociological thinkers than with seventeenth century contractarian thinkers.

Chapter Six   The Metaphysical Theory of the State

1. Hegel, *Hegel's Philosophy of Right*, trans. T.M. Knox (London: Oxford University Press, 1979), §257.

2. David Hume, *An Inquiry Concerning the Principles of Morals, with a Supplement: A Dialogue*, ed. Charles W. Hendel (Indianapolis: Bobbs-Merrill, 1957), 11–23, 46–58. For Hume, all moral rules are merely matters of utility and convention.

3. See Hume, *An Inquiry Concerning Human Understanding, with supplement: An Abstract of a Treatise of Human Nature*, ed. Charles W. Hendel (New York: Bobbs-Merrill, 1955), 72–89.

4. Ibid., 35.

5. See Immanuel Kant, *Critique of Pure Reason*, trans. Norman Kemp Smith (New York: St. Martin's Press, 1965), 44–55, for Kant's critique of Hume's analysis of "cause and effect."

6. See Immanuel Kant, *Critique of Practical Reason*, ed. trans. Mary Gregor, in series: *Cambridge Texts in the History of Philosophy*, ed. Karl Ameriks and Desmond M. Clarke (Cambridge: Cambridge University Press, 1997). The "categorical imperative," "the fundamental law of pure practical reason" in Kant's terms, is to "so act that in the maxim of your will could always hold at the same time as a principle in a giving of universal law" (28).

7. See Immanuel Kant, *Groundwork of the Metaphysics of Morals*, trans. H.J. Paton (New York: Harper and Row, 1964). Kant himself stresses that the "categorical imperative" can be framed as a natural law principle: "Act as if the maxim of your action were to become through your will a universal law of nature" (89).

8. See Immanuel Kant, "Peace Projects of the Eighteenth Century", *Kant's Political Writings*, ed. Hans Reiss, trans. H.B. Nisbet, in series: *Cambridge Studies in the History and Theory of Politics*, ed. Maurice Cowling et al. (Cambridge: Cambridge University Press, 1970), 100–101. Indeed, Kant's republicanism is linked to his prohibition against war, for not only is a republican system (as opposed to pure democracy lacking a separation of powers between legislature and executive) the ethically appropriate form of polity, it is the least likely to engage in war according to Kant. It should also be noted that Kant's objection to Hobbes' on the issue of war does not extend to other elements of Hobbes's political theory. Kant's political thinking was also framed as a theory of contract, and in agreement with Hobbes (and contrary to Rousseau with whom in other important respects he agreed), Kant conceived the hypothetical state of nature to be a state of war. See Hans Reiss, "Introduction," 27.

9. See Peter Singer, *Hegel*, in series: *Past Masters*, ed. Keith Thomas (Oxford: Oxford University Press, 1983), 3–4, for a general discussion of the growing dissatisfaction with Kant's treatment of theoretical and practical reason.

10. See *Hegel's Logic*, trans. William Wallace (Oxford: Oxford University Press, 1975). This translation is taken from Hegel's *Encyclopedia of the Philosophical Sciences*.

11. See Singer, *Hegel*, 80–83, for a brief but comprehensible analysis of the concept of the "absolute idea," and of some of its theological implications.

12. See S.J. Quentin Lauer, *Hegel's Idea of Philosophy with a new Translation of Hegel's Introduction to the History of Philosophy* (New York: Fordham University Press, 1983). In Hegel, "to know the *reason* why one is free is to be truly free" (30).

13. See ibid. As Quentin Lauer notes, in Hegel "the categories of thought reveal themselves as the categories of reality" (4). It must always be understood, however, that in Hegel, thought is reality, and what is revealed empirically is precisely that reality.

14. In his early phase, Hegel was influenced by subjective forms of idealism characteristic of the romantic movement of his times, but subsequently broke from this tradition. See editors "Introduction," *Fichte, Jacobi, and Schelling: Philosophy of German Idealism*, ed. Ernst Behler (New York: The Continuum Publishing Company, 1987).

15. Hegel, *Philosophy of Right*, § 357.

16. Ibid., § 360.

17. Shlomo Avineri, *Hegel's Theory of the Modern State* (Cambridge: Cambridge University Press, 1972), 116. At the same time, as Avineri stresses, Hegel himself rejected the notion that any state was adequate to the philosophical idea of it. Hegel's philosophical method is premised upon comprehending that which exists, not that which abstractly "ought to be." Certainly he cannot be interpreted, as he sometimes is, as positing an ideal theory of the state that is contrary to existing reality, or that predicts some future condition. See Paul Lakeland, *The Politics of Salvation: The Hegelian Idea of the State* (Albany: State University of New York Press, 1984), who expresses Hegel's intent best here: "the revelation of meaning will occur not where it is incarnated in its perfection, but where it is thought in its exactness" (69).

18. Hume's ethics were also utilitarian, but he did not share Bentham's crudely hedonistic concept of utility. By utility, Hume meant something like "usefulness" to society and the public. See Hume, *An Inquiry Concerning the Principles of Morals*, editor's "Introduction," xxxv.

19. Jeremy Bentham, "Principles of Morals and Legislation" in *The Utilitarians: An Introduction to the Principles of Morals and Legislation, Jeremy Bentham; Utilitarianism and On Liberty, John Stuart Mill* (Garden City: Anchor Press/Doubleday, 1973), 17–18.

20. James Mill *An Essay on Government*, ed. Currin V. Shields (Indianapolis: Bobbs-Merill, 1955).

21. While early utilitarianism was admittedly a crude and oversimplified doctrine, Plamenatz credits the utilitarians with finally liberating political theory from the last vestiges of the medieval political vocabulary. See John Plamenatz, *The English Utilitarians* (Oxford: Basil Blackwell and Mott, 1958), 159–160.

22. See T.M. Knox, "Hegel and Prussianism" and Shlomo Avineri, "Hegel and Nationalism," in *Hegel's Political Philosophy*, ed. Walter Kaufmann (New York: Atherton Press, 1970) for a defense of Hegel against those who attribute to him pro-Prussian and nationalist sentiments.

23. Hegel, *Philosophy of Right*, § 322. Hegel recognizes the power of a sense of national identity, and that it cannot simply be eliminated, but such identity is still only a "feeling of selfhood." Feeling is not a sufficient basis in Hegel for the state's legitimation.

24. E.J. Hobsbawm, *Nations and Nationalism Since 1870: Programme, Myth, Reality*, (Cambridge: Cambridge University Press, 1990). The bourgeoisie had come to see the state as a territorial structure enclosing a nation, the nation defined as the people within the territory (37–38).

25. That Mazzini is Italian deserves special note, because Italy did not become a unified state until the later nineteenth century, quite late for a West European state. The same was true of Germany that did not become a unified territorial state until the reign of Bismarck. A key part of the problem for Germany was its association with the Holy Roman Empire, and for Italy the existence of the autonomous papal states. These factors had slowed the consolidation of

subordinate political units into a centralized state structure. This was particularly the case in Germany which, even after the formation of the German Empire in 1871, was still a federation of twenty-five states. And in both cases nationalism proved to be an exceptionally powerful force, for it has been the history of nationalism, then as now, that it has been most ardently expressed in the weakest, least unified, states.

26. See Carlton J.H. Hayes, *The Historical Evolution of Modern Nationalism* (New York: Russell & Russell, 1968), 22–27.

27. For the impact of democratization on the evolution of nationalism from Mazzinian cosmopolitanism to ethnic and xenophobic radicalism, see Hobsbawm, *Nations and Nationalism*, 44, 101–130.

28. This is Marx's meaning of the term also, a meaning that he attributes to Hegel following in the line of eighteenth-century English and French thinkers. See Karl Marx, "Preface to a Contribution to the Critique of Political Economy" in *Karl Marx and Frederick Engels: Selected Works in One Volume* (New York: International Publishers, 1968), 182.

29. In G.W.F. Hegel, *Reason in History: A General Introduction to the Philosophy of History*, trans. Robert S. Hartman (New York: Bobbs-Merrill, 1953), Hegel explains this unity of the particular and the universal in reason thus: "Reason is not so impotent as to bring about only the ideal, the ought, and to remain in an existence outside of reality" (11).

30. See Lauer, *Hegel's Idea of Philosophy*, 54–56, for a brief but comprehensible exposition of Hegel's notion of the concrete universal. See also Lauer's explanation of Hegel's distinction between understanding and reason (23–29).

31. Hegel, *Philosophy of Right*, §126.

32. Ibid., § 135. Hegel emphasizes the purely abstract character of Kant's moral theory that leads to, in his words, a "never-ending ought-to-be."

33. Ibid., § 155.

34. See Patrick Riley, *Will and Political Legitimacy: A Critical Exposition of Social Contract Theory in Hobbes, Locke, Rousseau, Kant, and Hegel* (Cambridge: Harvard University Press, 1982), vii-viii.

35. Hobbes's concept of will, of course, abolishes any notion of a "free will". As he notes; "Neither is the freedom of willing or not willing greater in man than in other living creatures." See Thomas Hobbes, "De Corpore," in *The English Works of Thomas Hobbes of Malmesbury*, ed. Sir William Molesworth, Bart. (London: John Bohn, 1966), v. I, 206.

36. Riley, *Will and Political Legitimacy*, 199.

37. Singer, *Hegel*, 63. Singer notes appropriately that the "unhappy consciousness" of Christianity is a replication within the individual psyche of the Hegelian "master–slave" dualism.

38. Hegel, *Philosophy of Right*, § 258.

39. See ibid. § 108. Morality precedes ethical life for Hegel, but is the expression of a duty rather than a fully willed ethical life. This is so because morality is the manifestation of the individual will not yet united with the concept (universal principle) of the will as such.

40. That is, love of the nuclear family created by marriage, not of the extended family of the *gens*, which is an abstract product of understanding. See ibid., § 180.

41. Caring for and educating children requires the acquisition of property as well, a key function of the family for Hegel. For an analysis of this and other aspects of the family, See ibid., §§ 158–181.

42. Ibid., § 183.
43. Avineri, *Hegel's Theory of the Modern State*, 142.
44. Hegel, *Philosophy of Right*, § 183.
45. Ibid., § 75.
46. Hegel credits Rousseau with grasping that the state is based on will, but argues that he confounds the general will (the publicly interested will of a collectivity of individuals) with the universal will embodied in the state. Nonetheless, Hegel sees this as an advance over theories that posit instinct or divine authority as the basis of the state, that is, over most modern and medieval conceptions of the state. See ibid., § 258.
47. Hegel, *Philosophy of Right*, §§ 46, 185, 206.
48. Ibid., § 255.
49. Ibid., § 252.
50. Ibid., § 188.
51. Avineri, *Hegel's Theory of the Modern State*, 163.
52. Hegel, *Philosophy of Right*, § 252.
53. Ibid., § 295. This function of resisting state authority is developed less explicitly in the *Philosophy of Right* than the other functions of corporations, but it is crucial to Hegel's theory of the state nonetheless. For an excellent discussion of this and Hegelian corporation theory generally, See Avineri, *Hegel's Theory of the Modern State*, 161–167.
54. Avineri, *Hegel's Theory of the Modern State*, 48–49, 164–165.
55. See Alexis de Tocqueville, "What Sort of Despotism Democratic Nations Have to Fear," Part IV, Chap. 6, in Alexis de Tocqueville, *Democracy in America*, ed. J.P. Mayer, trans. George Lawrence (New York: Harper and Row, 1966). The problem of majority tyranny for Tocqueville, as developed in this chapter and throughout *Democracy in America*, is as much social as political. The mere force of public opinion carries with it despotic possibilities. See also his *The Old Regime and the French Revolution*, trans. Stuart Gilbert (Garden City: Doubleday and Company, 1955), Part II, Chap. 5, for the even greater possibility of democratic despotism in the case of postrevolutionary France.
56. There is a fundamental difference between Hegel and de Tocqueville, however, as there is between Hegel and contemporary pluralists. Hegel's intermediate groups are legal corporations integrated into the constitutional structure of the state. In this, Hegel was drawing upon a tradition of political thought, common in Germany at the time, which had its roots in late medieval corporatist views. It specifically aimed at rejecting liberal individualism, and was often combined with romanticism and nationalism. See Ralph H. Bowen, *German Theories of the Corporative State With Special Reference to the Period 1870–1919* (New York: Russell and Russell, 1971), 211–212. Some, such as Otto von Gierke, a thinker little read today but important in the history of state theory, went so far as to insist upon the real personality of the corporation (as opposed to the Roman law conception of it as a mere fictitious person) that ought to exist not merely in the positive law of the state, but in the law of nature itself. Gierke's concern, not without merit, is that groups were losing their autonomy as legitimate associations apart from the state. See Otto Gierke, *Political Theories of the Middle Age*, trans. Frederic William Maitland (Boston: Beacon Press, 1958).
57. Hegel, *Philosophy of Right*, § 273.
58. Ibid, § 275.

59. The acts of the legislature and executive combined (defined by Hegel as the "*universality of* the constitution and the laws," and "counsel, which refers the *particular* to the universal") constitute sovereignty for Hegel. These, however, are subsumed under the determination (the formal-legal affirmation) of the crown as the visible embodiment of the state. See ibid., § 275.

60. James Madison, "Number 51," in Alexander Hamilton, James Madison, and John Jay, *The Federalist Papers* (New York: New American Library, 1961).

61. Hegel, of course, expresses this in more complex language. "It is only the inner self-determination of the concept, not any other consideration, whether of purpose or advantage, that is the absolute source of the division of powers, and in virtue of this alone is the organization of the state something inherently rational and the image of eternal reason." Hegel, *Philosophy of Right*, § 272.

62. This correspondence of class to the moments of ethical life is true only in a general sense since the structure of Hegel's state incorporates all classes in its ultimate purpose. See, e.g., Hegel's discussion of the estates in ibid., §§ 303, 304.

63. See Avineri, *Hegel's Theory of the Modern State*, 160.

64. Hegel, *Philosophy of Right*, §§ 289, 303.

65. Ibid., § 307.

66. Ibid., § 301.

67. Ibid., § 303.

68. While Hegel defends basic liberal values within the context of his organicist concept of the state, there are certain limitations that he would put on freedom of speech, press, and so on that are contrary to the liberal position. This is particularly so in cases of libel or slander against the government and most importantly the person of the monarch. For Hegel's views in this regard, as well as his support for yet critique of public opinion in general, see ibid., §§ 314–319.

69. Ibid., § 286.

70. Ibid., § 256.

71. Ibid., § 331.

72. G.W.F. Hegel, "Lordship and Bondage," *The Phenomenology of Mind*, trans. J.D. Baillie (New York: Harper and Row, 1967), 229–240.

73. Hegel, *Philosophy of Right*, §§ 323–340.

74. Ibid., Surely Hegel's justification of the ethical basis of war has been the most controversial aspect of his political philosophy. While it is true that he has often been misunderstood as a "warmonger," it must be admitted that it is difficult to accept his view of war at face value, particularly in this century. A sympathetic but balanced discussion of this subject may be found in Avineri, *Hegel's Theory of the Modern State*, Chap. 10.

75. Hegel, *Philosophy of Right*, § 333.

76. See Avineri, *Hegel's Theory of the Modern State*, "One may paradoxically say that if *states*, in the plural, were to cease to exist, there could not, by definition, remain *a state* in the singular" (202).

77. Hegel, *Philosophy of Right*, § 278.

78. "We may . . . speak of sovereignty . . . residing in the people provided that we are speaking generally about the whole state and . . . (recognizing) . . . that it is to the state that sovereignty belongs." Ibid., § 279.

79. See Avineri, *Hegel's Theory of the Modern State*, 188–189. For Avineri, Hegel not only subsumes popular and ruler sovereignty under state sovereignty, but in his constitutional theory combines as well the parallel principles of classical democracy and classical monarchism.

80. Hegel, *Philosophy of Right*, § 200.
81. Ibid.
82. Hegel emphasizes in a number of different passages that poverty is not simply economic but affects the totality of human potentialities. Avineri has rightly noted that in this Hegel had a "strikingly modern and sophisticated description of the culture of poverty (that) parallels many much more recent attempts by social scientists to drive home the point that poverty cannot be described merely in quantitative terms." Avineri, *Hegel's Theory of the Modern State*, 150.
83. Hegel, *Philosophy of Right*, § 200.
84. Ibid, § 241.
85. Ibid, §.249.
86. See Avineri, *Hegel's Theory of the Modern State*, 151, for an excellent discussion of this dilemma.
87. Hegel, *Philosophy of Right*, §§ 246, 248. Hegel does not, however, dwell on the ethical propriety of colonizing for economic purposes.
88. Thomas H. Green, *Lectures on the Principles of Political Obligation* (London: Longmans, 1941), 32.
89. Ibid.
90. Ibid., 219.
91. The historically evolved forms of social democracy are so varied that it is difficult to sum them up in any one general definition. However, they have all essentially adopted those same or similar principles that characterize modern liberalism and its advocacy of the welfare state. This may certainly be said of Fabian socialism in the United Kingdom, as British liberals recognized early on See, e.g., L.T. Hobhouse, *Liberalism* (London: Oxford University Press, 1964), 112–113. It is true as well of the German socialist movement in the tradition of Eduard Bernstein. Bernstein's "revisionism" of the original Marxist position is particularly interesting because it draws again upon Kant and the importance of the "ideal," as opposed to a purely "scientific materialism," in the development of the socialist movement. See Eduard Bernstein, *Evolutionary Socialism: A Criticism and Affirmation*, trans. Edith C. Harvey (New York: Schocken Books, 1961), 201–224.
92. See Bernard Bosanquet, *The Philosophical Theory of the State* (New York: St. Martin's Press, 1965).
93. See L.T. Hobhouse, *The Metaphysical Theory of the State* (London: George Allen and Unwin, 1918), 1960.
94. Dewey was a pragmatist (instrumentalist) who understood democracy and liberal values to be justified in pragmatic terms. Much of his thinking on the social nature of human beings and the moral basis of politics, however, he derived from his early reading of Hegel. For an example of Dewey's liberalism, and its similarity to Green's analysis despite differing metaphysical assumptions, see John Dewey, *Liberalism and Social Action* (New York: Capricorn Books, 1963), 34–35.

Chapter Seven   The Sociology of the State

1. Max Weber, "Politics as a Vocation," ed. trans. H.H. Gerth and C. Wright Mills, *From Max Weber: Essays in Sociology* (New York: Oxford University Press, 1946), 78.
2. Ibid., 77–78.

3. See Anthony Giddens, *Capitalism and Modern Social Theory: An Analysis of the Writings of Marx, Durkheim and Max Weber* (London: Cambridge University Press, 1971), 76–81, for a good analysis of the otherwise confusing distinction between mechanical and organic forms of solidarity (the distinction seems at first glance backward since most social theorists are inclined to impute organic metaphors to more "primitive" societies," mechanical metaphors to more developed ones), and for Durkheim's dispute with Tonnies and Spencer over the nature of social solidarity under modern forms of the division of labor.

4. See Herbert Spencer, *The Man Versus the State*, ed. Donald Macrae (Baltimore: Penguin Books, 1969). Spencer's evolutionism led him to a radically individualistic and antistatist position and to an extreme interpretation of the classical liberal ideology.

5. While Tonnies is little read today, his distinction between *Gemeinschaft* and *Gesellschaft* was initially quite influential, and controversial. The problem, as Durkheim insisted, is that the distinction is too extreme. Modern industrial society cannot exist in rational-contractual terms alone; no society can. Some form of social solidarity beyond self-interest and legal relationships must continue to exist if society itself is to exist. See Giddens, *Capitalism and Modern Social Theory*, 77. While this debate may seem remote from contemporary theoretical concerns, it is in fact still important. The tendency to bifurcate the social world in *Geminschaft–Gesellschaft* terms remains a continuing issue. Primitive society versus civilization, modern society versus premodern, third world versus first world, industrial society versus agrarian society, and state society versus egalitarian society, are constructs that, unless employed carefully, stress only the differences involved. While these differences are very real, there are also continuities, including requisite forms of social solidarity.

6. For the primary example of Engel's "ontological" view of the dialectic, see Frederick Engels, *Herr Eugen Duhring's Revolution in Science (Anti-Duhring)*, ed. C.P. Dutt, trans. Emile Burns (New York: International Publishers, 1939). Engels argues, with some embarrassment to later Marxists, that the (materialist) dialectic works at all levels, "in the animal and plant kingdoms, in geology, in mathematics, in history and in philosophy" (154).

7. Karl Marx, "Theses on Feuerbach," in *Karl Marx and Frederick Engels: Selected Works in One Volume* (New York: International Publishers, 1968), 28–30.

8. *Verstehen* is not meant to replace the positivist approach for Weber, but simply to include the subjective element inherent in any social situation. See Frank Parkin, *Max Weber*, rev. ed., in series: *Key Sociologists*, ed. Peter Hamilton (London: Routledge, 2002), 19–27, for an analysis of this limited meaning of *verstehen* and for a critique of the concept.

9. It has been noted by numerous commentators that Marx possesses two theories of the state, and it is generally conceded that what we term the "primary theory" (class "determines" both the structure and ideological superstructure of the state) is, in fact, the dominant view, although Marx's initial analysis was much less deterministic. See, e.g., David Held, "Central Perspectives on the Modern State," *Political Theory and the Modern State: Essays on State, Power, and Democracy* (Stanford: Stanford University Press, 1989), 33. See also Bertrand Badie and Pierre Birnbaum, *The Sociology of the State*, trans. Arthur Goldhammer (Chicago: The University of Chicago Press, 1983), 3–11, for a different view.

10. Karl Marx, "Preface to a Contribution to the Critique of Political Economy," in *Karl Marx and Fedrick Engels: Selected Works*, 182.

11. Ibid., Marx and Engels, "Manifesto of the Communist Party," in *Karl Marx and Fredrick Engles*, 37.

12. Ibid. Marx, "Preface to a Contribution to the Critique of Political Economy", in *Karl Marx and Fredrick Engles*, 182–183.

13. Ibid., 183.

14. The concept of the "asiatic mode of production" and "oriental despotism" was never consistently developed by either Marx or Engels, and elements of it, not always consistent, can be found in a variety of their works. The fact is that the concept raises some serious issues for Marxian sociology in general, and for Marx's "primary theory" of the state in particular, for it presupposes that the state not only can be fully autonomous, but that the executive bodies of the state constitute a ruling class in a society without private property. See George Lichtheim, "Oriental Despotism," *The Concept of Ideology and Other Essays* (New York: Vintage Books, 1967) for the sources of and ideological issues surrounding Marx and Engel's analysis of the asiatic mode of production and oriental despotism.

15. The stalemate in the class struggle thrust Louis Bonaparte into the role of "representing" all classes which, given their mutually exclusive interests, was an impossibility. The consequence, Marx argued, was a government that could produce only a confused mélange of policies that had the effect of alienating all classes. See Karl Marx, "The Eighteenth Brumaire of Louis Bonaparte," in *Karl Marx and Fredrick Engels*, 177–178.

16. Frederick Engels, "The Origin of the Family, Private Property, and the State," in *Karl Marx and Frederick Engles*, 588.

17. Ibid., 587–588.

18. For a brief synopsis of Gramsci's views on consent, hegemony, the ideological role of the (organic) intellectuals, and the merging of substructure and super-structure, see Antonio Gramsci, "The Intellectuals," *Selections From the Prison Notebooks of Antonio Gramsci*, ed. trans. Quintin Hoare and Geoffrey Nowell Smith (New York: International Publishers, 1971), 12–13.

19. Ibid., 12.

20. Karl Marx and Frederick Engels, *The German Ideology: Parts I and II*, ed. R. Pascal (New York: International Publishers, 1947), 23.

21. Karl Marx, "Critical Notes on the Article 'The King of Prussia and Social Reform. By a Prussian.' " *Early Writings*, trans. Rodney Livingstone, Gregor Benton (New York: Vintage Books, 1975), 411.

22. Max Weber, "Domination," *Max Weber on Law in Economy and Society*, ed. Max Rheinstein, trans. Edward Shils and Max Rheinstein, from Max Weber, *Wirtschaft und Gesellschaft*, 2nd ed., 1925 (New York: Simon and Schuster, 1954), 322.

23. Ibid., 336–337.

24. Ibid., "The Economic System and the Normative Orders," 14.

25. See Weber, "Bureaucracy," *From Max Weber: Essays in Sociology*. Weber lists three key characteristics of modern bureaucracy that may be summed up as the regular and methodical performance of official duties within the framework of explicit legal rules (196).

26. Ibid., 205–206.

27. Ibid., 204–205.
28. Ibid., 225.
29. Ibid., 226.
30. Editor, "Introduction," in *From Max Weber*, 47.
31. Weber, "Politics as a Vocation," in *From Max Weber*, 82.
32. Ibid., "Bureaucracy," 239.
33. Ibid.
34. Ibid.
35. Weber, "Class, Status, and Party," in *From Max Weber*, 181.
36. Ibid., 193.
37. Ibid., 194.
38. Max Weber, *The Protestant Ethic and the Spirit of Capitalism*, trans. Talcott Parsons (New York: Scribner, 1958).
39. More radical socialist and communist ideologies and parties also arose, but Marxism had become the dominant revolutionary paradigm by the turn of the twentieth century, and it rejected the state as a viable mechanism for social reform.
40. Clyde W. Barrow, *Critical Theories of the State: Marxist, Neo-Marxist, Post-Marxist* (Madison: The University of Wisconsin Press, 1993), 4–5. Barrow argues that the emergence of the welfare state has shaped in fundamental ways the evolution of contemporary Marxist, neo-Marxist, and derivative theories of the state.
41. The issue of the autonomy of the state is not, however, an issue for Marxists and neo-Marxists only. See, e.g., Eric A. Nordlinger, *On the Autonomy of the Democratic State* (Cambridge: Harvard University Press, 1981), 203–207. Nordlinger argues that the democratic state is frequently autonomous, and rejects the "social reductionism" of empirical liberal-democratic theory.
42. Neither Marx nor the neo-Marxists deny the potential institutional autonomy of the state. Their point simply is that this autonomy does not obviate the ultimate basis of class domination. See Adriano Nervo Codato and Renato Monseff Perissinotto, "The State and Contemporary Political Theory: Lessons from Marx," in *Paradigm Lost: State Theory Reconsidered*, ed. Stanley Aronowitz and Peter Bratsis (Minneapolis: University of Minneapolis Press, 2002). "The problem of 'state power' is theoretically distinct from the problem of the 'state apparatus' " (64). That is, the institutional state may take a number of different forms, or be more or less autonomous, but the state remains a class state insofar as its policies favor a specific class. For Marxists and neo-Marxists, of course, state power is inherently in the interest of the capitalist class, however narrowly or broadly defined.
43. Ralph Miliband, *The State in Capitalist Society* (New York: Basic Books, 1969). Clearly the contemporary state is not dominated by a capitalist ruling class in the direct and obvious manner that Marx perceived in his time. Now managerial elites play a crucial role as well, but these, Miliband argues, come dispropor-tionately from the propertied and professional middle classes (66–67) and reflect the interests of the capitalist.
44. Held, *Political Theory and the Modern State*, 68. See also pages 67–76 for a brief but solid discussion of the debate between Miliband, Poulantzas, and Offe.
45. See Nicos Poulantzas, *Classes in Contemporary Capitalism*, trans. David Fernbach (London: NLB, 1975), for his rejection of "instrumentalism", his focus on superstructural factors in the crisis of capitalism, and his argument that ideo-logical and hegemonic controls will ultimately fail to resolve the crisis (169–171).

46. See Claus Offe, *Modernity and the State East, West* (Cambridge: The MIT Press, 1996). For Offe there is a fundamental contradiction inherent in the modern state. Its claims to ultimate authority (sovereignty) are delegitimized by the inability of the bureaucracy to meet increasing societal demands (loss of "rationality"), and corporatism, he argues, is a "solution" only in a limited number of states (63–70).

47. See Martin Carnoy, *The State and Political Theory* (Princeton: Princeton University Press, 1984). Carnoy notes the obvious influence of Weber in Offe's analysis, specifically of Weber's theory of bureaucracy, but with the continuing Marxist assumption that the bureaucracy ultimately reflects the interests of the capitalists (6).

48. Theda Skocpol, *States and Social Revolutions: A Comparative Analysis of France, Russia, and China* (Cambridge: Cambridge University Press, 1979), 29. While recognizing her debt to Weber, Skocpol also distinguishes her analysis from Weber's. See note 4, 304.

49. See Carnoy, *The State and Political Theory*, for an analysis of the correspondence between Skocpol's concept of the autonomous state and the increasingly autonomous theories of the neo-Marxists, and more generally of the emphasis on superstructural factors by Marxist theorists since Gramsci (250–261).

50. See Skocpol, *States and Social Revolutions*. Quite in line with Weber's analysis, Skocpol agrees that "of course, these basic state organizations are built up and must operate within the context of class-divided socioeconomic relations, as well as within the context of national and international economic dynamics" (29).

51. Ibid., 31–32.

52. Jurgen Habermas, *Legitimation Crisis*, trans. Thomas McCarthy (Boston: Beacon Press, 1975), 36–37.

53. Ibid., 37.

54. Ibid., 97–102.

55. See ibid., 102–117, for the general thrust of these arguments, and for a critique of contract theory that might otherwise appear to resonate with the concept of communicative competence (and the ideal speech situation). See also Thomas McCarthy's "Introduction" to this work for a good general overview of Habermas's discursively based ethical theory.

56. Ibid., 36

Chapter Eight   The State in Retrospect

1. Marxists have gone further than institutionalists in this regard, however, for despite the criticism of being "reductionist," they understand the state from a comprehensive perspective that includes class relations and ideological factors. For an excellent discussion of this and related critiques of the institutionalist framework, as well as critiques of various nonstatist and antistatist approaches, see *Paradigm Lost: State Theory Reconsidered*, ed. Stanley Aronowitz. Peter Bratsis (Minneapolis: University of Minneapolis Press, 2002).

2. See Andrew Vincent, *Theories of the State* (Oxford: Basil Blackwell Ltd., 1987), 219–224. Vincent correctly points to the conceptual basis of the state, and the need, therefore, to understand it "holistically" as both a structure of

governmental institutions as well as a set of values that, as he correctly emphasizes, are inconceivable apart from the state (rights, for example). In this book we
have emphasized that these values are derivative of the broader normative
domain of the state constituted by its ideology of legitimation and the system of
class stratification upon which it is based.

3. See Gabriel Almond, "The Return to the State," *American Political Science
   Review*, v. 82, no. 3, September 1988, 853–874. Almond's article, which generated much controversy within political science, constitutes a wholesale assault on
   the "statist" position in the discipline, and concludes that a return to a state-
   centered approach would merely cause a loss of "operational vigor." It is this
   potentially "destructive" ramification of a statist approach that really concerns
   Almond and others in the discipline who posses a more neo-positivist orientation.
   For a rejoinder to Almond by a variety of "statists," see "The Return to the State:
   Critiques" in this same issue of *American Political Science Review*, 875–901.

4. The argument being advanced here is that a state-centric approach is the
   necessary framework in understanding political behavior, not that the state
   should constitute the only subject matter of political science. This needs to be
   emphasized because there has been some unnecessary controversy in this regard.
   Apart from his concern that a "statist" perspective will result in a "loss of operational vigor," Gabriel Almond also points to what he feels will be a neglect of
   "non-statal variables such as political parties, interest groups" and so on
   (Almond, "The Return to the State," 871–872). But these are not "non-statal
   variables"; they are thoroughly implicated in the state, structurally and
   ideologically. A statist approach does not mean that political parties or interest
   groups are not valid objects of political analysis, simply that they cannot be
   properly understood apart from the state. Political parties, to take the most
   obvious example, are, as Weber emphasized, a historical by-product of the
   modern state and function within a constellation of social and political
   structures and ideological assumptions that precisely constitute the state. Even if
   the state is not to be treated as a distinct variable in political analysis, it needs to
   be included, particularly when empirical analysis leads, as it invariably does,
   to broader political and normative issues (see Nordlinger et al., "The Return to
   the State: Critiques").

5. See Robert O. Keohane and Joseph S. Nye, *Power and Interdependence*, 3rd ed.
   (New York: Longman, 2001), for an analysis of various transnational interac-
   tions that are shaping international relations into structures of "complex interdependence," but that does not deny the role of the state in world politics.

6. Even major trans-state regional organizations such as the European
   Community do not inevitably constitute a threat to the continued existence
   and viability of the state. At least this appears to be the case when major economic policy decisions by the EU are examined, for the role of the state clearly
   remains crucial in policy outcomes. See, e.g., Gaye Gungor, *The GE-
   Honeywell Merger: Irreconcilable Differences? A Comparative Study of
   Competition Policies of the United States and the European Union*, paper presented at the BMW Center for German and European Studies at Georgetown
   University, March 23, 2002.

7. See, e.g., Hedley Bull, *The Anarchical Society: A Study of Order in World
   Politics*, 2nd ed. (New York: Columbia University Press, 1977), 266–271. While
   not rejecting Nye and Keohane's thesis (as developed in their *Transnational
   Relations and World Politics*) that the modern state is implicated in a web of

transnational relationships, a fact Bull maintains has always been the case, he insists that this "in no way implies the demise of the state system."

8. See Charles W. Kegley, Jr. and Gregory A. Raymond, *Exorcising the Ghost of Westphalia: Building World Order in the New Millennium*, Prentice Hall Studies in International Relations, series ed. Charles W. Kegley, Jr. (Englewood Cliffs, NJ: Prentice-Hall Inc., 2002) for an example of this type of normative approach to international relations.

Bibliography

Allen, J.W. *A History of Political Thought in the Sixteenth Century*. rev. ed. London: 1957.

Almond, Gabriel. "The Return to the State." *American Political Science Review*, v. 82, 3 (1988).

Anderson, Perry. *Lineages of the Absolutist State*. London: Verso, 1979.

Aquinas Thomas, St. *The Political Idea of St. Thomas Aquinas*. ed. Dino Bigongiari. New York: Hafner Press, 1953.

Aristotle. *The Athenian Constitution*. trans. P.J. Rhodes. New York: Penguin Books, 1984.

———. *The Ethics of Aristotle*. trans. J. A. K. Thomson. Harmondsworth: Penguin Books, 1955.

———. *The Politics of Aristotle*. ed. trans. Ernest Barker. New York: Oxford University Press, 1962.

Augustine, St. *Concerning the City of God against the Pagans*. trans. Henry Bettenson. London: Penguin Books, 1984.

Avineri, Shlomo. *Hegel's Theory of the Modern State*. Cambridge: Cambridge University Press, 1972.

Badie, Bertrand and Pierre Birnbaum. *The Sociology of the State*. trans. Arthur Goldhammer. Chicago: The University of Chicago Press, 1983.

Baldwin, Marshall W. *The Medieval Church*. In series: *The Development of Western Civilization: Narrative Essays in the History of Our Tradition from Its Origins in Ancient Israel and Greece to the Present*. ed. Edward W. Fox. Ithaca: Cornell University Press, 1953.

Barrow, Clyde W. *Critical Theories of the State: Marxist, Neo-Marxist, Post-Marxist*. Madison: The University of Wisconsin Press, 1993.

Bentham, Jeremy. "Principles of Morals and Legislation" in *The Utilitarians: An Introduction to the Principles of Morals and Legislation, Jeremy Bentham; Utilitarianism and On Liberty, John Stuart Mill*. Garden City: Anchor Press/Doubleday, 1973.

Bernstein, Eduard. *Evolutionary Socialism: A Criticism and Affirmation*. trans. Edith C. Harvey. New York: Schocken Books, 1961.

Black, Anthony. *Political Thought in Europe: 1250–1450*. Cambridge: Cambridge University Press, 1992.

Bodin, Jean. *On Sovereignty: Four Chapters From the Six Books of the Commonwealth*, ed. trans. Julian Franklin. Cambridge: Cambridge University Press, 1992.

———. *The Six Books of a Commenweale*. ed. Kenneth Douglas McRae. In series: *European Political Thought: Traditions and Endurance*. ed. J.P. Mayer et al. New York: Arno Press, 1979.

Bosanquet, Bernard. *The Philosophical Theory of the State*. New York: St. Martin's Press, 1965.

Bowen, Ralph H. *German Theories of the Corporative State With Special Reference to the Period 1870–1919*. New York: Russell and Russell, 1971.

Bull, Hedley. *The Anarchical Society: A Study of Order in World Politics*. 2nd ed. New York: Columbia University Press, 1977.

Burckhardt, Jacob. *The Civilization of the Renaissance in Italy*. v. I, New York: Harper and Row, 1958.

Canning, Joseph. *A History of Medieval Political Thought: 300–1450*. London: Routledge, 1996.

Carnoy, Martin. *The State and Political Theory*. Princeton: Princeton University Press, 1984.

Chadwick, Owan. *The Reformation*. In series: *The Pelican History of the Church*. ed. Owan Chadwick. MiddleSex: Penguin Books, 1964.

Cicero, Marcus Tullius. *The Loeb Classical Library, v. XVI: De Re Publica-De Legibus*. ed. G.P. Gould. trans. Clinton Walker Keyes. Cambridge: Harvard University Press, 1928.

————. *On the Commonwealth*. trans. George Holland Sabine and Stanley Barney Smith. Indianapolis: Bobbs-Merrill, reprinted from the original edition, Columbus: The Ohio State University Press, 1929.

Clastres, Pierre. *Society Against the State*. trans. Robert Hurley. New York: Mole Editions, 1974.

Codato, Nervo Adriano and Renato Monseff Perissinotto. "The State and Contemporary Political Theory: Lessons from Marx" in *Paradigm Lost: State Theory Reconsidered*. ed. Stanley Aronowitz and Peter Bratsis. Minneapolis: University of Minneapolis Press, 2002.

Dahl, Robert A. *A Preface to Democratic Theory*. Chicago: University of Chicago Press, 1956.

————. *Who Governs? Democracy and Power in an American City*. New Haven: Yale University Press, 1961.

Dante, Alighieri. *Monarchy*. ed. trans. Prue Shaw. In series: *Cambridge Texts in the History of Political Thought*. ed. Raymond Geuss and Quentin Skinner. Cambridge: Cambridge University Press, 1996.

Dewey, John. *Liberalism and Social Action*. New York: Capricorn Books, 1963.

D'Entreves, Alexander Passerin. *The Medieval Contribution to Political Thought: Thomas Aquinas, Marsilius of Padua, Richard Hooker*. New York: Humanities Press, 1959.

————. *The Notion of the State: An Introduction to Political Theory*. Oxford: Oxford University Press, 1967.

Easton, David. *The Political System*. New York: Alfred Knopf, 1953.

Ehrenberg, Victor. *The Greek State*, 2nd ed. London: Methuen and Co., 1969.

Eisenstadt, S.N. *The Political Systems of Empires*. New York: The Free Press of Glencoe, 1963.

Engels, Frederick. *Herr Eugen Duhring's Revolution in Science (Anti-Duhring)*. ed. C.P. Dutt. trans. Emile Burns. New York: International Publishers, 1939.

Ergang, Robert. *Emergence of the National State*. ed. Louis L. Snyder. New York: Van Nostrand Reinhold Company, 1971.

Evans, Peter B., Dietrich Rueschemeyer, and Theda Skocpol. eds. *Bringing the State Back In*. New York: Cambridge University Press, 1985.

Fichte, Johann Gottlieb, et al. *Fichte, Jacobi, and Schelling: Philosophy of German Idealism*. ed. Ernst Behler (New York: The Continuum Publishing Company, 1987).

Foucault, Michel. *Discipline and Punish: The Birth of the Prison*. trans. Alan Sheridan. New York: Vintage Books, 1995.

Frankfort, Henri. *Kingship and The Gods: A Study of Ancient Near Eastern Religion as the Integration of Society and Nature*. Chicago: The University of Chicago Press, 1978.

Franklin, Julian H. *Jean Bodin and the Rise of Absolutist Theory*. Cambridge: Cambridge University Press, 1973.

Fried, Morton H. *The Evolution of Political Society: An Essay in Political Anthropology*. New York: Random House, 1967.

Friedman, Jeffrey. "Economic Approaches to Politics." *Critical Review: An Interdisciplinary Journal of Politics and Society: Special issue: Rational Choice Theory and Politics* v. 9 (1995).

Gaius. *The Institutes of Gaius*. trans. W.M Gordon and O.R. Robinson, with the Latin text of Seckel and Kuebler. In series: *Texts in Roman Law*. ed. Peter Birks. Ithaca: Cornell University Press, 1988.

Ganshof, Francois Louis. *Frankish Institutions Under Charlemagne*. trans. Bryce and Mary Lyon. New York: W.W. Norton and Company, 1970.

Giddens, Anthony. *Capitalism and Modern Social Theory: An Analysis of the Writings of Marx, Durkheim and Max Weber*. London: Cambridge University Press, 1971.

Gierke, Otto. *Political Theories of the Middle Age*. trans. Frederic William Maitland. Boston: Beacon Press, 1958.

Gilby, Thomas. The *Political Thought of Thomas Aquinas*. Chicago, University of Chicago Press, 1958.

Gilson, Etienne. *The Philosophy of St. Thomas Aquinas*. rev. ed. G.A. Elrington, trans. Edward Bullough. Freeport: Books for Libraries Press, 1937.

Gluckman, Max. *Politics, Law, and Ritual in Tribal Society*. Chicago: Aldine Pub, 1965.

Gramsci, Antonio. *Selections From the Prison Notebooks of Antonio Gramsci*. ed. trans. Quintin Hoare and Geoffrey Nowell Smith. New York: International Publishers, 1971.

Green, Thomas H. *Lectures on the Principles of Political Obligation*. London: Longmans, 1941.

Grotius, Hugo. *The Rights of War and Peace: Including the Law of Nature and of Nations*. trans. A.C. Campbell and A.M. London: M. Walter Dunne, 1901.

Guenee, Bernard. *States and Rulers in Later Medieval Europe*. trans. Juliet Vale. Oxford: Basil Blackwell, 1985.

Gungor, Gaye. *The GE-Honeywell Merger: Irreconcilable Differences? A Comparative Study of Competition Policies of the United States and the European Union*. Paper presented at the BMW Center for German and European Studies at Georgetown University, March, 23, 2002.

Haas, Jonathan. *The Evolution of the Prehistoric State*. New York: Columbia University Press, 1982.

Habermas, Jurgen. *Legitimation Crisis*. trans. Thomas McCarthy. Boston: Beacon Press, 1975.

Hamilton, Alexander, James Madison, and John Jay. *The Federalist Papers*. New York: New American Library, 1961.

Hammond, Mason. *City-State and World State in Greek and Roman Political Theory Until Augustus*. Cambridge: Harvard University Press, 1951.

Hammurabi. *The Hammurabi Code and the Sinaitic Legislation*. Port Washington: Kennikat Press, 1971.

Harrington, James. "The Commonwealth of Oceana." *The Political Writings of James Harrington: Representative Selections*. ed. Charles Blitzer. In series: The

Library of Liberal Arts, no. 38. ed. Oskar Piest. New York: The Liberal Arts Press, 1955.

Hayes, Carlton J.H. *The Historical Evolution of Modern Nationalism*. New York: Russell and Russell, 1968.

Hegel, G.W.F. *Logic*. trans. William Wallace. Oxford: Oxford University Press, 1975.

———. *The Phenomenology of Mind*. trans. J.D. Baillie. New York: Harper and Row, 1967.

———. *Hegel's Philosophy of Right*. trans. T.M. Knox. London: Oxford University Press, 1979.

———. *Reason in History: A General Introduction to the Philosophy of History*. trans. Robert S. Hartman. New York: Bobbs-Merrill, 1953.

Held, David. *Political Theory and the Modern State: Essays on State, Power, and Democracy*. Stanford: Stanford University Press, 1989.

Hinsley, F.H. *Sovereignty*. New York: Basic Books, 1966.

Hobbes, Thomas, "De Corpore." *The English Works of Thomas Hobbes of Malmesbury*. v. I, ed. Sir William Molesworth, London: John Bohn, 1966, 206.

———. *Leviathan or the Matter, Forme and Power of a Commonwealth Ecclesiastical and Civil*. ed. Michael Oakeshott. New York: Collier Books, 1962.

Hobhouse, L.T. *Liberalism*. London: Oxford University Press, 1964.

———. *The Metaphysical Theory of the State*. London: George Allen and Unwin, 1960.

Hobsbawm, E.J. *Nations and Nationalism since 1870: Programme, Myth Reality*. Cambridge: Cambridge University Press, 1990.

Hooker, Richard. *Of the Laws of Ecclesiastical Polity: Preface, Book I, Book VIII*. ed. Arthur Stephen McGrade. Cambridge: Cambridge University Press, 1989.

Hume, David. *An Inquiry Concerning the Principles of Morals with a Supplement: A Dialogue*. ed. Charles W. Hendel. Indianapolis: Bobbs-Merrill, 1957.

———. *An Inquiry Concerning Human Understanding, with Supplement: An Abstract of a Treatise of Human Nature*. ed. Charles W. Hendel. New York: Bobbs-Merrill, 1955.

John of Paris, *On Royal and Papal Power*. trans. J.A. Watt. Toronto: The Pontifical Institute of Medieval Studies, 1971.

John of Salisbury. *Policraticus*, ed. Lindsay Rogers. trans. John Dickinson. New York: Russell and Russell, 1955.

Johnson, Curtis N. *Aristotle's Theory of the State*. New York: St. Martin's Press, 1990.

Justinian. *Justinian's Institutes*. trans. Peter Birks and Grant McLeod. Ithaca: Cornell University Press, 1987.

Kant, Immanuel. *Critique of Practical Reason*. ed. trans. Mary Gregor. In series: *Cambridge Texts in the History of Philosophy*. ed. Karl Ameriks and Desmond M. Clarke. Cambridge: Cambridge University Press, 1997.

———. *Critique of Pure Reason*. trans. Norman Kemp Smith. New York: St. Martin's Press, 1965.

———. *Groundwork of the Metaphysics of Morals*. trans. H.J. Paton. New York: Harper and Row, 1964.

———. *Kant's Political Writings*. ed. Hans Reiss. trans. H.B. Nisbet. In series: *Cambridge Studies in the History and Theory of Politics*. ed. Maurice Cowling et al. Cambridge: Cambridge University Press, 1970.

Kantorowicz, Ernst H. *The Kings Two Bodies: A Study in Mediaeval Political Theology*. Princeton: Princeton University Press, 1985.

Kegley, Charles W., Jr. and Gregory A. Raymond. *Exorcising the Ghost of Westphalia: Building World Order in the New Millennium*. In series: *Prentice Hall Studies in International Relations*. ed. Charles W. Kegley, Jr. Englewood Cliffs: Prentice Hall, 2002.

Kelly, George Armstrong. "Who Needs a Theory of Citizenship?" *Daedalus*. v. 108, 4 (1979).

Keohane, Robert O. and Joseph S. Nye. *Power and Interdependence*, 3rd ed. New York: Longman, 2001.

Knox, T.M. *Hegel's Political Philosophy*. ed. Walter Kaufmann. New York: Atherton Press, 1970.

Krader, Lawrence. *Formation of the State*. Englewood Cliffs: Prentice Hall Inc. 1968.

Lakeland, Paul. *The Politics of Salvation: The Hegelian Idea of the State*. Albany: State University of New York Press, 1984.

Laswell, Harold. *Politics: Who Gets What, When, How*. New York: P. Smith, 1950.

Lauer, Quentin S.J. *Hegel's Idea of Philosophy with a New Translation of Hegel's Introduction to the History of Philosophy*. New York: Fordham University Press, 1983.

Lewellen, Ted C. *Political Anthropology: An Introduction*. South Hadley: Bergin and Garvey, 1983.

Lichbach, Mark Irving and Alan S. Zuckerman. *Comparative Politics: Rationality, Culture, and Structure*. Cambridge: Cambridge University Press, 1997.

Lichteim, George. *The Concept of Ideology and Other Essays*. New York: Vintage Books, 1967.

Locke, John. "Essay Concerning Human Understanding" in *John Locke: Works*, v. I. Germany: Scientia Verlag Aalen, 1963.

———. "Second Treatise on Civil Government" in *Two Treatises of Government*, ed. Peter Laslett. New York: New American Library, 1965.

Lowie, Robert. *The Origin of the State*. New York: Russell and Russell, 1962.

Machiavelli, Niccolo. "Discourses on the First Ten Books of Titus Livius" in *The Prince and The Discourses*. trans. Christian E. Detmold. New York: The Modern Library, 1950.

———. *The Prince*, 2nd ed. ed. trans. Robert M. Adams. New York: W.W. Norton and Company, 1992.

MacIver, R.M. *The Modern State*. Oxford: Oxford University Press, 1926.

Macpherson, C.B. *The Political Theory of Possessive Individualism: Hobbes to Locke*. Oxford: Oxford University Press, 1962.

Madison, James. "Number 51" in Alexander Hamilton, James Madison, and John Jay. *The Federalist Papers*. New York: New American Library, 1961.

Manicas, Peter T. *A History and Philosophy of the Social Sciences*. Oxford: Basil Blackwell, 1987.

Mansfield Jr., Harvey C. "On the Impersonality of the Modern State: A Comment on Machiavelli's Use of Stato." *American Political Science Review*, v. 77 (1983): 4.

Marsilius of Padua. *Defensor Pacis*. ed. trans. Alan Gewirth. Toronto: University of Toronto Press, 1980.

Martines, Lauro. *Power and Imagination: City-States in Renaissance Italy*. New York: Vintage Books, 1980.

Marx, Karl. "Critical Notes on the Article 'The King of Prussia and Social Reform. By a Prussian.'" in *Early Writings*. trans. Rodney Livingstone and Gregor Benton. New York: Vintage Books, 1975.

Marx, Karl and Frederick Engels. *The German Ideology: Parts I, II*. ed. R. Pascal. New York: International Publishers, 1947.

———. *Karl Marx and Frederick Engels. Selected Works in One Volume*. New York: International Publishers, 1968.

McIlwain, Charles Howard. *The Growth of Political Thought in the West: From the Greeks to the End of the Middle Ages*. New York: The Macmillan Company, 1932.

Miliband, Ralph. *The State in Capitalist Society*. New York: Basic Books, 1969.

Mill, James. *An Essay on Government*. ed. Currin V. Shields. Indianapolis: Bobbs-Merrill, 1955.

Mill, John Stuart. "On Liberty." in *The Utilitarians: An Introduction to the Principles of Morals and Legislation, Jeremy Bentham; Utilitarianism and On Liberty, John Stuart Mill*. Garden City: Anchor Press/Doubleday, 1973.

Morrall, John B. *Political Thought in Medieval Times*. London: Hutchinson University Library, 1958.

Nelson, Brian R. *Western Political Thought: From Socrates to the Age of Ideology*, 2nd ed. Englewood Cliffs: Prentice Hall, 1996.

Nelson, John S. "Education for Politics: Rethinking Research on Political Socialization" in *What Should Political Theory Be Now: Essays from the Shambaugh Conference on Political Theory*. ed. John S. Nelson. In series: *SUNY Series in Political Theory: Contemporary Issues*. ed. John G. Gunnell. Albany: State University of New York Press, 1983.

Nicholas, Barry. *An Introduction to Roman Law*. In series: *Clarendon Law Series*. ed. H.L.A. Hart. Oxford: Clarendon Press, 1962.

Nordlinger, Eric A. *On the Autonomy of the Democratic State*. Cambridge: Harvard University Press, 1981.

———, Theodore J. Lowi, and Sergio Fabbrini. "The Return to the State: Critiques." *American Political Science Review*. v. 82 (1988): 3.

Offe, Claus. *Modernity and the State East, West*. Cambridge: The MIT Press, 1996.

Olson, Richard. *The Emergence of the Social Sciences: 1642–1792*. In series: *Twayne's Studies in Intellectual and Cultural History*. ed. Michael Roth. New York: Twayne Publishers, 1993.

Overton, Richard. "An Arrow Against all Tyrants." *The Levellers in the English Revolution*. ed. G.E. Aylmer. In series: *Documents of Revolution*. ed. Heinz Lubasz. Ithaca: Cornell University Press, 1975.

Painter, Sidney. *The Rise of the Feudal Monarchies*. In series: *The Development of Western Civilization: Narrative Essays in the History of Our Tradition from Its Origins in Ancient Israel and Greece to the Present*. ed. Edward W. Fox. Ithaca: Cornell University Press, 1951.

Parkin, Frank. *Max Weber*. In series: *Key Sociologists*. ed. Peter Hamilton. New York: Tavistock Publications and Ellis Horwood Limited in association with Methven Inc., 1982.

Parkinson, F. *The Philosophy of International Relations: A Study in the History of Thought*. Sage Library of Social Research. v. 52. Beverly Hills: Sage Publications, 1977.

Plamenatz, John. *The English Utilitarians*. Oxford: Basil Blackwell and Mott, 1958.

————. *Man and Society: A Critical Examination of Some Important Social and Political Theories from Machiavelli to Marx*, v. I. New York: McGraw-Hill, 1963.

Plato. "Laws." *The Dialogues of Plato*. v. IV, Book XII. 4th ed. trans. B. Jowett. London: Oxford at The Clarendon Press, 1953.

————. "Republic." *The Dialogues of Plato*. v. II, Books VII–IX. 4th ed. trans. B. Jowett. London: Oxford at The Clarendon Press, 1953.

Plotinus. "Enneads." Book IV. viii. *The Philosophy of Plotinus: Representative Books from the Enneads*. ed. trans. Joseph Katz. New York: Appleton Century Crofts, 1950.

Pocock, J.G.A. *The Machiavellian Moment: Florentine Political Thought and the Atlantic Republican Tradition*. Princeton: Princeton University Press, 1975.

Pollard, A.F. *The Evolution of Parliament*. 2nd rev. ed. London: Longmans, Green and Co. Ltd., 1964.

Polybius. *The Rise of the Roman Empire*. ed. Frank W. Wallbank. trans. Ian Scott-Kilvert. New York: Penguin Books, 1979.

Poulantzas, Nicos. *Classes in Contemporary Capitalism*. trans. David Fernbach. London: NLB, 1975.

Pufendorf, Samuel. *On the Duty of Man and Citizen According to Natural Law*. ed. James Tully. trans. Michael Silverthrone. In series: *Cambridge Texts in the History of Political Thought*. ed. Raymond Geuss and Quentin Skinner. Cambridge: Cambridge University Press, 1991.

Reale, Giovanni. *The Systems of the Hellenistic Age*. 3rd ed. ed. trans. John R. Catan. Albany: State University of New York Press, 1985.

Riley, Patrick. *Will and Political Legitimacy: A Critical Exposition of Social Contract Theory in Hobbes, Locke, Rousseau, Kant, and Hegel*. Cambridge: Harvard University Press, 1982.

Rousseau, Jean Jacques. "Discourse on Political Economy." in *On the Social Contract with Geneva Manuscript and Political Economy*. ed. Roger D. Masters. trans. Judith R. Masters. New York: St. Martin's Press, 1978.

————. "Essay on the Origin of Language which Treats of Melody and Musical Imitation" in *On the Origin of Language*. trans. John H. Moran and Alexander Gode. New York: Frederick Ungar Publishing Co, 1966.

————. *The Government of Poland*. trans. Willmoore Kendall. New York: Bobbs-Merrill, 1972.

————. "Second Discourse: On the Origin and Foundations of Inequality Among Men" in *The First and Second Discourses*. ed. Roger D. Masters. trans. Roger D. Masters and Judith R. Masters. New York: St. Martin's Press, 1964.

————. *The Social Contract*. rev. Charles Frankel. New York: Hafner Press, 1947.

Sabine, George H. and Thomas L. Thorson. *A History of Political Theory*. 4th ed. Hindsale: Dryden Press, 1973.

Saxonhouse, Arlene. *Athenian Democracy: Modern Mythmakers and Ancient Theorists*. Notre Dame: University of Notre Dame Press, 1996.

Scaff, Lawrence A. *Participation in the Western Political Tradition: A Study of Theory and Practice. Political Theory Studies, no. 2*. The Institute of Government Research. Tucson: The University of Arizona Press, 1975.

Schapera, I. *Government and Politics in Tribal Societie*. London: C.A. Watts and Co., 1956.

Sealey, Ralph. *A History of the Greek City States: 700–338 B.C.* Berkeley: University of California Press, 1976.

Seidelman, Raymond and Edward J. Harpam. *Disenchanted Realists: Political Science and the American Crisis, 1884–1984.* In series: *SUNY Series in Political Theory: Contemporary Issues.* ed. John G. Gunnell. Albany: State University of New York Press, 1985.

Service, Elman R. *Origins of the State and Civilization: The Process of Cultural Evolution.* New York: W.W. Norton Company, 1975.

Singer, Peter. *Hegel.* In series: *Past Masters.* ed. Keith Thomas. Oxford: Oxford University Press, 1983.

Skinner, Quentin. *The Foundations of Modern Political Thought: The Age of Reformation,* v. II. Cambridge: Cambridge University Press, 1978.

Skocpol, Theda. *States and Social Revolutions: A Comparative Analysis of France, Russia, and China.* Cambridge: Cambridge University Press, 1979.

Smart, Barry. *Michel Foucault.* In series: *Key Sociologists.* ed. Peter Hamilton. London: Routledge, 1988.

Spencer, Herbert. *The Man versus the State.* ed. Donald Macrae. Baltimore: Penguin Books, Inc., 1969.

Springborg, Patricia. "Politics, Primordialism, and Orientalism: Marx, Aristotle, and the Myth of the Gemeinschaft." *American Political Science Review.* v. 80 (1986).

Spruyt, Hendrik. *The Sovereign State and Its Competitors: An Analysis of System Change.* Princeton: Princeton University Press, 1994.

Starr, Chester G. *A History of the Ancient World.* 4th ed. Oxford: Oxford University Press, 1991.

Strauss, Leo. *The Political Philosophy of Hobbes: Its Basis and Genesis.* trans. Elsa M. Sinclair. Chicago: The University of Chicago Press, 1952.

Strayer, Joseph R. *The Medieval Origins of the Modern State.* Princeton: Princeton University Press, 1970.

Thorley, John. *Athenian Democracy.* London: Routledge, 1966.

Thucydides. *The Peleponnesian War.* trans. John H. Finley, Jr. New York: The Modern Library, 1951.

Tierney, Brian. *The Crisis of Church and State, 1050–1300.* Toronto: The University of Toronto Press, in association with the Medieval Academy of America, 1988.

———. *Religion, Law, and the Growth of Constitutional Thought: 1150–1650.* Cambridge: Cambridge University Press, 1982.

Tocqueville, Alexis de. *Democracy in America.* ed. J.P. Mayer. trans. George Lawrence. New York: Harper and Row, 1966.

———. *The Old Regime and the French Revolution.* trans. Stuart Gilbert. Garden City: Doubleday and Company, 1955.

Ullmann, Walter. *Law and Politics in the Middle Ages: An Introduction to the Sources of Medieval Political Ideas.* In series: *The Sources of History: Studies in the Uses of Historical Evidence.* ed. G.R. Elton. Ithaca: Cornell University Press, 1975.

———. *Medieval Political Thought.* Harmondsworth: Penguin Books, 1975.

Van Steenberghen, Fernand. *Aristotle in the West.* trans. Leonard Johnston. Louvain: Nauwelaerts Publishing House, 1970.

Vernant, Jean-Pierre. *The Origins of Greek Thought.* Ithaca: Cornell University Press, 1982.

Vincent, Andrew. *Theories of the State.* Oxford: Basil Blackwell, 1987.

Wallace-Hadrill, J.M. *Early Germanic Kingship in England and on the Continent.* Oxford: Oxford University Press, 1971.

Weber, Max. *From Max Weber: Essays in Sociology*. ed. trans. H.H. Gerth and C. Wright Mills. New York: Oxford University Press, 1946.

———. *Max Weber on Law in Economy and Society*. From Max Weber, *Wirtschaft und Gesellschaft*, 2nd. ed. (1925). ed. Max Rheinstein. trans. Edward Shils and Max Rheinstein. New York: Simon and Schuster, 1954.

———. *The Protestant Ethic and the Spirit of Capitalism*. trans. Talcott Parsons. New York: Scribner, 1958.

Wittfogel, Karl. *Oriental Despotism; A Comparative Study of Total Power*. New Haven: Yale University Press, 1957.

Woolley, C. Leonard. *The Sumerians*. New York: W.W. Norton and Company, 1965.

Yolton, John W. *Locke and the Compass of Human Understanding*. Cambridge: Cambridge University Press, 1970.

Index

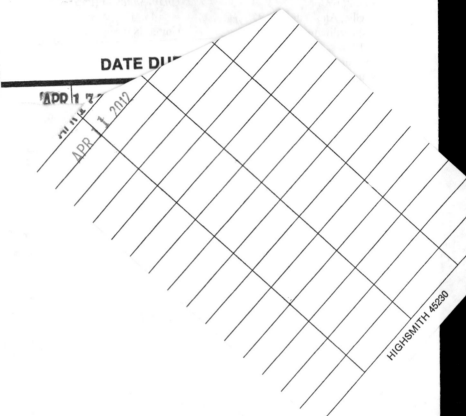